Masterful Coaching

Extraordinary Results by Impacting People and the Way They Think and Work Together

Robert Hargrove

Jossey-Bass
Pfeiffer
San Francisco

Copyright © 1995 by Jossey-Bass/Pfeiffer

Interior Design: Susan Odelson
Compositor: Judy Whalen
Editor: Susan Rachmeler
Production Editor: Dawn Kilgore

ISBN: 0-89384-281-8
Library of Congress Catalog Card Number 95-30092

Library of Congress Cataloging-in-Publication Data

Hargrove, Robert A., 1947-
    Masterful coaching: extraordinary results by transforming people and the way they think and work
together / Robert Hargrove.
      p.   cm.
    Includes index.
    ISBN 0-89384-281-8 (hard)
    1. Work groups.   2. Industrial efficiency.   3. Employee motivation.   4. Employees—Training of.
    5. Group relations training.   I. Title.
HD66.H37   1995
658.3'14—dc20   95-30092

Printed in the United States of America.

Published by

Jossey-Bass
Pfeiffer
    350 Sansome Street, 5th Floor
    San Francisco, California 94104-1342
    (415) 433-1740; Fax (415) 433-0499
    (800) 274-4434; Fax (800) 569-0443

    Visit our website at: www.pfeiffer.com

Printing   10

Table of Contents

Preface

A Coach's Odyssey

This book began with a quest on my part to find something to do with my life that would make a difference. In a sense, the desire to do this came from my spirit or the yearnings of my inner self. In another sense, it did not come from me at all. I was inspired by a handful of great leaders, thinkers, and achievers who became my spiritual parents as well as my teachers, coaches, and role models. They touched me with the idea that being human meant having a big dream or a purpose larger than oneself. Once touched with this possibility, my life was altered forever. I could never go back to what most people call a normal existence; I had to find my own way. This led to a long odyssey that has brought me joy and freedom. It has also brought me suffering and the need to overcome adversity.

One of my main issues was to find something to do with my life that would fulfill my dreams and sense of purpose and yet allow me to express my personal essence in the world. The route I chose to follow in making my way in the world was transformational coaching—unleashing the human spirit and helping people learn powerful lessons in personal change as well as expand their capacity for action.

My aim was not just to offer people advice about how they should think or to help them do what they were already doing better. It was to work with them in a way that produced a real alteration in their way of being. I didn't know how to do this when I started out but I knew I would find a way. For several years, I scanned the world for coaches, mentors, and role models. There is an old Zen saying that when the student is ready, the teacher appears. I found many. Then it was a matter of incorporating what I learned into my own person style.

I began by simply having conversations with friends, asking them about the future they wanted to create. I tried to elevate and release their dreams and aspirations and then looked for where their thinking and actions created a match or mismatch with their goals. Then I tried to find a way to help them align their thinking and actions with their goals. This took careful speaking and listening. In many cases, it was nothing more than my personal commitment to the person or group that led me to unlock whatever wisdom, intuition, and insight I had and helped me to find a way to help them. It was my commitment, together with their commitment, that became like an alchemical chamber in which transformation would occur, often in mysterious and magical ways. It definitely was not my formal training that led to this work having an impact with individuals, groups, and then later organizations of various kinds.

My colleagues and I currently operate under the name of Transformational Learning Inc. in Boston, Zurich, Montreal, and London. The idea behind transformational learning, which is a central concept in the book, is that whether you are an individual, group, or organization, your ability to achieve the results you truly desire is a matter of both real change and deep learning. Transformation is about creating a shift in viewpoint. Deep learning is about altering the habits that go along with old skills and capabilities that are no longer useful and learning new habits and developing new skills and capabilities.

In many ways, writing this book has been an odyssey of trying to articulate the tacit frames of reference and general knowledge in my own head—what I do but cannot say. In some cases, I have also relied on other practitioners from academia, business, and consulting who have already articulated various aspects of this tacit knowledge with clarity, inspiration, and power. The ideas, methods, and tools that you find in this book in regard to transformational coaching and learning are the synthesis of years of research and practice by many people. I view that group of people as a community of commitment, although many of the members do not even know one another. I pass these ideas, tools, and methods along to you on your journey toward becoming a masterful coach and invite you to become part of that community of commitment.

Introduction

Coaching is hot! Companies like EDS, Chrysler, and Herman Miller use coaching to create a culture of high performance, change, and learning. Xerox, IBM, Microsoft, and many others are training thousands of managers to become coaches. Even the United States Postal Service is applying coaching techniques to encourage its employees to think better and work better together. Personal coaches in New York, London, Paris, and Tokyo are helping CEOs, executives, and middle managers unearth their personal goals and aspirations and make better business decisions.

And yet coaching is a relatively new concept in today's organizations. It is different than managing by objectives where some poor soul is told what to do and then left to sink or swim. It is different than traditional training programs that pour tons of information into people's heads. It is different than traditional consulting that often provides piles of reports but does not necessarily change the way people in the organization think and interact. Coaching is about interacting with people in a way that teaches them to produce often spectacular results in their businesses.

We call this new style of management "transformational coaching" because it shows people how to transform or stretch their visions, values, and abilities. Today's business environment demands that both companies and individuals perform at much higher levels than in the past. To bring this about, coaches must learn to elicit greater commitment, creativity, and flexibility from people. The principle behind this work involves altering the underlying context that shapes, limits, and defines the way people think and act. All too often in transformational coaching you discover through the stories people tell that their thinking is based on arbitrary conclusions rather than on fact. Often, this crooked thinking leads to misfires and counterproductive action and leaves people stuck in their jobs.

But why should people change? After all, changing the way one thinks and shifting one's beliefs is not easy. Today, however, powerful historical forces are at work that suggest that tomorrow's winners will be those individuals and corporations that can constantly learn, adapt, and capitalize on sudden shifts in the marketplace. To understand the forces driving this change, it helps to look at economic history.

Three Rites of Passage

In the years between 1870 and 2000, American business will experience three rites of passage. The first passage encompassed the shift from crafts to high-volume, standardized production. The second passage involved the shift from high-volume to customers and quality. The third passage is presently underway and builds on, but goes beyond, volume and quality. Its focus is "perpetual innovation," creating "new" value, and continually searching for new ways to satisfy customers. Each time the context in which a company operates shifts, a new era is born, and the company must go through a rite of passage—whether it's to the Machine Age, the Quality Revolution, or the Virtual Corporation. This means that the company must launch a preemptive strike against its own most cherished beliefs, unlearn old skills, and set off in a new direction.

The First Rite of Passage: Standardization

In the first passage, the shift was from crafts and cottage industries to the factory and a newfangled philosophy called "management."

This new way of doing business involved high-volume, standardized productivity. Workers did the same thing over and over again while managers looked for ways to do tasks better, faster, and cheaper. W.F. Taylor and other management experts found ways to produce breakthroughs in worker productivity by scientifically designing jobs. Taylor found that a worker could load more coal onto a boxcar by varying the size of the shovel used—big shovels for processed coke, small shovels for heavy ore. Machines also had a mind-boggling impact. Within about five years of the invention of the cigarette-rolling machine in 1881, eighteen machines were supplying the needs of the entire country. To help those foundry workers light up their Lucky Strikes, Diamond Match designed a machine that produced and boxed matches by the billions. It's obvious that companies that didn't make this rite of passage were driven out of business.

The organization structure was hierarchical, bureaucratic, and often heavy-handed. As one worker in the Watertown Arsenal recalls from the 1940s, "If people didn't keep up the pace, the foreman would sometimes come along and give people a knuckle sandwich." The organization pretty much functioned as a giant machine for transforming raw materials such as steel, rubber, and glass into the finished products of trains, planes, and automobiles. Management was all about planning, organizing, and controlling. "Volume cures all ills" was the theme. The more that was produced, the more would be consumed, the cheaper the prices, and the higher the profits for the companies. An ad from Gimbels, the New York department store, declared in 1953 "Economic survival depends on consumption. If you want to have more cake tomorrow, eat more cake today."

While the high-volume economy placed a lot of value on consumption, it placed little value on people, treating workers as replaceable parts. The management attitudes were denigrating, the jobs were soul-stultifyingly boring, and the safety conditions abominable. In one steel plant, workers were often subjected to a blast furnace that had open pipes and that belched hot steam. In a major meat-packing plant, workers sometimes had to walk ankle deep through grease and sludge. The result of all this was anything but employee loyalty. In the early days of the Ford Motor Company,

35,000 workers had to be replaced in one year in order to maintain a work force of 50,000. Often, the only coaching people got was a few, simple instructions before the tedium began on the assembly line. Also, the notion of teams hardly existed except in reference to the national pastime: baseball.

The Second Rite of Passage: Quality

From the early 1970s on—in cars, consumer electronics, and other areas—foreign competition made it painfully clear that there was more to being successful in business than just volume. Joel Barker, author of *Future Edge*, describes the quality revolution sparked by consultant W.E. Deming as the major paradigm shift of the late Twentieth Century—a fundamental shift in the rules and regulations for success. The basic rule for companies in making this rite of passage was that they had to achieve quality based on world standards. Today, if you go into a Lechmere Sales, Circuit City, or Kmart, a polite sales consultant will tell you that the quality of the different televisions, video machines, and portable stereos is pretty much the same, adding "If they're not good quality, we wouldn't put them on the shelf."

In a company that is presently in this rite of passage, power and authority still rest with the management. Yet, a new power and authority begins to reside with those people throughout the organization who have the capacity to make improvements or to influence others to do so. In the corporations of the high-volume era, a business was described by functions and layered in levels. In the companies that adopt Total Quality Management, the phrase "business processes" begins to replace the whole idea of departments. Fascination with the boxes in the organization chart gives way to fascination with activities in the business process and how they link together. One of the greatest effects of the quality revolution happened on a social level, not on an economic one. The revolution gave people the chance to contribute more to the team and to the organization.

The Third Rite of Passage: Creating New Knowledge

The birth of a new economy, coming from the ashes of the old, came home one day to an entrepreneur named Rene Dury. It was the autumn of 1993 and Ms. Dury was moving her marketing and communications firm into a turn-of-the-century industrial building. As she arrived to inspect the newly renovated offices on the top floor, then bristling with computers, fax machines, and video-text-editing equipment, movers were wrestling the last of several heavy, ink-stained printing presses on cables down the fifteen-story elevator shaft and off to the nether world. The presses may well have been used to print the old union newspapers that were sent all over the country by truck. Dury said that an era passed before her eyes, yet it was also the start of a new one.

On February 18, 1994, the *New York Times* reported in the article "Economic Evolution: From Making to Thinking" that in places like New York, Boston, and areas of California less than one out of seventeen people are involved in mass production today. The work is no longer about making things, but about creating high-quality, customized products based on the unique needs of individual customers. Workers are now involved in designing, financing, advertising, and selling some of the most sophisticated goods in the world. They recognize that the economic value of the products they offer lies not in where they are built but in the creative thinking, complex problem solving, and collaboration that goes into them.

In the first rite of passage, power flowed to people like the CEO and entrepreneur who invested in and ran big factories. Today, power is beginning to flow toward people who can identify customer needs, put products and services together in unique ways, and act as strategic brokers with other companies. In the same sense, organizations are shifting from the image of the pyramid—top-down, bureaucratic—to what Xerox CEO Paul Allaire calls "productive work communities," which are made up of networks of movers and shakers and dozens (or even hundreds) of teams. Also, there is a fundamental shift taking place to what Ikujiro Nonaka, professor of management at the Hitosubashi University in Tokyo, Japan, calls a "knowledge-creating company." The reason for this is that creating new products and services requires creating new knowledge. In this kind of company, learning is not a separate activity but what Nonaka calls a "way of being."[1]

Thus, if the first rite of passage was a shift to high volume and the second rite of passage a shift to adding value to existing products, the third rite of passage is a shift to creating what never existed before. The products that are produced are usually high-quality, customized goods—jet engines, high-fashion apparel, specialty chemicals, industrial electronics with specific applications for almost every customer. At the same time, there are thousands of newer, dynamic companies that are producing goods and services tailored to the needs of individual customers: for example, Sam Adams, a lager microbrewery, and Shining Example, a shoeshine company that offers in-office visits, stress reduction massages, and instant tie repair.

This cannot happen without a special kind of management culture, one that is based on creating new knowledge. The crucial player in this new management culture is the transformational coach. His or her job is to provide the company's vision or direction while leaving plenty of room for people to pursue their own passions, personal interests, and projects. Transformational coaches unleash the creatively productive contribution of the individual. As Xerox's Allaire puts it, "The key to the new productivity is people—helping them do what they can do, what they want to do, what they inherently know is the right thing to do."[2]

The Context of Coaching

In coaching individuals within organizations, you eventually reach a crossroads.

The work of transformational coaching within organizations involves unleashing the human spirit and expanding people's capacity to achieve stretch goals and to bring about real change. This does not start with fiddling with the strategy, structure, or systems of the organization. Nor does it start with coaching techniques like setting goals, motivating people, and giving feedback. It starts with considering and altering the underlying context in which these occur.

The underlying context is made up of the sum total of all the conclusions people in the organization have reached in order to succeed. This context is shaped by the shared interpretations people make about the business environment, the existing theory of business, and the core competencies that have been built up over time. It is also shaped by the management culture that is inherited or self-imposed—a network of underlying assumptions, beliefs, and attitudes that are largely invisible but still felt. It is this basic cultural context that is important to consider in creating a framework for effective coaching.

For example, the prevailing context of most groups is based on hierarchy—the fragmentation of different people and groups into separate divisions and departments. Thus, as soon as you move from coaching the individual to coaching the group, especially in an institution, you have to talk about the context in which you are coaching. Is the coaching going to take place in the context of unilateral control, submissiveness, and dependency? Or is it going to take place in the context of internal commitment and involvement? These are the two contexts to consider before you embark on coaching in any group.

The Command, Control, and Coercion Model

The command, control, and coercion model has been the traditional model of organizations. According to Bill Walsh, former coach of the San Francisco 49ers, in this context "there is only one person who does all the thinking, makes all the decisions, and designs the game plan and that person is the dictator." There are still many managers whose need to pursue their own purposes, to "control" others, and to win is so strong that they use this model in subtle ways without even being aware of it.

Despite all the attention given to visionary leadership, culture change, empowerment, quality, and service in recent years, most of the changes have touched few people and have been largely cosmetic. Organizations are often dominated by people who place self-interest over service and who see their careers in terms of presiding over a sacred control ground as well as defining, watching, and determining what is best for other human beings. Today's organizations are also run by control systems, such as staff groups, accounting, budgeting, performance appraisal, and other human resource practices.

This often boils down to autocratic governance—getting people to do things that they ordinarily would not want to do. The price paid for this is enormous. Autocratic governance withers the human spirit and saps people of the motivation for high-level results and change. What is personal and sacred to people is usually either denied or treated as unimportant. In valuing stability, predictability, and control above all else, a norm is created that squashes creativity and is inconsistent with quality and adding value. In the end, people resist and everyone feels bewildered, frustrated, and resentful.

One of the major problems of this model is that it goes against human nature. That is to say that for people to work under this model they have to accept being dependent, submissive, and passive in the face of the leader. Since this goes against people's gut instincts, the command and control model gives rise to all kinds of defensive behavior. The boss ultimately is blocked, the shared view is lost as people try to win or withdraw from the conversation, the whole is sacrificed to the parts, and the organization becomes unmanageable and falls into a mood of resignation.

One of the other issues of this model is that people tend to perceive everything that comes from the top as another form of coercion. Thus, coaching people in this context by setting stretch goals will be seen as an attempt to dominate or to get more out of people after they are already past the breaking point. Motivating people with carrots and sticks will be seen as manipulation and observing and giving feedback will be perceived as checking up on people or trying to change someone who doesn't want to change.

Learning and training are resisted because people do not set their own learning agendas. This becomes a reinforcing cycle or vicious circle.

The Stewardship, Internal Commitment, and Learning Model

In attempting to realize high-performance goals and transformational change and to create higher levels of commitment from people, every organization reaches a fork in the road that represents a need to create a shift in context. The first approach is the road marked "command and control." The second road is marked "commitment and learning." Groups and organizations that operate under the commitment and learning context are a world apart from those that operate under the traditional command and control model.

In the personal commitment and learning context, people do not trade in their aliveness in order to earn a living. Rather they answer the two questions "Who am I?" and "What can I do that I passionately care about?" They then begin to look for a natural group of people to do it with and usually come together with others around a purpose larger than themselves. They choose their own goals, make their own plans, and work with disciplined intensity. The organization that results from this then takes its natural size, whether it turns out to be a small pizza shop, a multibillion dollar corporation like Microsoft, or a community of commitment and inquiry like the Organization Learning Center at the Massachusetts Institute of Technology. (See diagram I.1.)

In the new emerging organizations, the traditional staff and control functions may still be there but they exist to serve and to help create a focus on the vision and values that really matter to people. In a complex, rapidly changing world, the control infrastructure begins to be displaced by a new infrastructure that is based on human commitment and learning. Control is kept by people's involvement in their cause and through a community of commitment, communication, and support.

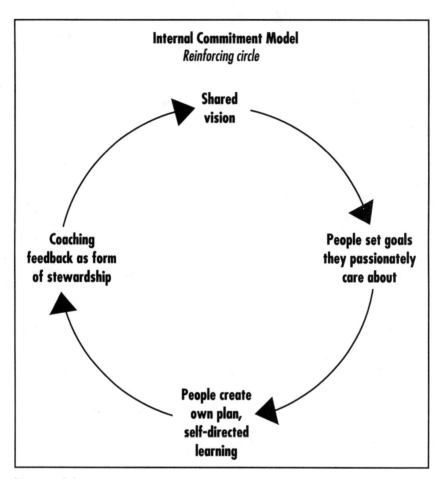

Internal Commitment Model
Reinforcing circle

Shared
vision

People set goals
they passionately
care about

People create
own plan,
self-directed
learning

Coaching
feedback as form
of stewardship

Diagram I.1

Learning plays a key part as people often do not know how to reach
the stretch goals or bring about change when starting out and often
need to learn and change in order to do so. The difference is that
instead of the learning agenda being determined by someone else,
it is learner-directed, determined by the person or group. It is not
a separate activity but something that happens in the context of
doing the job. As people reach the limits of their existing ways of
being, thinking styles, and habits, this naturally generates the need
for coaching.

Who is the coach in this context? The coach is an organization leader or manager, a front-line supervisor, a project manager, an internal consultant, an external consultant, or simply a colleague. In this context, the role of the coach is that of being a steward, facilitative leader, and teacher, not just the person with the biggest stick. He or she works with people to create a shared vision and values based on what matters to the institution, its demands and constraints, and what the people passionately care about. In this context, one of the coach's primary tasks is to help people create effective organizations that they believe in, where they can produce extraordinary results as an offering, not by demand. It is this model that *Masterful Coaching* is based on. (See diagram I.2.)

The Shift From Domination to Learning		
Context	Domination and Fragmentation	Learning and Primacy of the Whole
Direction Setting	Vision from "on top"	Shared vision
Thinking and Execution	Top thinks; local acts	Thinking and action merged at all levels
Nature of Thinking	Atomistic thinking	Systemic thinking
Conflict Resolution	Political mediation of conflict: person with biggest stick	Create dialogue; integrate diverse views (shared mental models)
Role of Leadership	• Set vision • Motivate people with carrot and stick • Make key decisions and create situations to control local actions • Delegate learning to training department	• Build shared vision • Empower and inspire commitment • Encourage team reflection and learning to make better decisions • Coach people in personal transformation and new skills

Diagram I.2

Part I

Personal Transformation

The journey to becoming a masterful coach is a lifelong process of self-development. It is a distinct field of inquiry, not just a search for a quick fix or a pat answer. It involves living inside questions such as "How can I help others realize their noblest visions, values, and ideas? What can I do to transform an 'organization' that is a complex web of competing forces into a community of commitment based on the primacy of the whole? How can I bring out the best in those around me and in the process forward inspired action?" Here you will find guiding ideas and specific methods and tools that can lead to powerful insights into these questions.

The focus here is on personal transformation, as this is the foundation for everything else. You will also find coaching strategies that will help you transform yourself into a facilitative leader, coach, and teacher. The key to becoming a masterful coach lies in having the dream, aspiration, and the bone-deep commitment to make a difference in the lives of individuals, groups, or entire organizations. It is that commitment that is the alchemical chamber in which great coaches are born. It is that commitment that unlocks your wisdom, intuition, and insight when mere technique fails.

In this section, you will learn how to engage people in conversations where people transform who they are in the face of their commitments. Transformation implies getting to the source of people's behavior and altering their frames of reference and ways of being, not just getting them to do something different. At the same time, when a transformation occurs, there is a sudden and dramatic change in human behavior. This is not a psychological, linear, or step-by-step process, but something magical and mysterious. As Sri Auribondo, an Indian sage, once said of transformation, "It happens in the hour of the unexpected."

CHAPTER ONE

The Journey to Masterful Coaching

Coaching is about challenging and supporting people,
giving them the gift of your presence.

Masterful coaching involves helping people in groups transform themselves, their communities, and their world. It involves impacting people's visions and values as well as helping them reshape their way of being, thinking, and actions. It involves challenging and supporting people in achieving higher levels of performance while allowing them to bring out the best in themselves and those around them. It means going through a deep learning process that results in embodying new skills and capabilities. In the simplest, day-in, day-out terms, masterful coaching involves expanding people's capacity to take effective action. It often comes down to making it possible for people to succeed in areas where they are most stuck or ineffective.

Masterful coaching is a journey, not just a destination. Whether or not you will embark on the journey depends not on whether you are a leader, project manager, or individual contributor; it depends on whether you dare to see and meet the calling to make a difference, whether in the life of one person, a group, or an institution. The journey is driven by passion. It asks for a person with a certain clarity of mind, heart, effectiveness, and, if possible, a touch of what the Buddhists call "crazy wisdom" (being colorful, dramatic, shocking, and wise). It requires someone who is willing to step back from preoccupations or the front lines and give someone the gift of his or her presence. "Got a problem? Let's talk about it."

Each of us can remember a handful, but only a handful, of coaches, teachers, and mentors who touched our lives with new possibilities or choices or who helped us achieve results that we never could have imagined. Perhaps our inspiration to take the journey comes from them.

The setting for the journey begins not in sports or the performing arts but in the workplace—whether one works in a business, school, or hospital. There are several reasons for this. First, there is a growing need for executive reinvention as well as collaboration between people with divergent views and perspectives. Secondly, to a large extent, coaching takes place in the domain of accomplishment and the workplace is where people go to accomplish something they have a lot at stake in.

A *masterful coach is someone who is a vision builder and value shaper.*

Thirdly, what Percy Barnevik of ABB calls the multidomestic corporation is perhaps the institution that has the greatest single influence on the world today. Still, the lessons to be learned about masterful coaching can be applied to the business of living—to a family or community group—anywhere people need help in improving their ability to learn and grow.

The time to take the journey is now. Today, organizations are faced with the need to produce high-performance results and introduce transformational change. Every business needs coaches who can help their organization learn about the most critical and difficult business issues confronting individuals and teams in the midst of action. Every school is facing a crisis in how to educate students that demands that teachers be less enforcers of *curriculum-directed* learning and more enablers of *learner-directed* learning. Our elected officials are often at legislative stalemates and need someone to facilitate them in building common ground. The world as a complex social and biological system is presenting us with ever more pressing dilemmas, and to solve them, we need coaches who can help us think and work better together. This is the domain of masterful coaching.

I. The Four Compass Points of Masterful Coaching: Mapping the Territory

A masterful coach is someone who is a vision builder and value shaper, not just a technician who helps people reach their goals. A masterful coach is someone who engages and enters into the learning system of a person, business, or social institution with the intent of improving it so as to impact people's ability to perform. However, this does not happen in a vacuum. One must discover his or her own humanness and humanity, as well as help others do the same. Then, one must shift his or her weight to the opposite foot, helping people in communities accomplish their goals by transforming who they are and becoming much more effective through whatever means possible.

To me, the lifelong journey toward masterful coaching is one of the highest expressions of what it is to be a human being even though it is fraught with challenges. Masterful coaching means taking a stand for breakthroughs for people as well as for breakthrough results, often when there is no evidence that this will happen. It involves holding forth that it is possible to make a difference, even when the mountain is high, the winds strong, the climate cold, and the road lonely. It is a journey filled with joy and pain, comedy and tragedy—all the ironies of life.

For those embarking on the course, the following compass points map the territory to be crossed in this journey, the cairns for the walk through the mountains, the street signs that let us know whether or not we are in the right neighborhood. The intent here is to walk the reader into a different world. At the same time, while there are no magic bullets, you will be provided with guiding ideas, methods, and tools that will help you develop as a coach and that can be put to practical and immediate use. The starting point is with the people you want to work with and in those areas where you have the most control.

Becoming a masterful coach is a developmental process. It takes striving to reach a certain level as a coach and then plateauing, striving, and reaching the next level—from individual to group, from group to organization.

Compass Point 1. Coaching as Stewardship

Stewardship is taking a stand for the future of the people, communities, complex social systems, and the world we care about.

Most of us act as if we were dropped on the planet from the heavens with the expressed purpose of living our lives as fully, successfully, and happily as we can. It seldom occurs to us that we are responsible for passing this world on to the next generation in better shape than we found it. It seldom occurs to us that our way of living is not sustainable and we are existing off the capital of future generations. It often doesn't occur to us that our legacy to our children should not just be a few material possessions but the raising of our collective vision from a foundation of socially constructive values deeply embedded in our society, communities, and schools.

The primary reason is that most of us have inherited a socially constructed reality that is based on an abundance of self-interest rather than a basic service orientation. The leaders of our institutions rarely see themselves as stewards of the planet, communities, and employees, but as voyagers on the road to personal and corporate success. We design organizations based on the idea of becoming more productive without taking into account the far-reaching conse-quences of a production culture. We lead, manage, and coach people out of this context, setting goals that do not take into account the purposes people hold as sacred, and we then cannibalize people's time and energy turning them into what the Japanese call a "salary man." As a result, people bury their deep feelings of caring for their organizations, their employees, and their work.

Masterful coaching doesn't start with setting goals, motivating people, and appraising their performances so as to get more out of them. It starts with looking in the mirror ourselves and asking about what really matters to us so as to unearth the fact that we do care. This naturally leads to stewardship, choosing service over self-interest, taking the longer and deeper view rather than just being concerned with next door or next week. It means seeing who we are in the context of taking a stand for the future of people, institutions, and the world. It means creating business enterprises that are not only outstandingly productive but that nurture the human spirit and allow people to learn and grow.

Any true leader, manager, or coach adopts stewardship and creating an environment of stewardship as a basic orientation. There are many opportunities in every organization to make stewardship real. For example, being an executive who makes strategic decisions that regenerate the company's future and the community and environment at the same time; helping a customer make his or her customer successful; serving as a mentor for an up-and-coming player; making sure the team gets the support, direction, skills, and capabilities it needs to succeed, regardless of the consequences to the coach. "What are your vision, values, and real goals? How do you see your next steps? How can I help?" People who truly embrace the quality of stewardship stand out.

Companies like Xerox, Royal Dutch Shell, Reebok, and Bally shoes have discovered that giving employees an opportunity to eliminate the artificial boundary between the things they care about at the office and the things they care about as human beings can create a context where people bring their whole selves to work. This starts with providing employees the windows of opportunity to not only impact the bottom line but to make a difference in the world.

A favorite example comes from Royal Dutch Shell. When many companies were divesting from South Africa, Shell decided to stay, both to do business and to try to help. This resulted in its gas stations being bombed in Holland. Shell sponsored a scenario planning process, similar to what they had done successfully during the OPEC oil crisis, with a group of South African business and community leaders.

They looked at the future possibilities and consequences of apartheid in South Africa and developed two scenarios. The end result showed a high road and a low road for the future of South Africa. The low road was that of becoming more entrenched in the apartheid practices, sinking deeper into a colonial-type economy based on raw materials without a modern infrastructure and resulting in exclusion from the rest of the world. The high road was to break down apartheid and to try to reenter the global community of nations and eventually become a modern economy.

The scenarios were presented in a neutral way by a man named Clem Suntner. He spoke to hundreds of audiences, black and white, in churches, schools, and government institutions. After each presentation, Suntner would facilitate a discussion with the idea of building a common understanding. This process is believed to have had a huge impact in eventually dismantling apartheid.[1]

Compass Point 2. Personal Transformation and Reinvention

Nothing happens without personal transformation.

W. Edwards Deming

Masterful coaching is about empowering people to create a future they truly desire based on unearthing what they passionately care about. It involves empowering people to create their lives based on what is deeply purposeful to them. The founders of some of our most successful organizations have benefited from a coach or mentor who encouraged them in this direction and so have the cultures that form their legacy: E.C. Johnson 2d of Fidelity Investments, Bob Galvin of Motorola, and Bill Gates of Microsoft to mention only a few. As Fidelity founder Mr. E.C. Johnson 2d told his son Ned (today's chairman), referring to his own father's unsatisfactory career, "Don't do what Pappy did; do what you love!"[2] This kind of coaching can be transformational as it naturally begins to alter the context out of which people come into the world, draw their identities, and make decisions.

Yet, transformation is not an event but a continual process of becoming. I have met many leaders who know what they passionately care about and are successful in building a shared vision with others. Yet, these leaders often don't realize that transforming and reinventing the organization is inseparable from transforming who they are and reinventing themselves. Masterful coaching is not based on analyzing people in a psychological way or focusing on what's wrong with them. It is based on altering the context that shapes the way people make decisions. The context is made up of people's particular perspectives and deeply held beliefs and assumptions. In most cases, people are unaware of the context or its consequences.

For example, I coached a leader of an entrepreneurial start-up group that was made up of people from the film, computer, and software industries. They had decided to launch a fabulous new educational product that they believed could reach $70 million in revenue in a year. The leader was very dedicated because, in his own words, "It is in my self-interest to be so." Yet there were certain aspects to his personal makeup that got in the way. Instead of looking for creative solutions to problems, he would look for what was wrong with every alternative. He would also make issues that were controversial but important to resolve undiscussable. When I spoke to him about these things, it was clear that he thought he was doing everything possible to forward the project. Yet, in reality, he was blocking the project at every turn.

Masterful coaching involves empowering people to transform who they are and reinvent themselves by helping them to see how their frames of reference, thinking, and behavior produce unintended consequences. This work involves encouraging people to surface and question the way they have framed their points of view about themselves, others, or their circumstances with the idea of creating a fundamental shift. For example, a shift from self-interest to stewardship, from being control oriented to being creative and generative, from seeing conflict as embarrassing or threatening to seeing conflict as a leverage point for building a shared view. When people's frames of reference shift, it allows them to see things in a new way and to act in a new way. (See diagram 1.1.)

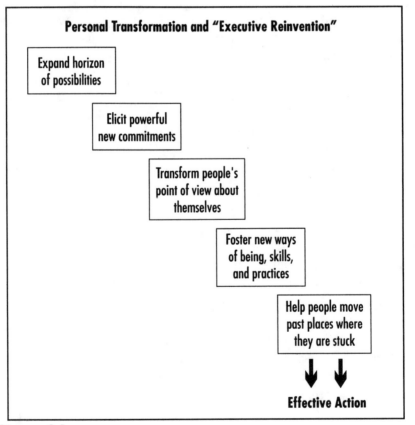

Personal Transformation and "Executive Reinvention"

Expand horizon
of possibilities

Elicit powerful
new commitments

Transform people's
point of view about
themselves

Foster new ways
of being, skills,
and practices

Help people move
past places where
they are stuck

↓ ↓

Effective Action

Diagram 1.1

Compass Point 3. Creating Communities of Commitment and Team Collaboration

Organizations have increasingly come to represent command and control, fragmentation and a piecemeal approach, an environment where people can't bring their whole selves to work. There are many leaders, managers, and coaching practitioners from different kinds of organizations who have made a quest for new metaphors. Peter Senge, from the Organization Learning Center at the Massachusetts Institute of Technology (MIT), speaks of "servant leaders," "communities of commitment," and the "primacy of the whole" versus the parts. Paul Allaire, CEO of Xerox, talks of "productive communities of practice." Philippe Chéhab, director of pilots and flight crews at Swissair, speaks of being part of "a living system" or "network." Juan Rada, head of strategic planning for Digital Europe, says, "I want to build a tribe."

In a community of commitment, there is a shared vision and purpose—a sense that the work people are doing is deeply purposeful. People draw their identities both from their individuality and from their profound connection to the whole. People usually have a true dedication to the "game" they are playing and work with passion and pride. At CNN, the game is covering the planet in real time so as not only to produce information but also to impact opinion shapers and movers. At Swissair, it is flying people to hundreds of destinations with personal service touches that give everyone a sense or real worth. At Ben & Jerry's, it is making ice cream, like Rain Forest Crunch, with the intent of changing the world. In our own small organization, it is making transformational coaching programs available.

In a community of commitment, the leaders are not reluctant to take a stand for what matters, yet leadership is often collective and can come from anywhere in the organization. People spend lots of time in communication with one another so that they are able to come to a shared view rather than fighting for their solitary views. The standards of excellence are usually challenging and rigorous.

There is an appreciation for how the parts of the organization must fit together to make a whole. Finally, there is a network of commitment, communication, and mutual support that gives people the feeling of having deep, intimate, satisfying relationships that mean everything to them. People look up from their desks and realize they are part of something larger. As Fred Kofman says, "They reach up and touch the web."[3]

Masterful coaching in the years ahead will increasingly involve transforming organizations into communities of commitment. One level of this is for leaders to offer guiding visions and values as well as to shift the context in which the job gets done—from following orders to working on causes. By and large, the leverage point for creating a community of commitment is a small group that comes together around a purpose larger than itself. This could involve a group of people that have had a lifelong dream to start their own business, a breakthrough product development group that has to work across functions, various people throughout an organization who are passionate about quality and service, or a team of people who want to build an infrastructure for a learning organization.

One of the keys to building communities of commitment has to do with empowering and enabling people to have collaborative conversations with one another that allow them to come together around a shared purpose, agree upon objectives, iron out conflicts, and generate a rallying momentum. Unfortunately, most groups do not know how to have a collaborative conversation. As we will see in later sections of the book, blocked mental models and defensive routines often prevent people from building shared understanding or coming up with creative solutions to bothersome problems and issues.

A masterful coach is one who can transform the situation by encouraging people's noblest aspirations and teaching them new skills while at the same time launching breakthrough projects that demonstrate the power of collaborative action. This starts with transforming the underlying structure of conversation from trying to persuade and convince others in order to win to building shared understanding or a sense of community across differences. On a very human level, it requires authentic communication. As Scott Peck says, "The very real steps in building community come when someone speaks at a level of authenticity and vulnerability at which no one in the group has spoken before."[4]

Compass Point 4. Expanding People's Capacity to Take Effective Action

One of the most important compass points of masterful coaching is helping people to take effective action. In many organizations, the effective person is rare. People work at jobs where there is a mismatch between their personal qualities of excellence and the slot they fill. In most groups, people set goals that do not stretch their minds or skills or inspire extraordinary levels of commitment. The level of thinking and communication at team meetings seldom leads to the ability to take coherent action. There are not many people who can create something that never existed before or produce results in difficult or impossible situations. Learning is a separate activity, an abstract training program, not something that happens in the context of doing the job.

Coaching people to be more effective starts with what Peter Drucker, in his book *The Effective Executive,* calls "making strengths productive." There is something that each of us was born to do and, if we can find the arena that fits our value system and a job where we can do it, our level of effectiveness will be greatly enhanced. According to Erich Weber, a masterful life/career planning coach and founder of Job Design in Switzerland, "The key is asking people about what it is they really want to do. What is their personal calling? What kind of work do they find fascinating? Until they can answer these questions, finding the right job is like looking for a button in a box. Even if they come across it, they would not necessarily recognize it."[5]

The next area that comes into play in coaching people to be more effective, as well as making sure that people are coachable, is setting challenging stretch goals that people are excited about and have something at stake in. It is amazing how much more effective people will be in situations that look difficult or impossible when they really do care and when they really do have something at stake. It is then that they discover the source of their own creativity and effectiveness and come up with new ideas, fresh approaches, and innovative solutions.

Coaching people to take successful action not only involves setting goals but also observing people on a daily basis, honestly acknowledging breakdowns, and intervening in some way with the idea of helping people to learn and improve. There are two ways to do this. The first involves a repackaging (more, better, or different) of what they are already doing. The second involves helping people learn to do something that is fundamentally different. A masterful coach is always asking penetrating questions: "What unintended results are you getting? How are you contributing to them? Where are you stuck in an old pattern? How could you look at the problem or solution in a different way? What's missing that could make a difference?"

II. Masterful Coaching Methodology: Transformational Learning

It is important to briefly state the governing values of masterful coaching before discussing methods. Masterful coaches establish governing values that are consistent with bringing out the best in people, individually and collectively.[6]

1. People set their own goals and learning objectives based on their personal aspirations and an appropriate challenge level so that there is an *internal commitment.*

2. The coach, in observing and intervening, is committed to providing *valid information,* illustrating all assessments with specific examples.

3. People make a *free and informed choice* about whether they want to change. If people do want to change, the coach

provides them with the knowledge and wisdom that helps them to do so.

These governing values provide a framework for how to coach people in real time as well as how people are likely to respond to being coached.

That being said, the primary methodology of masterful coaches is transformational learning. This kind of learning is necessary to transform who people are, to achieve breakthrough goals, and to introduce real and lasting organizational change. One way to understand how a masterful coach uses transformational learning as a methodology is to think of three learning loops.

Triple-Loop Learning: Transforming who people are by creating a shift in people's context or point of view about themselves.

Double-Loop Learning: Fundamentally reshaping the underlying patterns of people's thinking and behavior so they are capable of doing different things.

Single-Loop Learning: Helping people embody new skills and capabilities through incremental improvement.

In reality, all three learning pathways are interrelated. (See diagram 1.2.)[7]

Transforming Who People Are

When most people think of learning, they don't think in terms of having to change themselves. They tend to think of learning as being something that occurs on a transactional level by acquiring ideas, tips, techniques, and so on. Seldom does it occur to them that the problems they are facing in their work are inseparable from who they are or the way they think and interact with other people. Yet, in reality, this is often the case. Thus, enabling people to transform who they are often becomes an essential part of coaching them to produce the results they truly desire.

Coaching people in this loop means taking into account the context from which people draw their identities and basic patterns

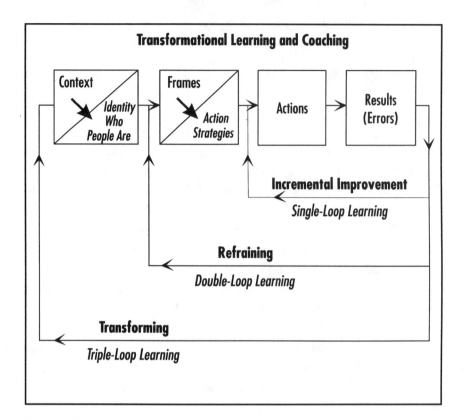

Diagram 1.2

of thinking and behavior. The context that people operate from is based on the sum total of conclusions they have reached as individuals. It is based on their particular perspectives and underlying beliefs and assumptions. The context shapes people's way of being, and their way of being shapes their characteristics, thinking, and behavior. It expresses itself in what I call people's winning formula (or generic solutions) for how to deal with a wide variety of problems, situations, and events. It is how a person shows up in the eyes of others.

For example, a leader who identifies with a command and control context will automatically adopt an autocratic style of governance and spend his time watching and checking up on people so he can get as much as he can out of them. This will tend to unintentionally produce an organization where people are passive, submissive, and dependent.

In the same sense, a team member who draws her identity from being nice, looking good, and knowing will tend to produce the unintended outcome of being inauthentic, managing impressions, and jumping to conclusions with a quick fix and a pat answer. As people tend to take their winning formulas for granted or as natural and needed and to be self-protective rather than reflective, the chances are good that they will bypass and cover up the problems.

> *Transformational learning is about creating a shift in context.*

Transformational learning is about creating a shift in context. In the case of our command and control manager, coaching him might involve enabling him to surface the underlying context he is operating from and understand its consequences and then helping him to create a new context that is consistent with his purpose and intentions. For example, he might draw his identity from a different set of governing values, like the "servant leader." This is not just an intellectual exercise but an emotional one. As Fred Kofman says, "Healing the universe is an inside job." [8]

For the team member mentioned above, the new context might be a commitment to being good rather than looking good, learning rather than knowing, self-reflection rather than self-protection. When the context shifts, it results in new ways of being as well as new thinking and behavior. It is not just that people begin to see the cracks in their winning formulas. "The person who was there before is not there now. The person that exists now was not there before." [9]

Learning to Do Fundamentally Different Things

People may be successful in personal transformation and reinvention by creating a shift in context and revising their winning formulas. However, they may still have managerial frames of reference that prevent them from producing desired results such as a marketing breakthrough or introducing change. The next loop of transformational coaching and learning has to do with helping people fundamentally reshape their thinking and actions in order to reach goals or solve specific problems. (In group settings, this involves helping people reshape the way they think and interact.)

In setting goals or learning to solve problems, people usually use their existing frames of reference, which often leads to trying to do the same thing better. All too often, the problem can only be solved by learning to do something fundamentally different. This requires questioning the frames of reference that led people to take the action in the first place. This can lead to seeing the goal, problem, or solution from a new angle and, thus, lead to new possibilities, choices, or insights. When people change their frames of reference, not only do they change the way they think but also the way they act. (This is what Argyris and Schön call double-loop learning.)

For example, I heard about a design and manufacturing company that, to reach its goal of increased sales, decided to make a new kind of industrial grinder. The company's mission was to build "the best grinder in the world." The engineers went off and assumed that this meant a grinder with a powerful motor. The marketing people assumed that this meant a grinder with a good price. Both sides had a lot of evidence to back up their views. The company tried to make a prototype of a grinder that satisfied both sides, but it didn't sell. A coach was assigned to the project and took both the engineering and marketing people to visit a key customer with the idea of testing people's beliefs and assumptions. It turned out that "the best grinder in the world," as far as the customer was concerned, was one that had a plastic cover over the grinding wheel. The people were concerned that their hands would slip and be damaged by the grinder.

As we can see from this example, learning often occurs when people are able to solve problems, eliminate mistakes, and produce desired results. A mistake usually reveals a mismatch between people's intentions and their theories of action or an inability to execute successfully. A masterful coach needs to develop "discriminating" awareness as to the nature of the mismatch in order to help people put in the correction. Does the solution require a fundamentally different approach or just incremental improvement and better skills and techniques?

A deeper learning cycle is usually called for when

1. *Going for a breakthrough.* For example, impasses in group problem solving can be transformed into opportunities for breakthrough thinking by using dialogue to surface and question beliefs and assumptions.

2. *Implementing change.* The tendency most people have to resist change and learning by camouflaging mistakes can be transformed by coaching people to reflect on the defensive nature of their thinking and how their actions produce unintended results.

3. *Doing the same thing but failing to get different results.* Coaching people in this situation often starts with interrupting their patterns of thinking and action and asking "What can you do differently?"

This deeper kind of learning can provoke resistance, as both individuals and organizations tend to identify with their professional knowledge and have a lot of psychological investment in their mental models and standard practices. For example, many companies invest materially in designing and manufacturing knowledge and do not catch on to the need to reframe their basic premises to marketing and service. Coaching people in groups to reframe their thinking and actions in these situations involves reflection and inquiry. "Let's adopt a beginner's mind and a learning orientation so we can learn something from this situation. Why did we set these goals in the first place? What is our thinking about solving this problem? How does it need to change? What assumptions do we need to test? How can we see the situation from a different perspective?"

Embodying New Skills and Capabilities Through Incremental Improvement

As people reframe their goals, problems, and solutions and begin to redesign their actions, new transformational learning needs begin to emerge. A person or group may be operating in the correct frame—leadership, team learning, collaboration and communication, a customer orientation—but not have any of the skills that allow them to take successful action. The first step is to identify the needed skill and provide some of the guiding principles and fundamentals (or action rules): for example, the four points of leadership, how to engage in a real quality of dialogue, or how to do consultative sales.

This kind of information is easy enough to come by, but it is often difficult to put into practice. There are two things that a coach can provide that will make a difference; one is the right ideas, methods, and tools. For example, I have found that having people "check in" and "check out" by saying what they are thinking and feeling before and after a meeting can be useful in freeing people of distractions. Similarly, I have found that having a meeting without an agenda can help to build the background of shared meaning necessary to build up a sense of community. There are other tools that can help people think together or raise controversial topics in a constructive way. Once people have the ideas, tools, and methods, the next step is to help them learn by making incremental improvements. (This is what we call single-loop learning.)

One of the main problems in teaching people new skills and capabilities is overcoming the popular notion of learning as being about knowing "what" to do. This interpretation of learning usually results in endless explanations and descriptions—"hand here, foot there" and so on. In reality, to be skillful at something means that we not only know "what" to do but also "how" to do it. To be skillful at a behavior means that we can carry it out without thinking about it, spontaneously and automatically. To put it another way, to be skillful at something is to embody the "know how" so that the "know how" is ready at hand. For example, when we ride a bike and come to a puddle, we instantaneously turn the wheel. If we tip one way, we intuitively correct the imbalance without thinking about it.

Enabling people to learn to embody the new skill or capability usually requires a continuous cycle of studying and practicing fundamentals and reflecting on the results in the context of getting the job done. This is a development process that takes place over a period of time, and an obsession with quick results can destroy the learning process. It is important to remind people that it is natural, in learning new skills and capabilities, for people to get "stuck." Being stuck means that they cannot find a way to move from the skills that they already have to what's required for taking successful action.

One of the problems that often happens is that people camouflage their stuckness and cover up their mistakes, saying they are doing one think when they are doing another. Or they avoid the coach or practice field because they are afraid to expose their ignorance or incompetence or they think they are improving when they are really not. The masterful coach's role is to cut through this camouflage. This involves providing guidelines to help steer the learning process: for example, (1) set goals and learning strategies, (2) find out guiding ideas, (3) take experimental action, (4) observe where you get stuck as well as what you do to get unstuck, (5) reflect on fundamental causes and solutions, and (6) look at mistakes as puzzles to figure out, as an opportunity to learn, and not as something to get depressed about.

> *While the "idea" of transformational learning can be electrifying, many people and groups resist it because it goes much deeper than most transactional learning processes where people simply acquire ideas, methods, or techniques.*

It puts people in touch with the arbitrariness of their beliefs and assumptions. It forces them to confront their blocked mental models and defensive routines in a group. It exposes their ignorance and incompetence as well as their mistakes. Masterful coaching involves helping people and groups produce desired results by inspiring a commitment to transformational learning in the face of their fear so that they can move beyond resistance and experience magic.

If you want to change the way someone thinks, don't tell them what to think, give them a tool.

In summary, there are three aspects of transformational learning.

1. **Transforming who people are (triple-loop learning).** Empowering people to alter the context out of which they make self-defining choices with the intent to helping them learn, grow, and produce the results they truly desire.

2. **Learning to do different things (double-loop learning).** Enabling people to fundamentally reshape their patterns of thinking or practices with the intent of helping them break through impasses and learn to do different things.

3. **Incremental improvement (single-loop learning).** Coaching people to continuously improve their current practices or do what they are already doing better.

III. Models and Tools for Transformational Coaching and Learning

This section provides some basic mental models for coaching as well as a toolbox of useful techniques that will be used throughout this book. As Buckminster Fuller said, "If you want to change the way someone thinks, don't tell them what to think, give them a tool."

Coaching Models to Learn From

The starting point for how to be a masterful coach is an authentic commitment to the person or group being coached. Commitment unlocks the wisdom, intuition, and natural knowing needed to coach people effectively in any situation. Without commitment, what you are left with is a bottomless quagmire of technique. At the same time, it is helpful to have a few mental maps. As with any model, the model should be the servant, not the master. It is important to do what is called for. Ask yourself, "How do I need to be in the matter?" and then don't get stuck in the technique.

The model most frequently used is the "doctor/expert model." This model is useful when people want to know the rules of the game or the fundamentals and are looking for a quick fix. The model is also useful in helping people produce a given outcome, such as facilitating a meeting so that conflicts are resolved or giving someone a tip or technique that help them perform a task. There are certain problems with this model. For example, a "patient" might not accept the "doctor's" diagnoses. Also, the expert may bring solutions but not implement them. The doctor/expert model often does not do enough to get the patient involved in the learning process necessary to eliminate the problem or create a remedy.

The "guru/catalyst model" is useful when people are seeking to create a powerful new future that requires personal reinvention. The coach as guru or catalyst must somehow get inside the person through inspiration or provocation and initiate the desire to learn and change. Edgar Schein of MIT has a good three-step process for promoting transformation.[10]

★ *Step 1. Unfreeze.* The "heat" of the guru or catalyst can help the "initiate" surface and call into question underlying thinking patterns or practices that get him or her into trouble.

★ *Step 2. Change.* The coach (guru/catalyst) provides guiding ideas with the intent of helping people make a fundamental shift in their thinking and practices.

★ *Step. 3. Refreeze.* This involves making the new ways of thinking or practices smooth and automatic through practice and study.

This model can backfire and create a rebellion in group situations if the guru or catalyst becomes too provocative.

Teaching coaching and training all too often means transferring knowledge from one person's head to another's. Fred Kofman of MIT suggests that a "learning enzyme" is a more appropriate metaphor especially where reaching high-performance goals requires creating new knowledge or building new skills.[11] The coach and coachee commingle and generate a new learning system between them that allows both to learn in the context of getting the job done. The coach is asking "How can I help?" The coachee is asking "How do I get unstuck?" Instead of giving people the answers or directly instigating change, the learning enzyme usually provides ideas, tools, and methods of inquiry with the intent of helping people expand their own capacity to learn. The drawback of this approach is that it can lack the heat of the guru or be too coolly intellectual to cause people to make a shift.

Personal Reflections on When to Use Which Models, Methods, and Tools

1. I use the doctor/expert model when indulging my own tendency to give advice, when people ask for help in an emergency, or in situations where there is little time to go into a deeper learning cycle.

2. I use the guru/catalyst model in executive reinvention or personal transformation programs. My methods and tools include guiding ideas, fluid framing, and role plays as well as crazy wisdom—being shocking, colorful, or humorous—to stimulate learning.

3. I use the learning enzyme model in group settings that require cool-headedness, basic sanity, and the development of team learning skills. My most frequently used methods and tools include creating a frame for team learning through the governing values and ground rules of collaborative conversations; dialogue to reach shared understanding, discussion to make decisions; fluid framing, working the "ladder of inference," and the left-hand column exercise;

and diagnosing and intervening to encourage observation and reflection.

Toolbox

The following list includes tools and methods that are most frequently used to foster transformational learning at the level of individuals, groups, and organizations.

★ *Beginner's mind.* Encourage coachees to look at each situation with a beginner's mind and from the premise that they can learn something from it. (See Chapter 3.)

★ *Personal stretch goals.* Encourage people to set stretch goals that are consistent with their highest aspirations, thus creating a context that enables people to achieve what's really possible, to think outside the box, and to bring out the best in themselves and those around them. (See Chapter 4.)

★ *Committed listening and speaking.* Speak with honesty and integrity and listen with empathy so as to step into the other person's frame of reference. (See Chapter 3.)

★ *Fluid framing.* Personal transformation, completing relationships, and breakthrough solutions require helping people to see things in a new way. "The way you see (XYZ) is.... The frames, opinions, and assumptions (XYZ) is based on are.... A more empowering way of seeing (XYZ) might be...." (See Chapter 2.)

★ *Effective action maps.* When people have gotten stuck or are ineffective, actions maps provide a useful tool for gaining both the incremental and the deep learning necessary to alter people's strategies and redesign their actions. (See Chapter 7.)

★ *Constructive feedback script.* "What I observe about you is.... My assessment is... and I feel.... What I want from you is...."

★ *Unwritten rules assessment.* Consider whether resistance to change is caused by people's disagreement with formal policy or by blocked mental models or because the unwritten rules of behavior make resistance the logical way to behave. (See Chapter 5.)

★ *Planned breakthrough projects.* A breakthrough project involves a group setting a short-term, measurable goal that can be achieved with existing resources, authority, and change readiness. People achieve extraordinary results and develop a "can do" attitude. (See Chapter 12.)

★ *Making powerful promises and requests.* Holding people accountable for making sincere commitments with explicit conditions of satisfaction can eliminate breakdowns and can forward action. (See Chapter 10.)

★ *Collaborative conversation ground rules.* These ground rules help generate shared understanding and coherent action by encouraging people to consider diverse views, to balance advocacy and inquiry, and to discuss the undiscussable in a way that does not harm relationships. (See Chapter 10.)

★ *Working the ladder of inference.* The ladder of inference is a tool that helps people with different views and perspectives build common understanding by both reversing and externalizing their thinking processes. (See Chapters 3 and 11.)

★ *Designing role plays.* Role plays are used to prepare for difficult conversations or to allow someone to take another person's view and argue that side of the conversation with the idea of learning from it. (See Chapter 7.)

★ *Distinguishing observations from assessments.* Help people to distinguish between witnessable observations and subjective opinions or judgments so that they can see where they have jumped to conclusions, made negative psychological assessments, or projected their judgments on others. (See Chapters 3, 7, and 10.)

CHAPTERTWO

A Coach Is Something That You "Be"

*I learned wisdom from all my teachers and
teaching from all my students.*

Ben Ezra, 2nd Century AD

A great teacher or coach often displays simple virtues like clarity of mind, basic goodness, basic wisdom, or fairness in dealing with others. When we meet people who possess such virtues, they automatically become coaches for us, whether they are teachers, bosses, or janitors. These people often distinguish themselves in our eyes because of their extraordinary genuineness. Sometimes, these people can be so direct, so real, and so true. Or they can have a big influence on us without saying very much at all.

The Japanese have a word called "korkoro" that has to do with perfecting one's inner nature. To be a great swordsman or tea master or Kojiki dancer, one must not only master the technique but perfect the way of being that is consistent with the discipline—having a calm and centered inner spirit. A student learns as much from the master's quality of being as from the master's knowledge and technical skills. To be able to teach people in "the way," one must perfect his or her own inner nature.

In the West, we tend to underestimate the importance of a person's way of being. We focus instead on his or her knowledge, skills, or techniques. Yet, whenever people stand out in a particular domain, they are recognized as "being" a leader, "being" excellent, "being" creative, "being" effective, or "being" understanding.

In most cases in our society, people don't ask the question "How do I 'be'?" when it comes to learning. They think in terms of "What do I do?" and "How do I do it?" This makes sense in teaching simple skills or practices. But it becomes limited when we try to apply the same principle to learning certain roles like leadership or coaching. Though we may be able to describe or explain what great leaders, coaches, or teachers do, the source of their actions often lies beyond such descriptions and explanations.

It's no accident that in many spiritual traditions, like Tibetan Buddhism or the martial arts, the master teaches the student both the spirit and the standard practices of the domain. Those who are able to embody the teacher's way of being, along with the skills and techniques, become part of the lineage. They become the next generation of masters, teachers, or coaches. It is their responsibility to pass on both the technical and mystical sides of the equation.

There is a story about a swordsman who went to study with a master in the mountains when he was just a young boy, and the master set him up in the kitchen washing pots and pans. The student begged the master to teach him how to use the sword, but the master didn't allow him to pick up a sword for over five years. Every time the master would enter the kitchen where the young boy worked, the master would pick up a stick, sneak up beside the boy, and whack him on the head.

One day the master silently walked into the kitchen and raised the stick to strike the student from behind, but the student picked up the top of a pot and blocked the stick. Soon it was almost impossible for the master to hit the student. The master had taught the student not only humility, but also how to defend himself from attack. The student went on to become one of the greatest swordsmen of Japan. He later said that it was the humility that his master taught him by making him work in the kitchen that developed his soul as a samurai. It taught him the spirit of true service and to be ready at all times.

For over 10,000 years, this is the way that most things have been taught in human culture; but in Western society we have separated the process of developing a way of being from the process of learning. In most management books, articles, and courses, there is little or no importance placed on how you have to "be" in order to excel at something; the emphasis, rather, is on skills and practices. The typical management seminar is more likely to lead to colorful plastic binders full of information and a list of "how to's" than to an alteration of a person's way of being.

Becoming a Masterful Coach

As the Japanese swordsman learned, becoming a masterful coach starts with making a commitment to being a coach. The first question to ask, then, is not "What do I do?" but "How do I 'be'?" You may say to yourself "I don't have those ways of being." Keep in mind that the essence of being a human being is to be able to create something. As Jacob Bronowski said in *The Ascent of Man*, "Man may be lower than the angels, yet he has a set of gifts which make him unique.... He distinguishes himself from the other animals by his imaginative gifts. He makes plans, inventions, and new discoveries by putting his talents together in more subtle and penetrating ways." Bronowski goes on to say that man's greatest inventions are not just the wheel, the telephone, and the printing press, but his "ability to reinvent himself."[1] This ability to reinvent ourselves is what makes it possible to learn new ways of being.

The Principle of Calling Forth

We have a particular approach to helping people develop new ways of being that we have termed "calling forth." The traditional approach to teaching people how to lead, coach, or teach is to identify certain characteristics, categorize them, put together lots of information about each one, and then present them to people, saying "Here, do this." People are often left hanging with the question "How do I become the kind of person who can do this? How do I get these characteristics inside me?"

With calling forth, the idea is to help you discover and express those leadership characteristics within you. Actor Robin Williams portrays this quality masterfully in the film *Dead Poets Society.* Williams coaches a student, whose self-image is meek and timid, to shout a "barbaric yawp!" from his belly. He then helps the boy to call forth his "poet inside" by visualizing Walt Whitman as a madman who is attacking him. The boy's poetry becomes striking and inspiring to the audience.

The traditional approach works from the outside in; this approach works from the inside out. Our intent is to help you trigger these new ways of being by "calling them forth" from yourself as opposed to trying to somehow get them inside of you. The first step in this process is to distinguish the characteristics of a masterful coach. (See diagram 2.1.)

Characteristics of Masterful Coaches

1. The ability to inspire

2. Setting higher standards

3. Honesty and integrity

4. Disciplined intensity

5. Forwarding action

6. A passion to help others learn, grow, and perform

Diagram 2.1

Characteristics of Masterful Coaches

1. The Ability to Inspire

We all grow up with lots of possibilities and opportunities before us, and then somehow circumstances close in and life becomes like a box. We become defined by the historical community we are born into, by our educations, mortgage payments, marriage partners, children, places of employment, and so on. Given all this, it's very easy for people to give up, and when people give up, their actions soon reflect their resignation.

> *Masterful coaches inspire people by helping them recognize the previously unseen possibilities that lay embedded in their existing circumstances.*

A good example of this is the story of James Escalante, a math teacher at an inner-city high school in East Los Angeles. Traditionally, the students from this school never went on to college because that wasn't even considered as a possibility and because the students were unable to pass the aptitude tests.

Escalante cajoled, pushed, wheedled, needled, threatened, and inspired eighteen students who could not do long division to become math wizards. When the students took the college aptitude tests, they passed with flying colors, but the testing board members were so surprised, they thought that the students must have cheated. The teacher suffered greatly because of this misperception and urged the kids to take the test again. Not only did they pass, but they did even better than the first time. Their success not only created the possibility of their going on to college but initiated a growing trend at the school of students going on to further education.

Where does the ability to inspire come from? It comes when we dare to dream about the possibility of a larger life—a life where ordinary people like you and I can make a difference. It comes when we are willing to stand up and fight for an idea when it is only a possibility. Finally, it comes when we are willing to risk everything and suffer in order to make that idea a reality.

Calling Forth Questions

Think about a time in your life when you were really inspired (or really inspirational). What was the source of that inspiration? Was it a leader, coach, or friend? Was it your own desire to make a difference? Was there a possibility that captured your imagination? Were you willing to take a stand for that idea? Were you willing to suffer the consequences in seeing the idea realized and still keep going?

---

2. Setting Higher Standards

Whether we are scientists, musicians, or businesspeople, most of us strive for excellence. This is why Mozart wrote beautiful music. It is what led Einstein to discover $e=mc^2$. It is what led Henry Ford to develop the assembly line. The same thing applies to people who are masterful coaches. The distinguishing factor is that they seek excellence by setting higher standards not only for themselves but for others.

In *A Season on the Brink*, John Feinstein tells how basketball coach Bob Knight of Indiana University set high standards for play and demanded stepped-up performance from his team. One day during practice, Knight lambasted Daryl Thomas, a player of huge potential who lacked the desire to make himself great, according to Knight. "Daryl, sometimes I think I want you to be a great player more than you want you to be a great player. And it just tears me up inside when you are not making the extra effort. There is no way you are ever going to be a great player unless you want it. You have the ability. But I can coach, scream, and tell you until Doomsday, and you won't be any good unless you want it as badly as I do. Somehow, I have to convince you to feel that way. Try, Daryl. If you try as hard as you can, I know it will be worth it. Don't try for me Daryl. Try for you." Thomas rose to the occasion during the next game and was Indiana's best player.[2]

Masterful coaches are not only stern taskmasters with others but also with themselves. This is often reflected in their willingness to take responsibility for mistakes, for lack of results, and for downright failure. John Wooden, former basketball coach at the University of California-Los Angeles, said "In all my years of coaching, I have never yelled at a player. If the player makes a mistake in a big game, my gut-level response is that I must not have given him enough coaching."[3] Can you ever remember hearing the president of an American company say that poor results were due to his or her lack of leadership? Did you ever hear a plant manager say that the high level of defects and subpar quality were a result of his or her management approach? Did you ever hear a project leader say that missed target dates were due to the way he or she ran the project?

Calling Forth Questions

Has there ever been a time when your coach pushed you beyond what you felt were your limits, and you found that you could do more than you thought you could do? Have you ever made unreasonable demands of people to perform to a higher standard? Are you able to balance toughness and holding people to a higher standard with compassion for what they have to go through to achieve it?

---

3. Honesty and Integrity

Masterful coaches hold themselves to the highest standards of honesty and integrity, not just because of expediency, but because these qualities really matter to them. *Integrity* is the consistency between what the coach wants for the team and what the coach says and does—"doing what you say you will do." If people see the coach treating others without integrity even once, they will expect to be treated the same way. Consistency is key. *Honesty* means not lying and having the highest ethical standards. Honesty and integrity have a very special meaning in terms of how a coach interacts with the people he or she is coaching. These words mean having a genuine commitment to the success of the people you are coaching and then, based on that commitment, being completely honest and forthright in all your communications with them. Masterful coaches never alter their communication to protect themselves.

Speaking honestly to people involves letting people know where they stand, questioning what people take for granted, and honestly acknowledging all mistakes. Though most managers might genuinely want to support someone, they often find it hard to be "straight" with people because they have been indoctrinated with social virtues like "be polite," "don't embarrass others," and "avoid saying something that might upset anyone." Though masterful coaches want to be liked, they learn to confront people for the good of the organization and out of a deep sense of caring for others.

Calling Forth Questions

Who is a role model for you in terms of honesty and integrity? How are you like them or not like them? Where are you doing what you say you will do? Where are you not? Recall a time when someone gave you straightforward feedback that had a positive impact, even though it was embarrassing or uncomfortable. Remember a time when you wanted to give someone some straightforward feedback and did not have the courage to speak up. What was the barrier?

---

4. Disciplined Intensity

Leon Royer summed up disciplined intensity very well when he said "Whenever anything significant is being accomplished, it is being done, I have learned, by a monomaniac with a mission." Disciplined intensity was present when Stephen Jobs built the first Apple computer, when a team of autoworkers at Honda's Maryville, Ohio, plant tried to beat the company record for assembling a car and succeeded, and when a mutual fund manager like Bob Beckwitt of Fidelity Investments brings his team together to bet billions of dollars in a single day in stock markets all over the world. By contrast, think about the average company on any given day. People stream into the office and make a phone call or two and then head for the coffee and doughnuts. They then go to a meeting and voice arbitrary opinions, without making decisions or taking action. Nothing seems to matter very much.

Though most people can rise to the occasion when there is a crisis, what distinguishes masterful coaches is their ability to elicit disciplined intensity using people's inner motivation rather than relying on outside pressure. When people work with a masterful coach, they are swept up by the "buzz" of purposeful activity that he or she creates. One of the characteristics of disciplined intensity is full participation—you are giving one hundred percent, totally focused on the task, and strangely unaware of yourself. Rock climbers report that the hardest climbs are the most difficult to remember because there is never an opportunity to think about what they are doing.

Calling Forth Questions

Think about those times when you were the coach of a team (or were part of a team) that worked with intensity and what you accomplished as a result. What was that experience like? What is the level at which you are willing to make demands of yourself and others?

---

5. Forwarding Action

Masterful coaches love action. They don't get stalled at the starting gate or bogged down strategizing, planning, or preparing. For example, I have seen Roger Servison, Fidelity Investments' head of worldwide marketing, immediately translate vague reports and recommendations into actions. He focuses on the next, most meaningful step to take by asking himself "What do we need to do to achieve the larger goal?"

> **M**asterful coaches know that an elephant can be eaten in small bites, even though the meal is huge!

Servison and other masterful coaches know that an elephant can be eaten in small bites, even though the meal is huge! They forward the action by identifying the openings that will allow them to get a meaningful result in the shortest period of time and, at the same time, will allow them to learn something that will provide new opportunities for action. Most people will only start a project after they've figured out all of the pieces. Forwarding action means acting even when you are uncertain of the outcome. It means building prototypes to see what you can learn, then refining them and trying again. Like putting together a puzzle on a rainy day, you're never sure where the pieces go; you just start making connections. Some pieces fit together and some don't, but eventually the picture is complete.

Calling Forth Questions

When someone tells you to do something, do you deliberate, plan, and organize? Do you ever feel overwhelmed by something that is just too big to tackle all at once? Do you break it into smaller tasks and allow the small accomplishments to propel you toward fulfilling the larger goal? Or do you procrastinate?

---

6. A Passion to Help Others Learn, Grow, and Perform

Masterful coaches have a burning desire to help others learn, grow, and perform. They are highly perceptive in discerning the gap between who people are today and their potential. They see leaders where others see followers. They see creative thinkers where others see those who can only follow conventional wisdom. They see players who can win the big games and actually make something happen where others see only the drones. They see hidden strengths in meek people where others see only weakness and timidity.

A masterful coach cannot stand to see someone who has potential but who is not being helped to fulfill it. It is the coach's job to make this happen. Coaches not only help people learn the skills they need to master today's job, but pay attention to people's development needs over the next few years. The way they do this can vary greatly. It is the urge to make a difference in other people's lives that sets them apart.

Calling Forth Questions

Do you have an irresistible urge to make a difference in other people's lives? Or do you frequently say to yourself "Who am I to say anything?" What is something that you could coach people on? Whom could you make the offer to?

A Methodology for Calling Forth New Ways of Being

We have a particular methodology to help you call forth the coach within you. (See diagram 2.2.)

I. Make a commitment to being a masterful coach. First declare that you will become a masterful coach and your reasons for wanting to become one. For the commitment to stick it has to be connected to

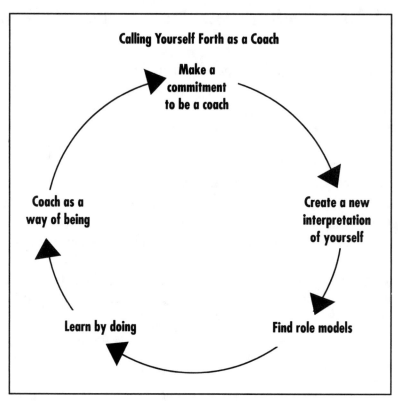

Calling Yourself Forth as a Coach

Make a
commitment
to be a coach

Create a new
interpretation
of yourself

Coach as a
way of being

Find role models

Learn by doing

Diagram 2.2

what you passionately care about. When you make such a commitment, you automatically start to alter your perceptions, the way you think about yourself, what you think is important, and what actions you take. A commitment is different from something you just say; it becomes a part of your identity. You can't always gauge people's commitment from their words, but you can always gauge their commitment from their actions.

II. Use fluid framing to create a new interpretation of yourself. Most of us draw our identity, as well as the way we think and act, from a particular perspective, deeply held beliefs, and assumptions. We don't just have our perspective; we become our perspective. We don't just have beliefs; we become our beliefs. We don't just have assumptions; we become our assumptions. Oftentimes, however, we forget that whatever our interpretation is, it is only one of many possible interpretations. Instead of seeing ourselves as an operations manager who gets his way by steamrolling others, we might create a new frame or interpretation based on seeing ourselves as a facilitative leader, coach, and steward. The challenge is that we not only have to learn a new frame, but to unlearn the old one.

III. Scan the horizon to find role models. One way to help alter the governing variables that determine your way of being, thinking, and acting is to search out role models. Identify role models that are a good match for you and your situation. Look within your group, organization, and community. Is there a coach, teacher, or friend that could serve this purpose? Once you identify the role model, it is important to observe him or her at work and ask questions about the characteristic you want to develop: for example, "Where do you draw your inspiration from?" or "How do you convey inspiration to other people?" or "How do you stay inspired when circumstances are tough?"

IV. Learn by doing. People learn through practice and performance. One way to begin to change yourself, to learn new mindsets, and to break old habits is to begin practicing within the new frames and to develop new skills or habits. You can do this by applying the new models in your normal on-line business meetings and interactions, as well as by creating special off-line situations for learning new skills. For example, you might attend a coaching program on facilitation on your own or with people in your group. Another way of doing it is to jump into a situation and learn through trial and error, drawing on role models and methods and techniques you've learned from being a coach in other areas of your life.

V. Just "be" it. All too often, people assume that being a coach or teacher is something that requires a long period of study and preparation, as well as specialized knowledge or skills. In reality, many leaders and managers know a lot about coaching but have never given themselves permission to do it. Look for opportunities where coaching is needed. Then make the simple declaration "I need to be a coach in this situation" and jump into action.

CHAPTERTHREE

Coaching Happens in Conversations

*A human being cannot resist the temptation to
express his personality and reveal himself,
which conversation gives him.*

Rainer Marie Rilke

A coaching relationship starts with engaging people in a conversation where they clarify their vision, goals, and ideas as well as their agreement to be challenged and supported. To put it simply, the coach needs the coachee's permission to coach him or her. A project manager once came to me with questions about coaching. He told me that he had started coaching the people on his team with the intention of supporting them in reaching their goals. To his dismay, however, instead of having his coaching skills confirmed, he heard statements like "Just tell me the result you want and I will bring it to you" and "Back off, you're crowding me." He learned from another manager that people viewed his attempts at coaching as just another way to dominate them.

Prior to establishing a coaching relationship, a coach and a team must have a conversation from which people gain a shared understanding of what it means to coach and to be coached. Setting the stage for this requires telling people what it is to have a beginner's mind and an attitude of learning. It can help to use a martial arts metaphor where the student surrenders to the master or to show a film from this genre that illustrates for people what it is like to let go and allow someone to coach them so that they can grow and learn.

It's important that people see that transformational learning is a double-edged sword. It swings one way and helps us cut through delusions and create new possibilities and new openings for action. Yet, when the learning sword swings the other way, it exposes our shortcomings, highlights our incompetence, and subjects us to the pain of trying to change.

One of the things that needs to come through in this preliminary coaching conversation is the coach's vision of what is really possible for the person, as well as a profound sense of caring. The coachee needs to show that he or she is really trying to create a new future, has a lot at stake in reaching specific goals, and is willing to be coached. The agreement to be coached is, in effect, a "coaching contract." Once this agreement takes place, the coaching relationship can begin in earnest. The coaching contract can take the form of this shared understanding of the coaching relationship or it can include more specific agreements with explicit conditions of satisfaction. For example, when working with groups, I create a coaching contract in which I specify that I will have the right to aggressively intervene at meetings.

> *The primary medium for all coaching interventions is conversation.*

Coaching also involves finding out what people's intentions are and aligning your intention with theirs. You agree to help cause their success and to let no other agenda get in the way. This is incredibly empowering and enabling for people. It is better to affirm people's sincere intentions, even when their thinking or behavior is inconsistent, rather than judge them or adopt a cynical attitude about them. This helps the coachee feel supported and creates the opening to give him or her feedback in a way that is tough and compassionate.

Coaching is not just about catching someone in the hallway and interjecting your advice, answers, or infinite wisdom. It is important in any coaching conversation to give someone the gift of your presence. This means giving someone your undivided attention when you are engaged in a coaching conversation. It can be helpful to set up a specific appointment for the coaching conversation. One contract I've created with individuals is to coach them three times a month for nine months with the purpose of completing the past and creating the future.

Creating a Coaching Relationship

1. Create a coaching contract that essentially says that you have permission to coach the person.
2. Find out what the person's sincere and honest intention is and align your intention with it.
3. Give the other person the gift of your presence by setting a time and place to hold a coaching conversation.

Coaching Conversations

Once the coaching relationship has been set up, it is important to understand that the primary medium for all coaching interventions is conversation. Coaching conversations are those where we speak and listen from a particular intent. In coaching conversations, we interact with the intention of helping people create a vision based on what they passionately care about; we speak and listen with the intent of helping people surface, question, and reframe assumptions; and we have the intent of impacting people's ability to perform. It is this intention that distinguishes a coaching conversation from all other business conversations.

One way to judge the effectiveness of a coaching conversation is by how people feel when you are finished. If people are coached properly, they will feel empowered and enabled. What do we mean by this? The sign of people being empowered is that they are more clear, more passionate, more powerful, and more "in action." The sign of being enabled is that people feel more capable of doing whatever it is that they have to do.

Let's use a metaphor. People are like a goldfish in the water. Just as the water is invisible to goldfish, people's thinking, practices, and environment are for the most part invisible to them. They are often so wrapped up in the routine of what they are doing that they may not be aware of the things they are doing that lead to unintended results. They may be working hard, yet not getting the results they want. Furthermore, they may not be able to figure out why or what to do about it. This can lead to all kinds of negative self-assessments, like "I'm not capable," "Others don't like me," "I can't win," or "I don't know what to do." The net effect is often very frustrating.

The purpose of a coaching conversation is to extract people from the water so that they can see the patterns of thinking and action that are getting them into trouble. A coach then helps people alter those patterns with wisdom, compassion and a sense of humor. When people go back into the water, you notice that they are clearer, freer, more powerful, and that their actions are more in line with where they want to go.

Committed Listening Is the Foundation

When people think of a coach, they often think of someone who has all the answers or who offers advice that tells people what to do. While it's useful to know something about the field in which you are coaching and to be able to offer advice, this kind of interaction with people can be very disempowering. Says Michel Renaud, a longtime friend and colleague who focuses on coaching chief executives and managers, "When you start giving people the solutions, it's easy to take away their power. You take away their game and you take away their accountability. You have to keep in mind that it is their game and their accountability."[1]

It is better to ask questions and to listen.

To have an empowering coaching relationship, the coach must recognize that people have the inherent creativity, intelligence, and tacit knowledge they need to succeed but may need help in gaining access to it.

A committed listener helps people think more clearly, work through unresolved issues, and discover the solutions they have inside them. This often involves listening beyond what people are saying to the deeply held beliefs and assumptions that are shaping their actions.

If you listen closely enough, you will discover that people's beliefs and assumptions are contained in almost everything they say and do. For example, someone might say "I think the problem in this group is that we need leadership, someone to take a position on issues and, if necessary, make a decision." This statement may reveal that the person's whole attitude about leadership is based on the idea of a single, solitary leader who has all of the answers rather than a leader who can help to harness a group's collective intelligence.

Listen for where people make observations and then make assessments that are completely arbitrary, or where they jump to conclusions. Listen for gaps and inconsistencies in people's thinking. Listen for where people have used defensive reasoning to protect themselves and distorted reality as a result. Asking questions that help people become aware of how their assumptions, beliefs, and attitudes may be helping or hindering them in getting the result they want can create openings for moments of true insight. These insights can be vital in penetrating individual or collective illusions.

When talking with the people you are coaching, it helps to create an atmosphere where people feel free to say whatever is on their minds. People may just need someone to talk to. They may say "I need to get things off my chest" or "I need to unload a bit." Being a committed listener at these times often means suspending judgment. In my experience, when people want to get things off their chest, they want someone to listen without agreeing or disagreeing so they can work through the unresolved issues for themselves. For example, a person may say "My boss is a jerk." If you agree or disagree, the communication can get stuck with the person either going on and on or trying to justify his or her point of view.

If you are willing to listen without agreeing or disagreeing, people will begin to see something that they didn't see before that allows them to disengage from their reactive thoughts or feelings. You might hear "You know what? I have been reflecting on this, and my boss really isn't that bad. I can see that I have really been upset with him and that I need to sit down with him and get clear about a few things."

When a coach listens deeply, people feel that at least one other person in their life understands. As Michel Renaud puts it, "I actually listen from the perspective of people being clear, that they are going to leave the conversation feeling clear and empowered. When I listen in this way, it's obvious that they don't need advice. I listen for their clarity and ask questions from that place. It is just magical."

Committed Speaking

The other side of coaching conversations involves committed speaking. Committed speaking starts with a sincere commitment to help people learn the lessons they need to take the next step in their journey toward excellence. If you have listened intently, you probably have some insights to share. Doing so, in a way that has impact, often requires being both tough and compassionate. This means speaking openly and honestly, while at the same time understanding what the other person is probably going through and not causing unnecessary upset. In most cases, however, openness and honesty take a back seat to not causing upset.

Though most people sincerely intend to speak with candor or "talk straight," they often wind up sugar coating their messages in order to avoid embarrassing or threatening the other person (or themselves). While this may seem natural and right, it can sometimes lead to sending mixed messages that prevent others from receiving the input they need to correct their errors and to learn. The other person may also interact with you in a defensive way that makes you feel cautious about being straight with them. If you alter your communication as a result of this, you become an accomplice to the individual's or group's defensive routines.

The reason we may be susceptible to doing this is that we have been conditioned to speak in ways rooted in certain social virtues—like getting approval, being nice, not upsetting people, minding our own business, and so on. Where most people tend to defer to others when they are stating their position in a way that makes it hard to disagree, or make face saving moves, or say things like "I don't want to discuss it," a coach has to operate in quite a different way. A coach has to be willing to discuss the undiscussable.

> *A coach has to be willing to discuss the undiscussable.*

I was once called in to coach a group of top executives in a large high-tech company. In the group, there was one person that had a distinct reaction every time he disagreed with someone—pounding the table, looking away, or talking to his neighbor. Most of the other members of the group appeared to be intimidated by his behavior. Over time, I observed that the group, at best, was only reaching superficial agreement. Every time the meetings got hot, the group would smooth the disagreement over or bypass the topic altogether. They had made this manager's behavior undiscussable and had colluded with one another in covering it up.

I gave some feedback to the group about what was going on, encouraging people to say what they were thinking about. I provided a model:

> *When you say ..., it makes me feel....*
> *I think it has this impact on the group....*
> *My request to you is....*

The result was that people started to open up and speak honestly about the situation. The manager had no idea how much disturbance he was creating by his unconscious behavior and began to work on it. In the next six months, the group's performance and team spirit improved dramatically.

Intervening Through Committed Speaking and Listening

To intervene is to step into the breach and help people reshape their fundamental patterns of thinking and practice that, if uninterrupted, will produce error. Intervening involves making certain observations and assessments of people and then giving them real-time feedback that allows them to learn. For example, when I am coaching an individual who has a tough goal and I see that person avoiding activities that take him beyond his comfort zone, I might say "Let's call a time out and talk." Or when I am coaching a meeting and I see some people advocating their positions to win while others who disagree silently withdraw, I say "Hold on a minute, let's freeze this conversation to look into what is going on."

As we have seen in Chapter 1, there are three kinds of interventions, whether we are talking about individuals or groups. The first kind of coaching has to do with *transforming who people are* (triple-loop learning) or altering the self-defining choices that result in people's way of being, winning formula, or defensive strategies. This type of intervention is used in "executive reinvention" engagements or anytime when people are producing unintended results and it is fairly obvious that a dramatic change in attitude or behavior is called for.

The second intervention has to do with coaching people to *learn to do new things* (double-loop learning). This involves reframing the governing variables around goals, problems, or solutions so that people see something that they didn't see before and thereby begin to redesign their actions. This is used especially with groups to transform impasses and defensive behavior into opportunities for breakthrough thinking and team learning.

The third kind of coaching is used to enable people to make incremental improvements, such as learning new skills. This involves *doing the same thing better* (single-loop learning).

Note: As both transforming who people are and helping them learn to do new things involve fundamentally reshaping underlying patterns of thinking and behavior, sometimes, for the sake of simplicity, I refer to them combined as transformational coaching. Transformational coaching is contrasted with incremental coaching, or doing the same thing better.

In this next section, we will look at two different applications of this distinction. The first approach involves *transforming people*, the second *transforming results*. The two coaching interventions are actually interrelated but have different focuses. *Transforming people* involves interacting with people in a way that produces a dramatic and fundamental change in their way of being, attitudes, and behaviors. *Transforming results* involves interacting with people in a way that expands their capacity to produce the results they need to achieve.

The time to focus on transforming people is when you notice that someone's way of being, attitude, or behavior is preventing them from getting the results they want or being satisfied, or is leading to breakdowns with other people. The time to coach people to transform results is when there is something that needs to be accomplished under conditions of time and pressure.

Here the focus is not on coaching attitudes and behavior, but on coaching actions.

The two kinds of intervention are related. Transforming people's frames of reference—the way they see things—directly impacts effective action. At the same time, coaching people to achieve results and to take successful action may require that you help transform their way of being, attitudes, and behaviors.

Transforming People

Personal transformation is a distinct domain with its own guiding principles and practices. Personal transformation involves helping people unearth what they care passionately about, as well as questioning their frames of reference, beliefs, and assumptions. As it is not possible to say everything about personal transformation in this chapter, the following metaphor will serve as a reference point.

Transformational Learning: Life as a Narrative

One way of looking at life is as a story that we tell about who we are. This story is our existential autobiography. As Jerome Bruner has pointed out, "The self is not a thing, but a point of view that unifies the flow of experience into a coherent narrative, a narrative striving to connect with other narratives and become richer." The way we tell our story about who we are is not just based on facts and events, but on how we interpret things. For example, you may think of yourself as a good leader because you are in a high position in an organization. Or you may believe that you are not a leader because of something that happened in the past that led you to conclude that you don't have leadership qualities.

It is important to understand that you and I do not just have a story, we are our story. Our story shapes, limits, and defines our way of being. It provides a frame of reference for our thinking and allows us to make sense of things. It tells us the rational way to behave.

Transformational coaching involves helping people surface, question, and reframe their stories when their current stories are disconfirmed or break down. For example, let's say you have a story about how you are a good leader. You collect evidence for that story in order to reinforce it. However, you get some coaching feedback that indicates that people at work think you are a stiff, humorless dictator. Your son also tells you you're a jerk for always trying to run his life. If you could hear that feedback without becoming crushed or defensive, you might start to surface and question your whole story about being a leader. You might reframe your point of view so that you see leadership in some way other than dominating people. Then one day you wake up and realize that you no longer have to draw your self-esteem as a leader from having to win; you can listen and be influenced. You no longer need to be right—you can say "I don't know"; you can become an inquirer.

There are three key points to keep in mind in setting the stage for transformational coaching.

1. It's important for people to make a free and clear choice to participate, as accepting transformational coaching may fundamentally change them.

2. It's also important for people to understand that the self is not something fixed, but something that is fluid and pliant, in a continual process of becoming.

3. People can transform who they are by reframing their point of view about themselves, their particular perspective, as well as their opinions and assumptions. This is always an emotional process as people have a lot invested in their old frames.

"Rut" Stories and "River" Stories

When engaging in a coaching conversation, a masterful coach understands that there are two kinds of stories people tell—rut stories and river stories.[2] Rut stories keep people stuck in old ways of being and thinking patterns and result in inaction. You'll recognize rut stories when there is no clarity and power in people's speaking and when they are looking at things in a crooked or distorted way that leads to individual or collective illusions. Rut stories often come from negative psychological assessments that result in taking things personally; from using defensive reasoning; or from inaccurate or obsolete paradigms or work practices that cause people to do the same thing even though the results are never different.

River stories are generally those of personal growth, self-renewal, and transformation. When people tell a river story, they speak with clarity, power, authenticity, and vulnerability regarding their growth edges, learning places, and breakdown spots. River stories are those where people reflect on and inquire into their way of looking at things, their deep beliefs, and their assumptions. This allows people to penetrate individual and collective illusions and to see things in a new way. It also leads to a new way of being and an expanded capacity to take effective action. River stories are always laced with wisdom, compassion, and humor and often contain a revelation of people's foolishness.

While river stories are born out of a commitment to learn and grow, rut stories develop when people use defensive reasoning to protect themselves. For example, people distort reality in order to save face, collude to avoid talking about any topic that could cause upset, and cover up errors by blaming others. These defensive stories and actions become so ingrained that people are hardly aware of them. They lead to unintended results, limited learning, escalating errors, and individual and collective illusions.

How do you transform rut stories into river stories? How do you speak and listen in a way that penetrates collective illusions? How do you break the grip of defensive reasoning when its self-sealing logic is leading to disaster?

Transforming Rut Stories Into River Stories

One thing is clear, transforming rut stories into river stories is not like a chat around the office water cooler. It involves engaging people in coaching conversations where you are dealing with them on at least four different levels of human experience:

1. Strengthening people's intention to create something in their lives that is not just an extension of the same old story
2. Reframing their mental maps
3. Using emotional energy as a source of transformation

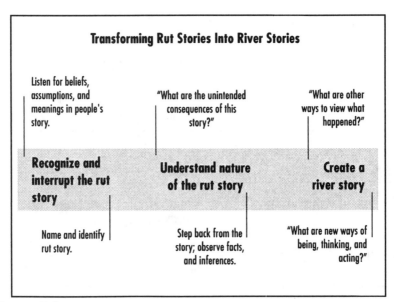

4. Letting go of physical blocks

The following methodology will help you transform rut stories into river stories. (See diagram 3.1.)

Transforming Rut Stories Into River Stories

Listen for beliefs, assumptions, and meanings in people's story.

"What are the unintended consequences of this story?"

"What are other ways to view what happened?"

Recognize and interrupt the rut story

Understand nature of the rut story

Create a river story

Name and identify rut story.

Step back from the story; observe facts, and inferences.

"What are new ways of being, thinking, and acting?"

Diagram 3.1

1. Recognize the rut story and interrupt it. There are many times when people will go on and on with their rut story. To break the spell of the story, pay very close attention to what people say with respect to what they want to create or the issues and problems they are having. Their story will provide lots of data from which to make observations and assessments about their way of being, beliefs, and attitudes.

I've found that the key is not just to pay attention to the plot line of the story, but to the structure of interpretation that people bring to it—the tacit beliefs, assumptions, meanings, and feelings that are there. There are times when the interpretation behind people's speaking, listening, or actions automatically throws up a red flag, and it becomes clear that the way they are looking at things will lead to unintended results.

This red flag is usually triggered by people speaking, listening, or acting in a way that is consistent with what I call a "classic" rut story.

The following archetypes will help you to understand the nature and consequence of classic rut stories. (See diagram 3.2.)

Rut Stories and Their Consequences	
The "I need other people's approval" story	People's intention to look good replaces intention to be good.
The "I'm afraid to lose what I have" story	People play it safe, take no risks.
The "artful victim" story	People give away their power and can't create what they want.
The "tranquilizing" story	People cover up incompetencies; no learning occurs.
The "Why bother?" story	People get stuck in resignation and do not create the future.

Diagram 3.2

- ★ **The "I need other people's approval" story.** People may not broadcast this story aloud, but they often tell it to themselves, constructing a whole series of pretenses and defenses in order to get other people's approval. The consequence is that the intention to look good often displaces the intention to be good (to perform and to create workable relationships).

- ★ **The "I'm afraid to lose what I have" story.** This story is often told by people who put off their visions, dreams, and aspirations in order to seek or keep their security. They often complain about their lives not being satisfying but, at the same time, they create lots of reasons to justify standing still. These people are generally nonplayers in the workplace, even though they may look like they are playing. The consequence is that they often spend their whole lives getting ready for everything to fall into place, only to discover that, like a seed, they have gone past their expiration date.

★ **The "artful victim" story.** This story is probably the most common. It involves people skillfully using defensive reasoning to create an open and shut case as to how other people or circumstances are doing them in. The consequence is that they often get stuck in this story, forfeiting all their power to other people or the situation, and then are unable to create what they want.

★ **The "tranquilizing" story.** Whenever people do not achieve a result, are incompetent at a task, or do something that gets them into trouble, they usually come up with a set of reasons and excuses. The purpose of the explanation is to tranquilize them and make them feel better about themselves. The consequence of doing this is that people do not highlight their own incompetence (which leads to limited learning), errors are covered up (which leads to more errors), and reality is distorted (which leads to individual and collective illusions).

★ **The "Why bother?" story.** People who tell this story say that they cannot create what they want because their possibilities and choices are limited. "I don't have the time. I don't have the authority. It's not in the budget." Oftentimes, this story is a cover-up for wanting to stay in their comfort zones or for not wanting to take responsibility. This often betrays an underlying attitude of resignation. The consequence is that people get stuck in this story and lose the ability to see the possibilities and options that they actually have.

When I hear people telling their particular version of a classic rut story, I intervene very aggressively: "Wait a minute. I think you are telling a classic rut story here and, in the process, digging a hole for yourself."

Intervening not only means interrupting the story in a literal sense, but more profoundly, speaking and listening with a strong intention to penetrate the illusions under which people may be operating. This involves breaking the grip of their existing structure of interpretation—frames, beliefs, assumptions, and meanings. Here are some examples of how to interrupt someone's rut story and promote reflection and learning.

> *Coach:* I am getting the impression that you are telling an "approval seeking" story. It seems that you want to accomplish certain things that are very important to you, but it appears that you are designing your actions to be reasonable and nice and perhaps to make yourself look good, rather than to create what you want.

> *Coachee:* Well, maybe you have a point, but I need approval to get my goals accomplished.

> *Coach:* Let's dig into this.

> *Coach:* You say you don't have enough time to create the strategic plan for your division because you are always in meetings. This could be an example of what I call a "tranquilizing story"—something you give as an explanation.

> *Coachee:* Well, it's true.

> *Coach:* Do you really need to go to all those meetings? Let me make a provocation. Is the problem really that you can't say no but you use the meeting story to justify your not having enough time to create your plan?

A coach should point out the difference between a rut story and a river story, as well as teach people to inquire into and reflect on stories in a manner similar to that illustrated above. After a time, people will intuitively understand whether or not their opinions, assumptions, and beliefs are going to help them produce the results they want: "Wait a minute. I hear myself telling a rut story. I'd like to step back and look at that for a moment."

2. Break the grip of the story by making people aware of its self-sabotaging nature and unintended consequences. Often when people are telling a classic rut story, they are not even aware of it. In effect, they are frozen into their story. At this stage, you need to say something that creates a meltdown or unfreezes the story and creates the readiness to change. By identifying and naming the story, you help people become aware of it. By making people more conscious of the unintended consequences of their story, you set the stage for them to extricate themselves from it.

> *Coach:* I hear you telling a "why bother" story about your efforts to introduce TQM improvements. You say you don't have the resources or budget. You sound resigned.

> *Coachee:* I could do something but first I need to have the resources and support. I feel like giving up.

> *Coach:* Do you realize that if you give up, you automatically forfeit your ability to create the future that you want or the difference you want to make.

> *Coachee:* Yes, that is true, but I am blocked in.

> *Coach:* There may be other ways to look at it. Instead of focusing on what you can't do, determine if there is anything that you can do with the resources you have right now that might bring a success.

★ ★ ★

> *Coach:* You and your colleague seem set on different versions of the story and you both seem intent on placing blame. What I hear is what I call the "artful victim" story.

You have a lot of reasons for why you are getting blocked. You're each very skillful in building your cases, yet is that getting either of you where you want to go?

Coachee: No, we seem to have backed each other into a corner and we can't move forward.

Coach: Perhaps, if you asked him to say more about his reasoning process, it might help open the lines of communication.

3. Transform rut stories into river stories by enabling people to revise their interpretations and see things in a new way. Coaching people to revise their stories often involves helping people to see that they are the authors of their stories. They may not have freely chosen what happened to them in life or work, but they constructed what the story meant to them. It's important to emphasize that people get stuck in their stories or become ineffective in their actions when they interpret things in an inflexible or rigid way. By seeing the self as fluid and by using "flexible framing," people can begin to see things in a new way. People can revise their stories and develop a new point of view about themselves, others, or the circumstances.

One way to assist people in revising their stories or being more flexible with their interpretations is to help them take a second look at their observations of what actually happened and the assessments they made about it. Observations are based on directly observable data; assessments are the judgments (inferences) made about those observations. Normally, people do not distinguish between the two and get into trouble when they take assessments as fact, when in reality they are only interpretations.

Assessments are often heavily influenced by the tendency to take things personally, blame others, or explain things away. Asking people to distinguish between their observations and assessments can help to put a crack in this structure of interpretation.

Coach: On what observations are you basing your assessment that the head of the other department doesn't like you and doesn't encourage others to cooperate with you?

Coachee: I know they are under the gun to complete their own projects, but they come late to meetings.

Coach: Do you see that you went from that observation to the assessment that it was personal and to the conclusion that they didn't want to cooperate?

(or)

Coach: Is what you are saying about the other group a fact or an interpretation?

Once people begin to step back a bit from their stories, the next step is to generate alternative interpretations. Your job as the coach is not to provide people with a better belief system than the one they already have. Yet, it would be foolish to forsake your wisdom, intuition, and insight. If you want to offer advice, it is better to say something like "I have a belief that..." rather than "I think this is how you ought to look at it." Another approach is to ask people to come up with their own alternative interpretations.

Coach: How else could you look at this?

Coachee: I see that I have to include other people's points of view a lot more in my reality.

Coach: What else?

Coachee: I also see that I tend to point a finger when something goes wrong, rather than to hold up a mirror.

Sometimes these everyday incidents can reveal the part of a person's existential narrative that is most narrow or constraining to them, as well as the classic stories they are stuck in. Doing the kind of work described above will often open up big cracks in the person's paradigms and give you the opportunity to do the inner healing work that needs to take place for personal transformation. As people expose their thinking, it's important to give them permission to express their emotions. Emotions can be a powerful source of transformational energy, and expressing them can help people to let go of a point of view that keeps them stuck, helping them to see something they didn't see before.

There are appropriate ways to elicit emotions even though the cultural environment in business doesn't always encourage it. Let's say a person is full of righteous indignation about the boss not listening and seems sad and angry about it. The coach might say "I welcome your emotions about this." Another simple approach is to say "Tell me about your emotions as you speak." When people get things off their chests, they often drop defensive reasoning and the wall of arguments they have constructed to protect themselves. This can suddenly create an opening for moments of true insight.

> *Coachee:* I always say that my boss doesn't listen. Now that I've got this fear and anger off my chest, I am starting to see that I go to the table already assuming he won't listen and thus don't put my ideas across.

It's important to acknowledge people for their vision, courage, and commitment as they open up new possibilities for themselves.

> *Coach:* Your commitment to self-improvement is really inspiring to me and I am sure it will pay off in terms of results.

Transforming Results

Thus far the focus has been on how to transform people's ways of being, attitudes, and behavior with the idea of helping them create the results that they really want. Yet this kind of inside work needs to be balanced with coaching people to accomplish the tasks that need to be done. Transforming results comes into play when people have to achieve something that they or the organization has a lot at stake in, but it seems that they are not able to do it on their own, at least not in the given time frame. In other words, people's goals have taken them to the borders of their way of being, competence, and skills, and they need help to proceed.

In coaching people to achieve better results, you obviously have to have a clear sense of what the goals and objectives are. However, the key thing is to manage people's actions. The intention is to empower and enable people to take successful action, action that is directly related to producing concrete results. This may involve expanding their capacity to act in ways that perhaps they have not even imagined or to act in ways that they know are necessary but which they have not previously been able to do. Experience shows that if you manage people only on their goals, the coaching process becomes too loose: "Here's the goal. Come back to me when you have the result." Also, managing people only on big or long-term goals can be overwhelming or even paralyzing. It's like taking a young baseball player to the ballpark and saying "hit home runs, hit home runs, hit home runs" without talking about how to grip the bat, stand, or swing.

> *One of the most important action steps a coach can take is to simply keep people in action, even if they are not successful at first.*

The question is on what specific actions can you manage people that will help them reach their objectives. A coach needs to think backward from the objective, through the major milestones, key tasks, and action steps that need to be taken, and then assess the coachee's ability to accomplish these. You can do this simply by observing where people's attempts to take committed action lead to breakdowns. Next, assess what people may need to be able to take successful action—a new way of being, mental map, attitude, behavior, skill, or action prescription. Then work with them on whatever the next step is.

One thing to keep in mind is that learning to do things that are fundamentally different than what has been done before is tough because it puts people in touch with their ignorance, highlights their incompetence, and is potentially embarrassing. Therefore, in asking someone to accomplish something new or different, a coach must take into account that people will tend to avoid any action that puts them in an embarrassing or upsetting situation. One of the most important action steps a coach can take is to simply keep people in action, even if they are not successful at first. For example, in coaching people to make enrollment calls for our personal transformation seminars, we noticed that many people would get uncomfortable and create lots of ways to avoid this task. When people are coached to stay in the action, however, they eventually pass through their fear, fine-tune their skills, and get results.

Coaching in this way requires a much tighter kind of management than most people are used to. In today's organizations, management by objectives, autonomy, and independence have become sacred cows, and have resulted in a loose style of management, which is actually a disservice to people. What is often required, especially when people are stretched, is a tight style of management or at least a balance between loose and tight styles. It's important for anyone doing coaching to observe and assess their own resistance to managing people in this way. "I don't want to step on people's toes," "I will tell people what, but not how," and "He has to learn to think for himself" are the standard refrains. As one top coach once told me, "I found that to bring a player through to the next level, I had to be all over him like flies on honey."

Once you get people in action, it's important to keep them there by teaching them the new skills and capabilities they need to succeed. One key is to make sure that you set attainable short-term goals with people that will give them the experience of winning.

The coach has to be constantly observing and assessing what people need to take effective action and to provide what's missing. It's important at these times to be able to step back from it all and have a coaching conversation.

Coaching People to Take Successful Action

Coaching people to take successful action starts with focusing on the places where they have been unsuccessful. As Sara Schley, a coaching practitioner, says, "I tell people that for me to coach in a way that makes a difference, they'll need to focus on those areas where they are most stuck or ineffective. Though exposing one's learning edges, growth spots, and breakdown places can be embarrassing, to do so can create the opening for people to take a big step forward in their lives. I ask people to take on a beginner's mind and look at what they can learn rather than to protect themselves. For me as a coach, it's important to be compassionate with people as they wrestle with these areas of personal challenge and breakdown."[3] (See diagram 3.3.)

- ★ **Ask people to tell you about a recent time when they were stuck or ineffective.** It's important to be as specific and concrete as possible. These "small" incidents can reveal gaps or inconsistencies in people's thinking or where their action didn't work. The idea is to gain insight into the patterns of thinking and behavior people are unaware of that will lead to repeated mistakes. Ask people to recap what happened: "What was your intention in the situation? Who did what? How did that make you feel? Then what did you do?"

- ★ **Penetrate illusions by asking people to give examples of the assessments they have made.** It's important to listen not only to what happened but to the assessments people made about it. Oftentimes, when people do not get the results they want, they start making all kinds of subjective interpretations that they treat as fact. For example, "We made a great presentation but didn't get the boss to sign off. He says he cares about quality but he is a liar and a phony. On the other hand, I feel like a failure." This is what is called being "high" on the ladder of inference. The ladder of inference is a useful tool for helping people become aware of their often automatic reasoning processes. It helps people

MAP: Coaching People to Take Effective Action

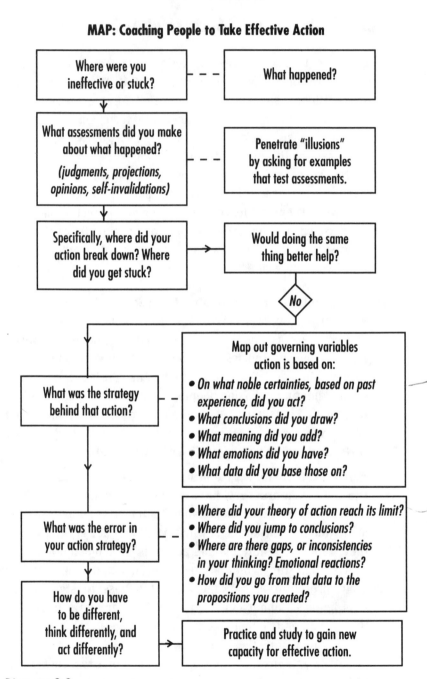

Diagram 3.3

see the places where they have jumped to conclusions, been inconsistent in their thinking, or camouflaged error with defensive reasoning.[4] (See diagram 3.4.) What the coach needs to do is walk people down the ladder with the intent of "grounding" assessments that might lead to self deception, lack of learning, or escalating error. In this example, a coach might ask "What led you to conclude you made a good presentation? What witnessable data or examples do you have to support your contention that the boss is a liar and a phony? Does this really mean you are a failure?"

★ **Ask people to be specific about where their actions seemed to break down or where they got stuck.** Asking people to be specific about where they got stuck or where their actions started to misfire is very important in determining the kind of coaching you will give. It could be that a person was taking the right action and only needs coaching for incremental improvement on how to do the same thing better. For example, a person might say "I was being diplomatic and it was working, but the person suddenly started acting like a fish and I got mad. I need some ideas on staying cool." Or a person might require transformational coaching that helps to alter a way of being, thinking, or practice so that his or her capacity for effective action is expanded. A person might say "I have always been diplomatic. But in this situation, I was not able to get any commitment from Fritz. Being diplomatic just was not effective. I need to learn to be more forthright and confrontive."

★ **Help people reveal the strategies behind their actions.** Let's assume that you have determined that people need to go beyond fine-tuning their existing approach and do fundamentally different things. This often involves helping them break through old thinking patterns and practices that seem natural and right. Start by asking people to map out the strategy behind the action, taking into account such things as their personal preferences, reasoning processes, or

Ladder of Inference

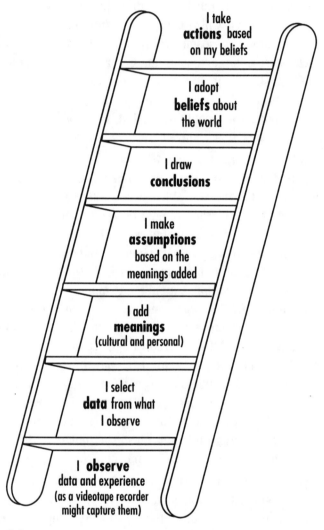

I take **actions** based on my beliefs

I adopt **beliefs** about the world

I draw **conclusions**

I make **assumptions** based on the meanings added

I add **meanings** (cultural and personal)

I select **data** from what I observe

I **observe** data and experience (as a videotape recorder might capture them)

Diagram 3.4

emotional reactions. Taken as a whole, these things represent an internal framework or "structure" that is often triggered by a situation. The ladder of inference is helpful in identifying these structures.

A coach might ask the following questions to elicit a person's framework: "What do you see as the sensible way to act in such situations? What conclusions did you draw? What was the witnessable data that influenced you? What emotions did you have?" A coachee may map out this scenario: "I felt attacked and took it personally. I then defended myself by explaining what I thought had really happened. I see at that point that I was no longer driven by closing the sale but by protecting myself and avoiding losing."

★ **Help people discover where there are errors in their action strategies.** Often when the strategy for action becomes clear, its limits or errors become clear as well. However, if not, ask more questions that help reveal the errors and breakdowns of the strategy. "Where did you jump to conclusions? Where were there gaps or inconsistencies in your thinking? How did you go from that data to your proposition that...? Where did your theory of action reach its limits?" Taking the time to draw out the answers to these kinds of questions can allow people to gain insight into the often automatic and unconscious behavior they have.

Coach: You say your natural tendency is to ask a lot of questions and draw out the people in the group. You have a theory that says to involve people and not to dominate them. In this situation, do you see where this course of action might have caused unintended consequences?

Coachee: Yes, I believe in this situation people were waiting for me, as the boss, to say where I stood and were probably getting suspicious of me because I was not revealing what I thought. Now that I think it through, I might have appeared wishy-washy and indecisive to them.

★ **Have people reflect on how they have to be different, think differently, and act differently.** As people begin to see the error in their theories of action, they can begin to declare new ways of being, discover how they need to think about things differently, and design new actions.

Coach: You've been ineffective in getting people to enroll in your project. You believe that to win people over you have to convince them with the logic of your arguments. You have seen that while this provides rational reasons for people to participate, it does not touch them in a way that aligns what is important to them with the project. How do you need to think about things differently and act differently? How would you have to be different to do that?

Coachee: It is clear that I have to spend more time with people and open up more to them, asking lots of questions and really listening. Then, to enroll them in my project, I need to show people how participating can help them fulfill their own purpose and intents.

The coach may also offer suggestions. It is important to do this in a way that does not disempower people.

Coach: I have a belief that in order to get people's voluntary emotional commitment, you have to show how being involved will help them realize their own visions or purposes. Finding out what is important to people demands that you spend some time talking with them. This is often a very intimate conversation and will require your asking questions and listening carefully to what people say. Have you had a conversation like this before?

Coachee: Yes, I have. But I have had some difficulty asking people personal questions.

Coach: It takes a lot of coaching and practice to learn how to ask questions and listen in a way that draws out what really matters to people. Jack in marketing is really good at this. How would you feel about working with him for a while and using him as a model?

It is important to emphasize here that knowing what to do is not the same as knowing how to do it. The person mentioned above may have difficulty being open, asking questions, and listening. It often takes lots of practice and study over a period of time to take on and stabilize new ways of being, thinking, and acting. (We will look more closely at this in Chapter 8, "Teaching New Skills and Capabilities.")

The Myth of Icarus

In Greek mythology, Icarus, seduced by his own power after putting on wax wings, flies too close to the sun. As he does, his artificial wings melt and he falls into the sea and dies.

There is a good lesson here for all of us that gets to the heart of this book. Like Icarus, many of us have great strengths that seduce us. These strengths often lead to our early successes. But eventually we become so enamored of them or overly reliant on them that we cover up our weaknesses. Or we fail to recognize the need to change something that seems natural and right. To expose our weaknesses or to change something with which we have been successful and then to do something new is difficult, especially if we are full of pride. It requires not only a commitment to change, but to learning.

Coaching is having both the toughness and compassion to skillfully intervene in people's learning processes. A successful coaching relationship is always a story of transformation, not just of higher levels of performance. It's a story that takes people beyond their immediate passion and pride and helps them to come to grips with the fact that to reach what is really possible and achievable for them, they must be willing to fundamentally question who they are, what they do, and why they do it.

To challenge and support someone else in their story of transformation goes beyond doing something for others and extends to ourselves. To have someone invite us to participate in his or her transformational learning process is not just an opportunity but a gift, a gift to the human spirit. It's the opportunity to look up from what we are trying to accomplish and the mundane aspects of daily affairs and to see the hidden meaning behind all that we do. It's learning not only to recognize who other people are and what they are magnificently capable of but also to know ourselves at the same moment.

Part II

Coaching for Team Learning: The Fundamentals

This section focuses on a small group of people that come together around a purpose larger than themselves. This is the generative point for transformation and learning at the organization level. I have found that people who have had more personal transformation experience are more likely to be creative and productive group members. They have the skills to reframe problems and solutions, they are more conscious of the way they think and interact, and they tend to be reflective rather than protective.

At the same time, I have found that just coaching people for a personal transformation does not have enough impact on overall group or organization performance, on the way people think and interact, or on group defensive routines. People who are otherwise creative, productive, and learning oriented often cling to static ideas and become counterproductive and defensive when in group settings.

Most approaches to improving organizations focus on team building and changing processes, yet do not go deep enough to yield sustainable results in terms of team learning or changing the way people think and interact. This section, then, focuses on the coaching practitioner applying the governing values and the coaching fundamentals to creating productive work groups and communities of practice.

As we shift our focus from transforming individuals to transforming groups, one thing that can have enormous impact on the way people think and interact is reeducating people in the governing values. This happens through the coach's or facilitator's application of these values in practice sessions or during performance-oriented meetings. People build shared vision rather than just pursue their own purposes, develop a shared approach rather than just fight in their own corners, and optimize the whole, not just the parts. Again, the governing values are

1. Foster internal commitment to goals and learning

2. Provide valid information, illustrating assessments with specific examples

3. Give people free and informed choice in deciding whether or not to change

That being said, this section is squarely focused on the fundamentals of coaching. While we will be looking at coaching teams, the same principles apply to coaching individuals. In discussing the topics in this section, it is impossible to say everything. What I have tried to do, instead, is to provide some navigation points that can have direct and immediate impact as well as provide direction for further learning. I see this book as just a thread in a tapestry that many people are working on today with the intent of creating transformation and learning in groups and communities. The coaching fundamentals are

1. Setting stretch goals

2. Eliciting internal commitment and motivation and self-directed learning

3. Creating a successful theory of action

4. Practicing the fundamentals

5. Observing breakdowns

6. Providing meaningful feedback

7. Teaching new skills and capabilities

CHAPTERFOUR

Stretch Goals, Yearning, and Learning

Ah, but a man's reach should exceed his grasp, or
what's a heaven for?

Robert Browning

Setting Stretch Goals

Five days after Russian cosmonaut Yuri Gagarin's historic flight in space, President John Kennedy summoned Lyndon Johnson for a no-nonsense talk in the Oval Office. "I want you to tell me where we stand in space. Do we have a chance of beating the Soviets by putting a laboratory into space? Or by a trip around the moon? Or a rocket to the moon and back with a man? Is there any space program which promises dramatic, breakthrough results?" President Kennedy knew that what was needed was a bold step and that now was the time. By creating a clear and compelling vision of landing a man on the moon, Kennedy was able to rally the will of the people, as well as the knowledge and resources, to beat the Soviets to the moon.

What can you do to create a future for your organization and get a jump on the competition? To your dismay, you see your company vision isn't based on a point of view of the future, rather it's based on doing more of the same. And you see people operating in the comfort zone and the company being pushed along by the momentum of the marketplace. The same question needs to be asked if you are a team leader or coach. Your team's performance is good enough, but you have a gut feeling that good enough isn't good enough.

One thing you can do is set some stretch goals. More and more executives are realizing that setting incremental goals, worthwhile or not, invites people to carry out the same comfortable processes year after year. Stretch goals force people to develop new products and services and reinvent their current business processes. To reach a stretch goal, people have to think and learn "outside of the box."

> **S**tretch goals force people to develop new products and services and reinvent their current business processes.

Company leaders, like Frank Shrontz of Boeing, GE's Jack Welch, and L.D. DeSimone of 3M, realize that if you don't demand something out of the ordinary, you won't get something out of the ordinary. In fact, there is a lot of evidence developing that shows that setting ambitious goals provides people with the leverage to accomplish more. Judith Rosen, a consultant with CSC Index, notes, "Our data showed that one key difference between companies that win or lose at reengineering is that the winners aim high at the outset. High achievers hit the target, low achievers missed it by half. This was true for all goals—market share increases, reduction in cycle times, quality and productivity improvements."[1]

Dennis Gormley, CEO of Federal Mogul Corporation, an auto parts manufacturer, used stretch goals to increase productivity and create value. He says, "Setting an impossible goal forces everybody to sit down, rethink everything, and break away from all the old traditions and habits. Goals that don't force that kind of exercise miss a tremendous opportunity."[2] (See diagram 4.1.)

According to Gormley, stretch goals are a good way to create a sense of urgency from within rather than waiting for the problems to create that urgency from the outside. To do this, Gormley set goals to slash lead times to days instead of months, to generate the flexibility to build whatever auto parts the market demands (whether millions of pieces or one piece), to improve productivity by 30 percent,

Stretch Goals Demand

New knowledge
and resources,
New ways of being

Existing knowledge
and resources,
Old ways of being

Today's Results

Diagram 4.1

and to reduce scrap and rework by half—all to be accomplished in three years.

At Boeing, CEO Shrontz found that while the company's planes were sleek and trim, the manufacturing process was slow, primitive, and cumbersome. Shrontz set targets of cutting the manufacturing costs by 25 percent and cutting the cycle time needed to build a plane from eighteen months to eight months, all within four years. Likewise, at GE, Chairman Jack Welch says "We used to nudge the peanut, moving along from 4.73 inventory turns to 4.91, now we want the big stretch like ten turns or fifteen turns."

3M has traditionally had a goal of generating 25 percent of its revenue from products developed within the previous four years. This led to products like Scotch™ Tape and Post-it™ Notes. In recent years though, the goal has seemed to lose its magic. So CEO DeSimone increased the goal to 35 percent, encouraging managers to look for possible blockbuster products and rush them to market. He asked for breakthrough thinking and got it. A team developed a never-rust "scouring pad," made from recycled plastic bottles, to replace steel wool. 3M put up a plant and launched the product in one year, capturing a stunning 22 percent of the $100 million market.[3]

The Principle of Stretch

"Stretch" is not just about setting goals but is a core principle of coaching that applies to implicit goals, intentions, visions, and purposes. Many people are more motivated by fundamental visions and values than goals. As Miami Dolphin's coach Don Shula says, "I think goals are often overrated." Though we will be talking about goals here, the primary thrust is to coach people in groups to achieve extraordinary results consistently by stretching their minds and their skills. I have found that there is a place that people stop in trying to produce the results they really want, and often some coaching can help people move past that point and produce a breakthrough.

Years back, I was coaching someone in our office in making enrollment calls to executives for an upcoming Transformational Leadership seminar. After making a call, the enroller got off the phone and said that the person didn't want to do the seminar and had given various reasons and excuses. I sensed from what the enroller said that the person very much wanted to participate but just had cold feet. I challenged the enroller to get back on the phone and not get off until the person signed up. The conversation that followed took exactly five minutes. The person showed up at the coaching program, which made a big difference for both himself and his group.

The fact is that most people are capable of achieving more than they think is possible to achieve. The only reason that they don't is that they get caught in limiting beliefs and assumptions or because they get discouraged and want to give up.

The same principle applies to organizations. They, too, are capable of achieving more than they thought possible. Gary Hamel and C.K. Prahalad write "Think of General Motors versus Toyota. CBS versus CNN. Pan Am versus British Airways. RCA versus Sony. Suppose you had been asked 10 or 20 years ago to choose the victor in each of these battles? Where would you have placed your bets? With hindsight, the choice is easy. But at the time, GM, CBS, Pan Am, and RCA all had stronger reputations, deeper pockets, greater technological riches. Only a dreamer could have predicted that each would be displaced by a competitor with far fewer resources but far greater aspirations."

As Hamel and Prahalad point out in the article, "Strategy as Stretch," by coaching people to stretch, you consciously and intentionally create a gap between your group's aspirations and the knowledge and resources that are available.[4] This gap produces what Bob Fritz, author of *Creating*, calls "creative tension"—something that people naturally seek to resolve.[5] (See diagram 4.2.) If the goal is really meaningful to people, it releases their personal and collective aspirations and mobilizes them into action. The goal is a leverage point for both personal and organizational change and learning. As people strive to reach the goal, it becomes part of their personal process of becoming.

Four Principles for Setting Stretch Goals

★ *The principle of aspiration: "Who do we want to be?"* We each have personal aspirations and a desire to excel. Our aspirations are often embedded in the work that we do in groups, organizations, and communities. For example, we may want to be part of a group that comes up with a landmark biotechnology medicine or part of a group that is known for the highest quality or outstanding service. Yet, oftentimes, the bar of excellence is too low to release the collective

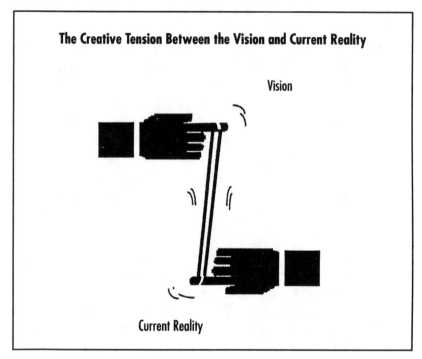

The Creative Tension Between the Vision and Current Reality

Vision

Current Reality

Diagram 4.2

aspirations of the group or to inspire people to bring their whole selves to work. The role of the coach is to inspire people to raise the bar of excellence. Creating a stretch goal is one way to release the collective aspirations of the group and inspire extraordinary levels of commitment from the individual. The examples of the Apollo moon landing and 3M bear this out.

★ *The principle of lever: "How do we apply our resources so they can make the biggest difference?"* One of the defining characteristics of a stretch goal is that it is something that, while exciting, seems difficult or almost impossible to achieve. As mentioned, for the goal to be a stretch, it should create a deliberate mismatch between the group's aspirations and ambitions and its present knowledge and resources. This means that to achieve the goal, people need to learn to get more out of what they have. One of the functions of a coach is to help people do just that. This not only applies to deriving more from material resources, but to tapping the hidden reserve of creativity and effectiveness that is usually available in any group. When you create a deliberate mismatch between what needs to be achieved and what people already think and know, you force people to think outside the box and to move beyond the limits of their existing paradigms.

★ *The principle of convergence*: "What can we create together?" There is an old Greek saying: "Alone we can be great; together we can be greater." Stretch goals allow people to come together to create something larger than themselves. The coach's role is often to act as a steward in this process of convergence. It helps if the group is a natural group with a common calling, like wanting to design and implement a learning approach rather than a bureaucratic one. It also helps if each person has something to contribute that makes the group more powerful.

★ *The principle of concentration*: "What are one or two goals to focus on?" Peter Drucker, in his book *The Effective Executive*, has said that the single most important principle of human effectiveness is concentration. My experience shows that there need to be one or two long-term, inspirational goals that become navigation posts to the future and that ensure different people and departments are focused on the same thing. The principle of concentration also is applied to concentrating resources on key strategic goals where they can have the most impact. I have found that in small teams, people cannot hold their focus on goals that are too big or too long. The coach can help by getting the team focused on measurable objectives that can be done in weeks, not months. (Chapter 12 will detail coaching strategies for designing breakthrough projects that do just that.)

Several years ago, I was doing a consulting project for Adidas. The company was slipping behind Reebok and Nike and it didn't have the advertising dollars to compete. The company's marketing chief, Rob Strasse, and ex-Nike man, decided to spearhead a breakthrough by focusing actions in a small area. His theory was to create a new image for the company through a "mark" called "adidas, equipment." Then he asked the product development people to develop a small range of "equipment" shoes and textiles in the different sports categories. The last step was to focus all advertising dollars on the adidas equipment line. The theory was that by making this part of the line successful, even though it only represented 15 percent, the rest of the company would be turned around. Not only were the results extremely successful, but the idea energized people, moving them from feeling like they were caught in the discouraging complexity of the situation to feeling like they had a reason to wake up in the morning and conquer the world.

Guidelines for Setting Stretch Goals

1. Get key stakeholders together; talk about stretch goals and why they are important. Stretch goals are seldom achieved through the organization chart but rather through a network of turned-on, talented people throughout the organization. Emphasize that people can't really succeed in today's competitive environment by looking for ordinary or predictable results or by being run-of-the-mill in their approach. People can only succeed by looking for creative, entrepreneurial, breakthrough results. To validate this claim, use some examples from other groups or companies. In the earlier example, Toyota, CNN, British Airways, and Sony were all challengers who set stretch goals to become the leaders. The companies they challenged sat back, rested on their laurels, and acted as if leadership was a natural birthright. Stress that once challengers become leaders, they must continue to set stretch goals to maintain their leadership. (See diagram 4.3.)

2. Perform a team audit of future opportunities and today's breakdowns. Have a dialogue on the opportunities and issues the group is facing in order to assess where to set stretch goals. Prahalad and

---

Setting Stretch Goals

1. Get key stakeholders together; talk about stretch goals and why they are important.

2. Perform a team audit of today's breakdowns and opportunities.

3. Create one or two stretch goals.

4. Create a "case for action" that explains the importance of the goal and that builds motivation.

5. Explore how the goal is personally meaningful to individual players.

6. Emphasize that reaching the goal will require learning.

Diagram 4.3

Hamel emphasize the importance of helping people think in terms of regenerating their company, not just reengineering its processes. It is, therefore, important to ask questions that help develop a point of view about the future, as well as to recognize performance opportunities in today's processes. Some sample questions are "What assumptions is the organization making about strategy or customer needs that are no longer valid? What breakdowns are showing up and in what functions of the organization? Do we have new products in the pipeline that will give us a future? What are our key customers saying about us or our competitors? What are marginal customers asking for that may represent a key to the future?"

3. Create one or two stretch goals. Whether you are coaching an individual, a group, or a business will determine what kind of stretch goals you set or aspirations you unleash. At the same time, a useful framework is to think in terms of setting one goal in the area of creating a new future and another goal in the area of improving today's problems. The following questions might stimulate some dialogue and discussion in choosing a goal.

★ Are our goals based on a point of view of the future? What are we doing to break new ground in our products and services?

STRETCH GOALS, YEARNING, AND LEARNING   ★ **93**

★ How can we make it much easier for our customers to do business with us?

★ How would we redesign a process from scratch, knowing what we now know?

★ Do we have any goals that would force our business processes to breakdown and, out of necessity, force us to reinvent them?

4. Create a "case for action" that tells why the goal is important and that builds commitment. People are often overwhelmed by a stretch goal because it doesn't "fit" their existing knowledge or resources. Instead of reducing the goal or trying to answer the question of how it will be achieved, create a compelling and urgent reason to achieve the goal. The thing to focus on is why the goal is important. This is done by building a "case for action" that is based on facts, not just interpretations, and real business needs, not just personal preferences. Start by asking each person in the group to take a piece of paper and write one or two paragraphs on why reaching the goal is important. After the group has done this, ask people to review what they have written. Then the group as a whole should write a one page case for action about why accomplishing the goal is important. Going through this process gives people the reasons why the goal should be a real focus. It helps to generate a sense of urgency about the goal; for example, "If we don't change, we will go out of business in eighteen months."

5. Discuss how the goal is personally meaningful to the individual players. The case for action represents the rational side of getting people involved. To enroll people to make a voluntary, emotional commitment to the stretch goal, hold a discussion about people's feelings about the stretch goal, as well as the challenges and opportunities in it for each of them. The coach should emphasize that the difference between internal commitment and the lack of it is the difference between real goals and pseudo goals or a real team and just a bunch of people sitting in a circle. Ask "How does going for the goal affect people's basic values?" Allow plenty of time for people to express what they are thinking and feeling. Help them to see the personal challenge and opportunity in going for the stretch goal. Make sure people understand what is being requested of them. At some point, each person must choose to be either in or out. Give everyone the opportunity to stand up and declare his or her own commitment.

6. Emphasize that reaching the goal will require learning. The coach needs to make it clear that stretch goals are those where the path to the result is unclear. Achieving the goal could require breakthrough thinking, team learning, and organizational change. It is important to carefully encourage and build on people's internal commitment to learning. Ask people to remember a time in their lives

> *O*ne misconception is that the coach is responsible for motivating people.

when they wanted to reach a goal and were willing to go through the bewilderment, frustration, and awkwardness of learning to reach it. At the same time, make people aware that learning is a double-edged sword, fascinating and exhilarating on the one side, potentially threatening and embarrassing on the other. A stretch goal not only requires people learning to question their frames, but developing new skills and unlearning old ones, and having patience with themselves and others. Ask people to adopt a beginner's mind and a learning orientation. Ask people what their personal stretches will be in reaching the goal and how they will have to think, speak, and act differently. (Chapter 9 includes an interview with Stephen Pook on using stretch goals to create a company breakthrough.) (See diagram 4.4.)

A Stretch Goal Requires Yearning

In order for people to go for a stretch goal, they have to have a hunger; they have to have a thirst; they have to have a yearning. No one is going to go for a stretch goal unless this is present. What we are really talking about (and it applies to coaching people in any context, not just stretch goals) is the whole issue of motivation—and this is often clouded by misconceptions.

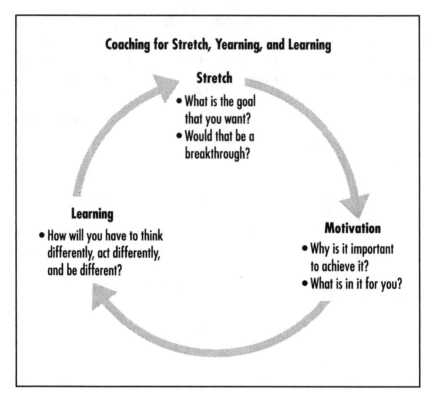

Coaching for Stretch, Yearning, and Learning

Stretch
- What is the goal that you want?
- Would that be a breakthrough?

Motivation
- Why is it important to achieve it?
- What is in it for you?

Learning
- How will you have to think differently, act differently, and be different?

Diagram 4.4

One misconception is that the coach is responsible for motivating people. In reality, the coach cannot really motivate anyone, and to think that he or she has to places a tremendous burden on the coach. A better way to frame the issue of motivation is that people are always already motivated by who they aspire to be and what is important to them. One of the things that a coach can do is to find out what it is that intrinsically motivates people and use that to help them reach personal or group stretch goals.

Many managers assume that people have to be motivated from the "outside in" with carrots and sticks, punishments and rewards, in order to get them to work. In most organizations, it is as if a compact exists that says that *extrinsic motivation* is the only kind of motivation there is. Yet, there is another kind of motivation that comes from the inside out, *intrinsic motivation*, that has to do with the people's need to express their real identities, dreams, and aspirations. What a masterful coach does is help people reveal their aspirations and find opportunities to use their inner motivations.

Unearthing What People Care About

The things that people care passionately about—their visions, values, personal aspirations—are often buried in their psyche. Most of us are born into a society that asks us to trade in our passion for life in order to earn a living. We are trained to get good marks in school, not for the sheer joy of learning, but to go on to become a doctor or lawyer or to get an MBA. The organizations that we join are geared to fulfill the first level of Abraham Maslow's "hierarchy of human needs"—food, clothing, and belonging—and rarely encourage us to think beyond that. Yet, at the same time that we are seeking these symbols of success and security, we have an inner yearning and questioning that asks "Is this all there is?"

A masterful coach can help people unearth what they care passionately about by asking them questions like "What is your vision?" "What is your purpose?" and "What really matters to you?" In our Transformational Leadership seminar, when we ask "What is your vision?" people most often talk about material success. When we ask "What is your purpose?" they often respond "to have a challenge" or "to find something interesting to do."

Regardless of what people say when I ask these questions, I provoke people by raising the stakes and getting them to think of themselves and their vision and purpose in larger terms: "You have a lot of potential. Do you really think your goals are ambitious enough?" Or I might use an inspirational quotation to help people think about their lives in terms of the contribution they want to make. For example, Albert Schweizer said "Though it's not always possible to know what your destiny will be, of this you can be certain. The only ones amongst you that will be truly happy, will be those that have sought and found how to serve."

Enrolling the Players

How does a coach think and operate when setting a stretch goal to create a team of fully motivated players? The first thing that the coach needs to do is to recognize that success in business today is largely a function of enrollment. In the past, as workers did the same thing over and over, they could more or less be told what to do. However, Peter Drucker has pointed out that, in today's business environment, everyone is a volunteer. People can't be told to be committed to a stretch goal or to think creatively or to act with initiative; they have to be enrolled. To enroll in this context means to elicit people's voluntary, emotional commitment to participate in a project by speaking to what they care passionately about or hold important. This is different than trying to convince them through force of argument or pressure.

> **A** coach must learn to ask people to do something in such a way that they will be delighted to do it.

The coach, as an inside person, can play a key role in enrolling players in the group or, as an outside person, in teaching people in the group how to enroll. I have observed that, while managers may enjoy creating strategic stretch goals, they often don't align these with people's personal visions or sense of real purpose. They often unconsciously operate from a command and control model rather than a commitment model while trying to get people to do things that they would otherwise not want to do. The result is that these managers never really elicit people's committed participation and then wind up frustrated when it seems that people don't care.

Enrolling people is not about making a demand, but about making an offer. In the movie "The Godfather," the Godfather said "I want to make you an offer you can't refuse." A coach must learn to ask people to do something in such a way that they will be delighted to do it. In enrolling people in a goal, project, or action request, find out what is important to them and frame your invitation in those terms rather than in terms of what is important to you or to the organization.

Obviously, you have to practice some deep listening in order to be able to determine the other person's frame of reference and what is important to him or her. For example, everyone wants to have the opportunity to be significant, to make a difference, and to have an impact. Thus, if you frame your offer in these terms, you are much *(handwritten star)* more likely to succeed. Of course, you must be sincere in your offer. Any attempt to manipulate people will likely be detected and backfire.

There are different levels of enrollment. At first people may be *(handwritten: See family)* in agreement intellectually, but not in alignment emotionally. Later, people may be aligned to the point of taking committed action, but they will only be capable of sustaining that action in the presence of the leader or with group support. The highest level of enrollment is when people can self-sustain committed action to a breakthrough goal or a transformational change effort, independent of the leader or group and in the absence of immediate results. At this level, people's enrollment is usually connected to their noblest aspirations and is deeply purposeful.

Steps in the Enrollment Process

★ Ask people what matters to them—their visions, purpose, aspirations.
★ Listen deeply with the sincere intention of drawing out what matters to people.
★ If you feel there is a match between what someone feels is important and what the team feels is important, tell that person your team's stretch goal.
★ Ask if people can see how being part of the team going for this stretch goal can help them to realize their own visions, goals, and purpose.

A Stretch Goal Requires Learning

One of the most important roles the coach has to play in reaching stretch goals or in helping people realize their aspirations is to encourage a basic attitude of learning in the group.

However, many business organizations have a corporate culture that puts a premium on "knowing." A manager is supposed to know in the same way that one's father or mother is supposed to know. The result is that managers are often uncomfortable with what they don't know and tend to protect their mistakes rather than see them as a learning experience. All of this has led to what Peter Senge has called *knowing organizations*, rather than *learning organizations*. A learning organization is one where people are continually expanding their capacity to create the desired future.[6]

In reality, this kind of learning organization cannot be formed without personal transformation on the part of a critical mass of people. This kind of personal transformation is a shift from the "attitude of knowing" to the "attitude of learning." Once this transformation occurs, a change occurs in people's behavior. They display a willingness to disclose their unresolved issues and uncertainties. They no longer act like they have it all together, assume that they know it all, or are certain that they are on the right track.

Encouraging a Basic Attitude of Learning

I have found that it is personally challenging to communicate to people what it is to have a basic attitude of learning, where people approach life as a learning opportunity rather than as a series of linear checkpoints on the calendar. A study at the University of Virginia showed that managers who approach their key events and tasks with this attitude are three to four times as successful as their colleagues who do not. In many cases, people agree with the idea of learning but resist when it leads to questioning their views or starts to highlight their ignorance or incompetence. They also tend to see learning as acquiring new content knowledge, such as ideas, tools, and methods, rather than as attempting personal change.

Again the kind of learning that we are encouraging in this book is transformational learning. This learning is based on the principle that the problems that need to be solved in organizations are inseparable from who people are and the way they think and interact. It involves questioning assumptions, not the least of which is the tendency to draw self-esteem from having the answers. It also involves a long-term commitment to continuous learning and improvement.

I once worked with a group of managers in a large European pharmaceutical company who were grappling with a major product development goal. In addition to being technically challenging, the goal required a much higher level of interdisciplinary teamwork than they were used to. Nonetheless, the managers acted as if they would be able to accomplish their goal using the expertise that was already in people's heads, as well as their routine work practices. It was clear that these managers, who behaved as arrogant know-it-alls, were going to have to change their viewpoint and begin seeing themselves as learners who were capable of saying "I don't know."

I asked them to write down on one side of a white board what it was they had to accomplish, breaking the goal down to key tasks and problems to be solved. I then had them write down on the other side of the board the kinds of approaches they would use to reach the goal, as well as everything they knew and didn't know about achieving the tasks. I then started asking them questions about how they would solve the various problems. One of the managers soon stood up and said "There is a big gap between who we are today and how we need to develop as human beings to reach this goal." From that point on, the managers stopped acting like they had all the answers and adopted a basic attitude of learning.

Designing an Environment for Learning

To be sure, once stretch goals are set that people care about, conditions are created in which learning should naturally ensue. Project teams with high goals tend to take on a learning organization environment as people are pushed to a state of "zero information" where prior knowledge does not apply. Here are some other ways that a coach can design an environment where learning occurs:

Make sure the goal leaves a lot of room for passion, commitment, and a sense of ownership. In Japan, top management makes sure that the goal leaves ample room for people to shape it according to their own personal interests. Seldom does top management hand out a razor-sharp product development concept or business process blueprint. For example, a team at Honda was given the challenge of designing a new concept car based on the figurative language "Let's Gamble." This created an atmosphere where people had to define their own goals and set their own agendas.

Encourage self-directed learning. Don't tell people what to learn. Instead, provide them with learning opportunities. For example, the Honda team that was building the new concept car was invited to spend a summer "look[ing] around at what's happening in Europe."[7] At Canon, the project manager for an innovative camera noticed that people in his department were spending time reading technical journals. As the group members would frequently get together to talk about what they were learning, the manager knew that he would have to do something to keep up. He read books on marketing, but they were too dry and abstract. Reasoning that cameras were like toys, he decided to spend his lunch hours in a nearby toy store in order to understand the kinds of products that both children and adults were interested in. Says he, "It was the only way I could keep up my end of the learning curve."[8]

Promote team learning through the cross-fertilization of people and ideas. Most projects of any significance in companies today are carried out by people from different functional specialties with different views and perspectives. Normally, people look at another person's point of view as the enemy and try to squelch it. One of the primary roles that a coach plays is to honor different views and perspectives. This can lead to new ideas, methods, and tools. The coach has to ensure that the members not only have enough time to spend together, but that they do so in a qualitative way. A Fuji Xerox team leader ensured cross-fertilization by putting all the players in one large room. He explains "You start thinking in terms of what's best or second best for the group at large, not only about where you stand. If everyone understands one another's positions, then each of us is willing to give in or at least to talk to one another. Initiatives emerge as a result."[9]

Set a good example by engaging in questions. The people who produce the most extraordinary and tangible results in business are those who are likely to say "Let's inquire into that" or "This is not a trivial conversation" rather than those who say "I'll tell you what my opinion is" or "I think I have the answer to that" or who make snap judgments. When a coach takes the questioning attitude, he sends a signal to everyone on the team that what counts is *learning* as opposed to *knowing*. Point out to people that inquiry is not an abstract intellectual exercise but part of an experimental mind set where people ask questions, formulate ideas, do experiments, and ask more questions until they see something they didn't see before that allows them to produce the desired result.

Have a dialogue on how the group can think and work better together. In a project set up to reach a stretch goal, the primary unit of learning is the team. Team learning requires some degree of structure. A group whose members go about their tasks but never stop for a period of time to ponder and reflect on how they could think better and work better together does not really have much opportunity to learn. To encourage an attitude of learning, have a dialogue with the project team on the following questions: "How do we learn as a group?" "What successful learning experiences have we had?" "What are the things that are helping learning?" "What are the issues that are getting in the way?" "What problems have we had with learning?"

Encourage the group to view mistakes as learning opportunities. Gathering the group and inquiring into how people deal with mistakes is another way to encourage an attitude of learning. Have an open, candid conversation around the issue, starting off by talking about general attitudes and then getting into specifics. A question to ask is "Do people in the group generally look at mistakes as learning opportunities or as a reason to get discouraged and give up?" One way to start a discussion about learning from mistakes is to use an example from outside the company. One example, from Tom Peters' book *Search for Excellence,* is about Howard Head, the inventor of the fiberglass ski. Howard Head would go out to his shed, mix up a big batch of black plastic goop and mold it into a pair of skis. He would then take them to Tuckerman's Ravine at Mount Washington in New Hampshire to have the ski instructors try them out. The skis broke on the rugged terrain over and over again. After thirty-three trips back to the shed over a period of months, the thirty-fourth pair of skis worked.[10] If Howard Head had been afraid to make a mistake, perhaps we would not be skiing on fiberglass skis today.

Capture the learning. Ask on a weekly and monthly basis what is working and what isn't working in regard to achieving the stretch goal. Then use this feedback to correct mistakes.

*T*he attitude around mistakes needs to be that
a mistake is a breakdown on the path to
accomplishment rather than something that
represents a personal failure.

Breakdowns, in turn, trigger creative and effective thinking, new ways of being, and the invention of new tools. The questions to ask when you make mistakes are not the psychological ones like "What's wrong with me?" "What's wrong with what I did?" "What's wrong with the others?" Rather, you should ask "What was the breakdown?" "What correction do we need to make to eliminate the breakdown in the future?" "What is missing that would make a difference?"

CHAPTERFIVE

The Unwritten Rules of the Game

Don't fight forces, use them.

Fuller Sheller

The Rule of Rules

While encouraging the people you are coaching to set ambitious goals and challenge conventional thinking, remember that every job has boundaries. There is a difference between "pushing the envelope," as the pilot Chuck Yeager talks about, and sailing off into the heavens without any boundaries at all.

Whatever the game is, the rules establish what the limits or boundaries of the field are and tell us how to be successful within those boundaries. From a very early age we are subjected to all kinds of explicit and implicit rules. For example, to get the acknowledgment we want from parents and others, we have to try to please. Later in school, we realize that to succeed, we have to memorize information, get an "A" on the test, and stay on good terms with the teacher.

For the most part, the rules represent physical reality and are unsentimental. As Lao-tzu, the great Chinese philosopher, once said, "The universe treats all men like straw dogs." The rules don't care what or how you think or whether you agree with them or not.

Finding out what they are and following them generally supports your well-being. If you don't, there are consequences.

Of course, we have the power to challenge and bring about new rules. Yet to do so we have to be prepared to suffer, as most systems resist change, especially if our efforts are seen as an attack on the rules. In most companies, we can't simply do whatever we want. To be successful, we have to find out what the rules are and make a committed attempt to play by them. One of the keys in coaching people is to help people in this process.

A "Shared View of the World" Is Essential

In sports, like tennis and golf, the rules are obvious and do not change very much. In business, however, the rules of the game are always subject to change. Success is often determined by your ability to figure out the rules of the game in the midst of change, complexity, and ambiguity.

As a coach you must help people develop a view of the world that gives them an accurate picture of the reality in which they are operating. Failing to do so can result in strategic drift, significant operation problems, and a backward management culture. The difficulties that companies like IBM, General Motors, Pan Am, and others experienced in the early 1990s can be attributed to their having a view of the world that was far from accurate.

Paul Allaire, chairman of Xerox, spent months with his team of top executives trying to come up with a shared view of the world that fit the reality of the business environment and that all could agree on. Xerox stumbled badly in the mid-1980s, allowing Canon to take its place as number one in the personal copier market. Xerox hadn't realized that the Japanese had changed the rules of the game by seeking fundamentally different ways of doing things.

Today, Allaire often speaks in terms of understanding the rules of the external business environment. He says that at Xerox the rule was to do the same thing over and over again, better, faster, and cheaper. Then the company, realizing it had forgotten about the customer, started paying attention to quality and to improving what it was already doing. In the future, the rules of the game will be to satisfy customers by finding out their real needs and to create new value for customers by learning to do entirely different things.[1]

Unwritten Rules Determine Behavior

Why do so few chief executives succeed at making their vision statements come alive, even when people agree with them intellectually and emotionally? Why do seven out of ten attempts to achieve stretch goals or introduce real change fail in today's business organizations? Why are so many managers and employees frustrated, skeptical, and even cynical about their own ability to make something happen? According to Dr. Peter Scott-Morgan, a top Arthur D. Little consultant whom I interviewed for this section, the answer lies in a lack of awareness of the unwritten rules of the game.[2]

Every organization has formal rules. For some this could mean the vision of the company: to be number one or two in your business or be sold or to make sure you have innovative products and smooth delivery. It could involve being given a mandate to increase sales, cut costs, and improve profit margins. Yet, in addition to these espoused rules, there is often another set of rules that are not so clearly stated but plainly felt. These are rules that no one really seems to be in control of and that may be difficult to even clearly articulate, let alone change.

Understanding how the unwritten rules apply is essential for anyone coaching an individual or group to reach high performance or to introduce change. The key is to find out how you can use the forces generated by the unwritten rules to get where you are going. If you try to avoid them, you may wind up bumping into obstacles you didn't know were there.

The Unwritten Rules at Ford Motor Company

In 1990, Ford Motor Company started a project in cooperation with the Organization Learning Lab at the Massachusetts Institute of Technology. The purpose of the project was to create the next generation Lincoln Continental, while at the same time practicing new "learning disciplines" like reflection and inquiry and group dialogue. The story of their success is very impressive. The project team broke, by a wide margin, nearly every speed record for product development at Ford.

Quality defects in the Lincoln prototype were 20 percent lower than usual for a new car. Also, as a result of the atmosphere of learning that took place, the team was able to return some $65 million of budget money that had been allocated for fixing engineering glitches. By all objective standards, the project was a huge success. However, the manager of the project, Fred Simon, was recently passed over for promotion and given early retirement.

The reason, although nobody said it outwardly, was that the learning organization environment that was created broke the unwritten rules of the Ford organization. In the past, if managers asked people how a project was going, people would say "It's going according to plan—no problem." In reality, this was just a cover-up for date slippage and other mistakes. It was an unwritten rule of the culture not to talk about problems. In the Ford/Learning Lab case, however, a norm was created where problems were openly talked about. People could thus resolve problems quickly, rather than wait for the otherwise inevitable crisis to emerge.

When upper management found out that three hundred engineers were talking about problems, not only to the people in the project, but to other people and departments in the organization, they went into a state of high anxiety.

One of the things that Simon might have explained to his boss was that learning organizations can lead to a lot of chaos. When building a new model, a process that usually takes at least three or four years, automakers typically expect 150 or so engineering problems to be outstanding early in the design stage. Simon found, as people began to talk about the problems, that they had over five hundred. One of his colleagues went to top management who wanted to know how the Lincoln was going and said "If green is go, yellow caution, and red danger, Simon's project is purple."

But Simon felt he was on the right track, hoping to solve more problems earlier in the process and therefore avoiding costly rework at the end. However, regardless of the outstanding results, this went against the organization's culture and norms. Had Simon taken into account the unwritten rules of the game, he might have made some adjustments and been promoted to the next level rather than forced into early retirement.[3]

Unwritten Rules and Their Consequences

As the people at Ford found out, the discrepancy between the formal policies, the company- or team-stated objectives, and the unwritten rules presents very serious consequences. Imagine that you are working in an organization where the CEO is a visionary who talks about the importance of empowerment and teamwork, yet various "barons" of the company see their success associated with being empire builders. The barons amass their empires by developing their own unwritten rules: "build up fiefdoms," "guard your territory," "withhold information." These unwritten rules get passed down to other employees who, even though they agree intellectually with teamwork, don't see it as a real possibility. Other people see this and say that the bosses are not walking their talk.

Unwritten rules can arise when a CEO or manager tells people to do one thing and then pays them for another. For example, I was involved in a company where the CEO had a vision of cross-selling products and services from different areas. The managers agreed intellectually and even emotionally with the idea of cross-selling but basically resisted it because, in the words of one person, "There is nothing in it for me." It turns out that the compensation system was designed to reward people for the performance of their individual areas. The managers saw that cross-selling would lead to loss of control of accounts and to a poor bottom line.

The CEO was very frustrated and told everyone that unless they changed their behavior, people would be fired. Though the CEO was upset, the unwritten rules of the game made it perfectly logical for the executives to behave the way they did. As Peter Scott-Morgan has pointed out, "Though people sometimes complain about resistance to change, once we see the unwritten rules, we can see that people's behavior is perfectly logical."

> *The way to create an opening for real change is to close the gap between the formal policies and the unwritten rules.*

In most cases, executives are unaware of the unwritten rules that they establish. Take the case of the CEO of an oil company whose objective was to grow the business by discovering more oil. To help implement that vision, the CEO decided to embark on a Total Quality program. One of the program's dictums was that of "doing it right the first time," which meant designing business processes so that a lot of energy wouldn't be wasted in making mistakes.

The executive took a stand for quality at public gatherings and said "do it right the first time" on many occasions. The result: People stopped discovering more oil because the CEO had unknowingly established an unwritten rule that told people not to get involved in something that might result in them being associated with failure. In this case, when the executive became aware of the unwritten rule and its consequence, he called a special "town hall" meeting and acknowledged that he had been sending the wrong message.

A Methodology for Uncovering and Realigning the Unwritten Rules

Peter Scott-Morgan points out that the way to create an opening for real change is to close the gap between the formal policies and the unwritten rules. To do this, a coach must understand that most people have a good reason for following the unwritten rules. Seen this way, it becomes possible to understand people's behavior and to deal with the real impediment to change rather than to reduce the vision, to abandon the project, or to simply wind up hurling accusations at people.

1. Consider the Unwritten Rules That Could Affect a Goal's Outcome

Once a goal has been set, it is important to talk to people about the unwritten rules and their influence on human behavior. This helps to inject an element of pragmatism into strategies that you set, plans you make, and actions you take. Here's an exercise that should help people to recognize the gap between the written and unwritten rules. Start by selecting a controversial issue. Tell people what the formal policy is and then ask them to list some of the unwritten rules. Finally, ask them to look for the "disconnects" between the unwritten rules and the formal policy.

It is important that people understand not only the unwritten rules, but also the logic behind them. In other words, a coach might help people to see that "Jack isn't acting the way he does because he doesn't want to do a good job or because he doesn't want to cooperate. He is acting the way he does because of the signals he gets from his boss or because of the way, say, the reward system is influencing his behavior. As a result he has formulated certain unwritten rules that he follows in order to be successful."

Once people start to go through the exercise above, they will see that there are many cases where people's behavior may look selfish or even ridiculous, but once the unwritten rules are clear, it is easy to see that the behavior makes perfect sense and honestly represents a commitment to doing a good job.

2. Talk to People About Business Issues

To find out why someone is behaving in a particular way, Scott-Morgan suggests identifying your key stakeholders (people who could influence the outcome) and then having an informal talk with them. For example, say something like "We are trying to implement a new program. Can you tell us how it does or doesn't tie in to what you do?" You are not trying to get them to talk about the formal policies or the unwritten rules, but about the business issue that they feel is important to them.

As they are talking, listen for any disconnects between the goal and the behavior that is showing up in the organization. These might be comments such as "The bosses don't walk their talk," "There are turf battles," or "There is a lack of teamwork." It is important to understand that, for the most part, these are just symptoms. Most people in the company could write them down on the back of an envelope in a few minutes. Instead of stopping at this point, you need to work your way back and ask "Why? Why is it that those are sensible ways to behave?" You have got to understand the logic behind the unwritten rules. If you don't understand this, you will never be able to change the unwritten rules or work around them.

3. Cluster Comments Under Three Major Headings

Scott-Morgan suggests that "After you talk to each person, go back to your office and write down each of the following categories: motivators, enablers, and triggers."

Motivators. The first category is the motivators, which answer the question *"What is important to this person or group?"* It is important to distinguish the difference between the things that people are supposed to be motivated by and what they are actually motivated by. For example, people are supposed to be motivated by making the organization successful or by making the company's vision of TQM a reality when, in fact, they may be motivated by making themselves successful or by gaining more power and influence. Most people do not wake up in the morning and say to themselves "I really feel like I have to do something to improve quality today." They wake up thinking about what they can do to create more opportunity for themselves, to get whatever it is that is important to them: it might be to do something significant or to feel like a member of the team or to get a promotion or a raise in pay.

Enablers. The second category involves the enablers. To find out who the enabler is, ask *"Who can help this person or group get what is important to them?"* It is important to distinguish between who the enabler is supposed to be and who the enabler really is. If you want acceptance from other people on the team, the person who can give you that may be the person whose approval matters most to you. Or, if you are looking for a promotion or a raise in pay, the person who can give you that may be your boss.

Triggers. Triggers answer the question *"What are the conditions that will trigger the enabler to grant a reward or impose a penalty?"* Now that you have determined what is important to people and who is important to them, you need to determine how the triggers work. For example, let's say Bill wants a chance to lead a big project and the person who can give him that chance is his boss, Jim. If we also say that Jim likes people who think for themselves and can manage others, then that is the trigger, and the sensible way for Bill to behave becomes obvious.

Questions That Help to Distinguish Unwritten Rules

★ What are the people I am coaching trying to achieve?
★ What do they think and feel about the project?
★ What are the motivators? Who are the enablers? What are the triggers?

---

4. Build a Chain of Logic

Once you have had enough conversations with people, you can begin to look at the way the unwritten rules combine to affect behavior.

For example, imagine a company where the CEO has been communicating a new mandate for teamwork. When you begin to talk to people and listen for the motivators, enablers, and triggers, you see that the key motivator for people might be career advancement. Now, let's say that the formal policy is that, based on performance, 10 percent of the managers can be promoted by the boss in two years. That would immediately indicate that the key enabler is the boss and that the trigger is whatever the boss is looking for—in this case, profit and loss.

Now, let's also say that there is a formal policy that says "to become a top manager, you need to become a well-rounded individual, with experience in many areas of the business." Thus, if career advancement is the number one motivator, and people get that from breadth of experience, then one of the unwritten rules is to job-hop as fast as possible. It is a sensible way to behave given the formal policy and people's desire to advance.

If the boss is the one person who can grant that advance, another sensible way to act is to keep the boss happy and to stand out from the crowd. People have to be seen to be doing well, so they can't afford to submerge their egos. They also know that the boss is going to look for profit and loss in each area, therefore another sensible way to act—the unwritten rule—is to "protect their turf" and to "watch their quarterlies." There will be no rewards for growing someone else's empire. No matter what the top management says about teamwork, if people don't have their quarterlies, the memos start coming down. You can see as this scenario plays out how the unwritten rule is going to contribute to teamwork problems. (See diagram 5.1.)[4]

5. Change the Rules or Go With the Flow

When you find out the unwritten rules that are driving people's behavior, there are different things you can do depending on your level in the organization.

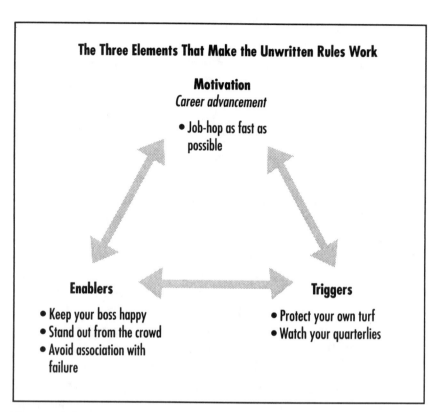

The Three Elements That Make the Unwritten Rules Work

Motivation
Career advancement

• Job-hop as fast as possible

Enablers

• Keep your boss happy
• Stand out from the crowd
• Avoid association with failure

Triggers

• Protect your own turf
• Watch your quarterlies

Diagram 5.1

When you are in charge, do what is necessary to alter the rule. If you have control over the company, area, or unit, you can change policies and procedures and encourage new behaviors in your area. Say you are trying to encourage teamwork across functions and the unwritten rule is not to speak candidly for fear of embarrassing someone. You might say "In the future, people will be measured by their openness and candor in discussing the undiscussable." Then you might create an open discussion and ask questions like "What are the issues we haven't addressed with one another?"

If you then find out that one of those issues is the compensation system and that people are protecting their turf because they will only be measured or rewarded on the performance of their area, you may want to review the compensation system.

When you're not in charge, find a sponsor. Let's say in the process of talking with people, you find out that the previous management system fostered an unwritten rule to "share information with people from other areas, but not too much." Now, if you are accountable for a key project that involves getting cooperation from people you have no control over, and those people are resisting because of unwritten rules, what do you do?

This is when you need to find sponsors who are higher up in the organization who can change procedures and policies and encourage new behavior. The way to persuade the sponsor to support you is not to hurl accusations at other groups, but to start by saying that you are not getting enough information, citing two or three examples. Then explain to your sponsor that people's behavior is perfectly logical given the unwritten rules that have been created by formal policy or encouraged by management behavior. Once the manager sees the logic of this, he or she will find a way to intervene, and your problem will be a step closer to being solved.

When you don't have a committed sponsor, go with the flow. If you are in a situation where you are unable to get a sponsor, you can still use the understanding of the unwritten rules to come up with solutions. As Peter Scott-Morgan says, "Just having knowledge of the unwritten rules means that you can come up with a pragmatic design that treads on as few toes as possible and creates as much of a win-win situation as possible."

CHAPTERSIX

From Theory of Action to Practice

First ponder, then dare.

Helmuth Moltke

Designing a Theory of Action

The word theory comes from the Greek word theo-ros, which means spectator and has the same root as the word theater. People in groups often create theories to put into play in the public arena, ideas that might better help them understand their world and gain the insights to be more effective within it. Though theorizing is sometimes looked at as "up in the clouds," cold and abstract, it can also be looked at as something that is related to practical concerns, human interaction, and day-in, day-out, bothersome issues and problems.

> *In reality, a strategy or theory is a mental map that helps guide us through the mazeway of time and space so that we can reach our intended destination.*

Creating a stretch goal involves coming up with a strategy or theory of action to achieve it. In simple terms, a goal tells you what you are trying to achieve; the theory of action tells you how you are going to achieve it. The purpose of an action strategy is not to go through an intellectual exercise, but to frame a problem and come up with implementable solutions. This could involve helping people understand what is driving the unwritten rules of the game or breaking the grip of paradigms (existing theories) and defensive reactions.

All plans, whether we realize it or not, are based on a theory. The plan creates either a match with the intended results or a mismatch. Usually, if we do not reach our goal, it is because our theory of action was wrong in the first place or because we did not do what we said we were going to do. If the theory is wrong, it's often a result of inconsistencies in our thinking and not enough inquiry into our underlying assumptions, beliefs, and values. (See diagram 6.1.)

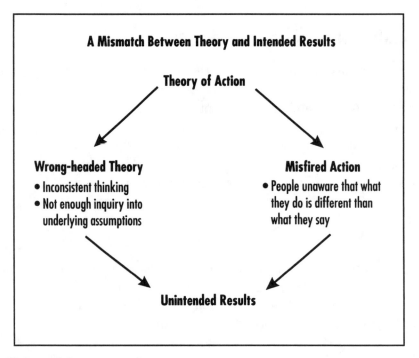

A Mismatch Between Theory and Intended Results

Theory of Action

Wrong-headed Theory
- Inconsistent thinking
- Not enough inquiry into underlying assumptions

Misfired Action
- People unaware that what they do is different than what they say

Unintended Results

Diagram 6.1

Dilemmas Require a Community of Inquiry

To be sure, when you set a stretch goal, you place yourself in a situation where there are complex problems, dilemmas, and puzzles. There are no simple or obvious solutions. One of the first steps to take is to create a community of inquiry amongst your peer group to help you ponder the dilemmas you are facing. This involves taking the time to really think deeply about the problems you are facing rather than just jumping to conclusions. (Some guidelines for building a shared approach through collaborative conversations and group dialogue are included in Chapter 10.)

One of the first things to do in meetings with the inquiry group is to frame the problem. This will determine the kind of solution to look for. For example, is the problem to create a new future or is it to fix operation problems today? Is the problem to produce a breakthrough result or just some small improvements in an ongoing way? Does the problem involve stretching your resources and knowledge or does it involve using what you already think and know?

After you have framed the problem, the next step is to look at any existing theories you have for dealing with such problems to see if they are a match. This often involves reflecting on your paradigms or frames of reference. For example, if you are using a total quality approach and you are looking for a breakthrough result, to solve the problem, you may have to find new tools and methods that are consistent with breakthrough thinking. Or perhaps the problem lies in creating a marketing breakthrough and you are operating from a design and manufacturing mentality rather than a marketing and service one. Oftentimes, people in groups get trapped in old paradigms that are socially constructed and reinforced.

Reflecting on Underlying Frames and Existing Theories of Action

Although each person in a company may see the world somewhat differently, due to a dominant person or managerial frames within the company people will typically think alike. The lessons from the past become like a DNA code that gets passed from one group of managers to the next. This can prevent people from recognizing changes in reality, seeing the big picture, or seeing alternative ways of solving complex problems.

I heard a story about a group of monkeys. One monkey runs up a pole in a shower to get some bananas. When the monkey gets to the shower head, the bananas turn out to be plastic decorations and instead of a bite to eat, he gets a cold drenching. He does this four times. The other monkeys watch him and repeat the same procedure. Eventually, they stop climbing the pole. Then, one of the monkeys from the group is removed and a new one replaces him. The monkeys teach the newcomer never to climb up that pole. Eventually all the monkeys from the original group are replaced, yet the new monkeys quickly learn to never go up that pole, even though none of them have gotten a cold shower. They just accept that pole climbing is discouraged.

A coach, using a story like the monkey story, can help to illustrate that people often do not question conventional wisdom. It can also help you to point out that, in most cases, people are not even aware of the frames that define their possibilities and choices. And what makes matters worse is that these frames prevent people from seeing that other possibilities and choices exist for solving the problem. Thus, important questions to ask the group are "Is the problem/solution we are deliberating one that will require double-loop learning or single-loop learning? Can we solve the problem by doing the same thing better or by doing something different?" (See diagram 6.2.)

Double-loop learning is usually suggested in situations where people keep doing the same thing even though they do not get different results. It is also suggested in cases where people take actions to avoid embarrassment or threat and where actions lead to unintended results. As we know from tennis, golf, or skiing, the old theories that are stuck in our heads often prevent us from learning

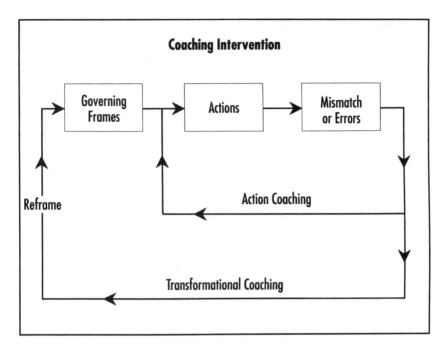

Diagram 6.2

new skills. The key to double-loop learning lies in a reflective stance rather than a protective stance.

Stretch goals usually imply doing something different. This often requires that people break the grip of old frames. Designing a new theory of action involves being able to surface and question the frames people are operating from. Here are some "paradigm accelerator" questions that can help.

1. Does the solution require doing something different or doing the same thing better?
2. What does our language say about our assumptions?
3. What are our pet theories for doing something?
4. What are the standard practices that we act on?
5. What could we do that is fundamentally different?

Generic Solutions for Complex Problems

In most cases, when people have to solve a new problem, they don't invent a new theory from scratch. What they do is adopt a generic theory from a book or from a conference. In the past ten years or so, there have been several new theories that have had a significant impact. The following are examples of generic management theories that promise high leverage. (The theory is generic in that it does not carry a particular brand or label and might be used by any organization.)

- ★ *Stretch as leverage.* This involves creating a new future by developing a strategic intent or long-term goal where people deliberately create a mismatch between ambitions and resources.

- ★ *TQM and reengineering core processes.* To improve efficiency and productivity, set organizations up so that they are based on cooperation rather than conflict and on core key business processes rather than fragmented functions.

- ★ *Learning organization.* To create lasting change requires more than big goals and restructuring; it takes transforming people's ability to think and interact.

- ★ *Relationship marketing.* Intertwine with customers to define problems and solutions that neither you nor the customers could have come up with separately.

- ★ *Combinations of the above.* The following chart from Arun Maira of Arthur D. Little, Inc., shows a good attempt to integrate generic management theories in a way that creates more leverage for high performance, change, and learning. (See diagram 6.3.)[1]

What frequently happens is that managers adopt one of these theories and try applying it to their situation, preaching stretch goals, quality, learning, or whatever. They then run into problems. However, the real problem in implementation often occurs because people's theory of action is silently displaced by another theory that they are unaware

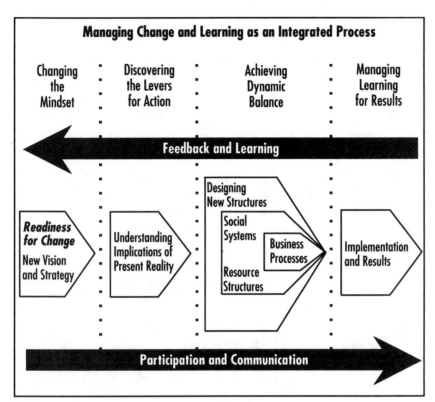

Managing Change and Learning as an Integrated Process

Changing the Mindset · Discovering the Levers for Action · Achieving Dynamic Balance · Managing Learning for Results

Feedback and Learning

Readiness for Change New Vision and Strategy

Understanding Implications of Present Reality

Designing New Structures
Social Systems
Business Processes
Resource Structures

Implementation and Results

Participation and Communication

Diagram 6.3

of. In other words, instead of people following through with their theory or ideas, they drop them and start behaving according to a theory that is designed to help them manage impressions or to protect them from threat or embarrassment.

"Espoused Theory" Versus "Theory-in-Use"

Chris Argyris has written that while people may have an *espoused theory*, their *theory-in-use* is the one they act on. This is a little more complex than saying that people do not practice what they preach—although that is part of it. The new espoused theory often gets dropped when it doesn't match the theory that people have been successful with or the skills that come naturally and automatically. For example, a person may start trying to lead others to think together about a complex problem and then get frustrated with the group process and start to do everyone's thinking for them because that's what he or she knows how to do. (See diagram 6.4.)

In large part, the espoused theory gets displaced when people find themselves in situations that are embarrassing or threatening and adopt another theory based on defensive action strategies. This often leads to unintended consequences that people are not aware of. According to Argyris, this is rooted in a Model I or "master program." In this model, people (1) pursue their own purposes, (2) control others, (3) maximize winning and avoid losing, and (4) don't

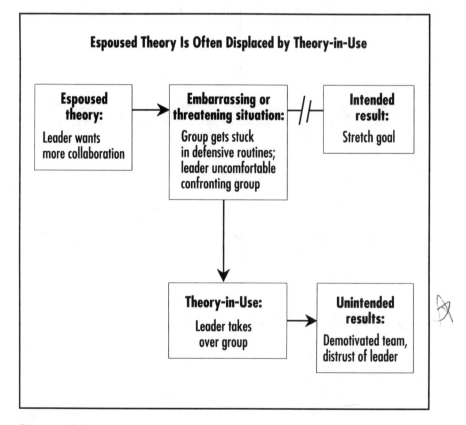

Diagram 6.4

show vulnerability by talking about problems. This, in turn, creates action strategies such as (1) saving face, (2) persuading and convincing, (3) looking good rather than being good, and (4) confronting, avoiding, and accommodating. (These will be discussed in greater detail in Chapter 11, "Recognize and Disperse Defensive Routines.")

One of the issues is that managers are often unaware when their espoused theories fall into the background and their theories-in-use take over. This is due to the fact that defensive reactions are almost second nature and that people's reasoning processes are so skillful and quick that they do not see that they have changed tracks. For example, someone goes to a big meeting deciding to take a stand for a stretch, reengineering, or organization learning and then winds up altering her position because she feels the need to accommodate others. Yet, because she doesn't want to feel like she compromised herself, she deceives herself into thinking that the position that she took is actually the same position that she began with. Suddenly, the advocate of change and learning becomes caught in her own patterns of self-deception. It is part of the coach's function to help people be aware of these patterns. (See Chapter 7, "Observing and Giving Feedback.")

The Dilemmas of Implementation

Imagine a business situation that presents technical, organization, or marketing problems. On top of this, there may be problems to do with the organization processes. Underneath this, there may also be problems resulting from the unwritten rules of behavior. Then this is overlaid on patterns of personal or organizational defensiveness that become highly routinized. The result of all this is that the initial dilemmas have not become simpler but, in fact, more complicated.

This is the point where most managers reach their cognitive, as well as their personal, limits. They may feel blocked by their own paradigms and may be operating from a wrong-headed strategy. They may be entangled in a chess game with others due to their own defensive strategies or Model I theory-in-use. At this point, people may feel frustrated, bewildered, and downright scared, doubting themselves and others in the group. They have reached in their minds a point of maximum contraction from analyzing the situation to death and seeing that they may have no possibilities or choices. They may feel dull and depressed and not know where to turn.

Creating an Opening for Possibilities and Action

When people feel that there are no possibilities or choices, it has been my experience that there is usually some kind of blindness or illusion in place. In other words, there are possibilities and choices, but people do not see them. The coach's role in this situation is to try to help people to create some kind of opening in a situation that is growing increasingly contracted. The following are some generic strategies that can help to create an opening for possibility or action.

1. Get people to take a reflective stance rather than a protective one. One way to help people gain some insight into their situation is to "tell it like it is" and speak to them authentically or to make provocative statements to encourage self-reflection. For example, a coach might say "In this situation, it seems to me that you are just protecting yourself from the other department heads, rather than being willing to understand what they say and be influenced by it." Another approach would be to reeducate people so their response is to take a reflective stance rather than a protective stance. Taking the reflective stance helps people see where their problems are caused by their own foolishness and can lead to insights that create an opening for possibilities or action. For example, people start to observe their thinking rather than defend it and see where their paradigms may be blocking them or where their defensive behavior is getting in the way. Instead of asking people to reflect when they are having an emotional reaction, give them the room to go through their reaction and then ask them to reflect.

2. Encourage people to mull. Oftentimes, people's thinking processes are so fast, compulsive, and obsessive that they cannot see that they are just moving down the same channels of thought. The result is that, despite intensive deliberation, they cannot create any new strategies that might come from thinking laterally and they wind up reapplying the old strategies without any change in results. If you see people or a group becoming bewildered, frustrated, and confused in their thinking, suggest that they take a break or even a few days to mull things over. As a result, the brain "airs out" and people in the group naturally loosen up on their positions, embrace one another's views, or see things from different angles. This can lead to shared understanding or a good new idea. Some good questions to mull over might be "What do we know about this? What is our thinking now? How does it need to change?"

3. Ask "What does crazy wisdom and intuition tell you to do?" The intuitive approach is especially useful when the rational one has reached its limits. The analytical mind tends to run on old paradigms and focuses the spiral of our thinking down to a fine point of deliberation. This can be good in being exacting about a decision, but it can also lead to all alternatives looking equally bad. Get people's creative and intuitive minds to focus upward and laterally toward free space, breaking existing paradigms and creating new possibilities. Sometimes a way to help people tap their intuitive minds is to ask "What are the 'crazy things' to do?" These often turn out to have wisdom. Crazy wisdom is often an antidote to overrationalization and can create an opening where before there was only analysis paralysis.

4. Ask "What is the most simple and logical thing to do?" Ask people what can be done in the situation that is the most plain, simple, direct, and obvious, keeping in mind that the intention is to create an opening by taking some action. For example, managers often fret themselves into a very worried state about interpersonal relationships because dealing directly with these issues often leads to upset or threat. So they confront, avoid, or accommodate instead of doing the simple and obvious thing which would be to go and complete the relationship. Or another action might involve doing something to enroll the players or to get the nonplayers off the field. Enabling people to identify the simple and obvious thing involves asking them what they can do that requires the least degree of speculation, the least number of assumptions, the least number of inferences.

5. Use small, well-placed actions to make a big difference. One of the most important parts of mounting a strategy is producing some results and learning from them. These coaching questions are useful in that regard.

- ★ What can we do now based on existing resources, change readiness, and authority?

- ★ What are the high-leverage areas for reaching this stretch goal, where focused action and concentration of resources could create an opening for further progress?

- ★ What are the easy things that we could get started on right away to build some momentum?

Action as Strategy

One of the best ways to encourage people to evolve a new strategy is to take action and look at that as an inquiry in itself that can lead to more insight into the means to end deliberation.

- ★ *Get outside the box.* People are likely to see something that they have never seen before that gives them penetrating insight into the situation. Sitting in the office thinking about your company's market position or what product to come up with may not lead very far, but spending a day in the life of a customer may lead to a very clear-minded strategy.

- ★ *Experiment and reflect.* When people take experimental action they discover the validity of their existing theory in practice and can begin to alter it or change it altogether. This is the PDAC cycle: plan, do, act, and check (reflect and adjust your actions).

- ★ *Tap tacit knowledge in action.* Action allows people to tap tacit knowledge or subjective insights, hunches, and automatic skills that cannot be accessed just by talking or thinking. In other words, people discover the correct strategy in the process of execution.

★ *Use anomalies to discover revolutionary new theories.* One of the most potent aspects of action inquiry is that it can lead to breakthrough ideas. Thomas Kuhn, who introduced the idea of paradigms, said that most of the time scientists practice normal science, extending their existing paradigms. But sometimes what happens is that a scientist will notice an anomaly, something that doesn't fit the existing theory, and this leads to a new paradigm or frame. This is where most breakthrough ideas in science and management come from. For example, C.K. Prahalad and Gary Hamel noticed that while the conventional notions of strategy were that of fitting strategy to existing resources, the strategic winners were practicing stretch rather than fit and creating a deliberate mismatch between ambitions and resources. This led to a powerful theory: strategy as stretch.[2]

CASE STUDY:
Get More Out of the Resources You Have

In this day of tight budgets, smart coaches design strategies that leverage what they have. A good example is John O'Rourke, president of Pony USA, a small athletic footwear company.[3] O'Rourke's task was to help the brand recover from a mistake the previous owners had made by selling the shoes through discounters like Kmart and Wal-Mart. The result of this strategy: Pony had a mediocre product that didn't appeal to upscale retailers like Footlocker and Athlete's Foot.

When I talked to O'Rourke, he said his task was to generate a new range of athletic footwear that could be sold in upscale stores and that was fashionable enough to attract consumers. I asked O'Rourke about his strategy or theory of action. "I knew that if we were going to bring the brand back," said O'Rourke, "we needed some new breakthrough products across all lines." The problem was that he had no in-house designers and no budget for hiring top designers from the outside. To leverage his limited budget, O'Rourke went to three different design houses and asked to work with some young, talented designers whom he could engage very inexpensively.

"I told each of the three design houses that I would give them the opportunity to design our basketball line and that I'd pick the best one. Then I said, 'Here is the money. I'm paying each of you for a year. This, however, will turn into a long-term relationship for somebody.'" He knew that just giving the young designers the opportunity would produce results, but his theory was that introducing a competitive aspect would create a situation where people would be challenged to bring out their absolute best. O'Rourke also gave each designer one of his other lines in addition to basketball. One would be doing cross-training, one would do indoor shoes, and one would do outdoor shoes.

This worked great, as the young designers rose to the opportunity. Before long, people back in the office were wondering where all the designs were coming from.

Practice Allows Us to Test Our Theories of Action

Saying is one thing, doing another.

Montaigne

We are now at the point where we have set a stretch goal, calculated the unwritten rules, and developed a theory of action. Now we have to put our theory into practice and start to take action. Practice is where we learn by doing. We can have a beautiful theory about how to play the piano but until we raise our finger in the air and press a key, we do not even know what a piano sounds like. The beautiful thing about practice, especially if there is coach around, is that it gives us an opportunity to get some feedback. We either get good notes or sour notes. If we take our theory of action and put it into practice and it doesn't produce desired results, we can see that something is off.

Obviously, a key coaching role is to observe what happens as people begin to practice. If people are not getting desired results, we can help them by questioning the assumptions behind their theories or we can coach them on the specific actions they are taking so that they can develop more competence. Practice is what makes observation possible and allows people to adjust their actions according to the feedback they are getting. In the next chapter, we will look at observing and giving feedback but for now let's look at how to make our theory real in the world of action.

Making adjustments as people move from theory to action could involve either transformational coaching (intervening in people's frames of reference) or coaching for incremental improvement (intervening in what people do). As the coach, you have to make observations and assessments of individual and group behavior. Are people taking wrong-headed actions? Do they have the wrong theory of action? Is what they are doing different than what they think they are doing? Do they need to take more time out to study and practice new skills and capabilities that will help them to solve these problems? Are people managing impressions in order to look good or are they talking about problems and trying to learn from one another?

Move Between Performance and the Practice Field

In most groups, getting the job done happens in one box; training and learning happens in another. Because the traditional training situation is often separated from what really needs to be done, there is often no way for people and especially teams to learn on the job. There is no place where managers can go to reflect on what they are doing and learn new skills in the context of getting the results that they need. In the next ten years, I predict that there will be many innovations in regard to creating a learning organization infrastructure so that learning happens by design, not by chance. One of these innovations is coming from Peter Senge and his colleagues at the MIT Organization Learning Center. It has to do with an idea called the "managerial practice field."[4] For example, in the field of competitive sports and in the performing arts, players continuously move back and forth between the practice field and the performance field. The idea is to expand people's capacity. It is difficult to imagine a football team learning without practice or a symphony orchestra learning without rehearsal.

Yet, this is precisely what is expected of managers and teams. Managers frequently have to act on their strategies when there is no chance to test them, when the fear of personal failure is great, and when there is no way to develop new team skills or replay an important decision.

> *The basic idea of performance and practice fields is to make sure that learning occurs in the context of doing the job rather than as a separate activity.*

This idea comes out of distinguishing those environments where learning and work are integrated from those environments where they are not.

Examples of Practice Fields

The MIT group has set up a number of different managerial practice fields with prominent companies like Ford, EDS, and GS Technologies. In the Lincoln Continental division at Ford, in a project that focused on speeding up product development and quality, managers set up regular one- or two-day learning labs to deal with the issues that were coming up. These learning labs helped managers discuss problems that would normally be undiscussable.

At GS Technologies, a practice field was created by Bill Isaacs to solve the problems between labor and management. Business conversations can easily escalate into a hot debate, with people reacting to one another and not thinking with clarity, logic, or deep insight. Isaacs suggests "cool inquiry" as a way to balance this tendency. It means stepping back from the heat of the debate, allowing people to move through their emotional reactions without trying to change or fix them, and reflecting deeply on the nature of thought as well as the issues and problems that are on the table. Isaacs taught people dialogue skills and after a number of meetings the dialogue heated up so much that someone compared the room to a container of hot molten metal. Isaacs said, "I like it that way" and stayed with the group until a breakthrough occurred that led to a new basis of cooperation between labor and management.[5]

EDS decided that it wanted to create a learning organization infrastructure. A learning lab was developed by Fred Kofman that focused on developing twenty or thirty coaches that would be proficient in the skills of a learning organization, such as shared vision, team learning, and systems thinking. These coaches would later be "seeded" into the organization. The infrastructure consisted of (1) special conferences where new skills and practices could be developed, (2) concrete projects where the skills and practices could be applied to key performance criteria, (3) practice and reflection assignments, and (4) personal coaching meetings. Today a high number of EDS employees report directly or indirectly to these program participants.[6] (See diagram 6.5.)

In each case, in order to help the process along, various coaches were used, along with learning methods and tools that were appropriate to the different issues that were arising. "The Learning Lab," according to one participant, "wasn't structured like most training environments we are used to. [The boss] didn't begin with an overview of 'the ten things we are going to tell you.' Instead, he said 'We're going to learn together as we go along.'"[7]

Practice and Reflection Go Together

According to Senge, 90 percent of the learning that occurs in these learning labs is on the personal and interpersonal level. "When people

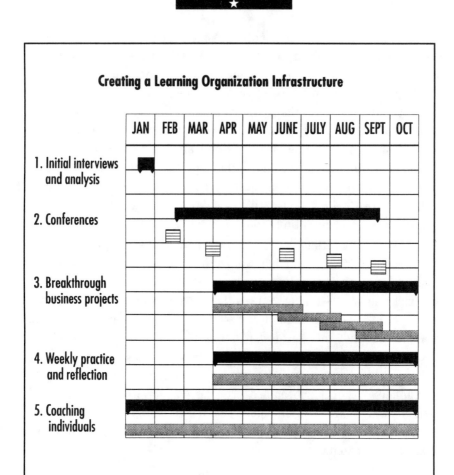

Creating a Learning Organization Infrastructure

	JAN	FEB	MAR	APR	MAY	JUNE	JULY	AUG	SEPT	OCT
1. Initial interviews and analysis										
2. Conferences										
3. Breakthrough business projects										
4. Weekly practice and reflection										
5. Coaching individuals										

Diagram 6.5

In most companies have a problem, they normally blitz right by it by coming up with ten solutions, picking one, and implementing it. American managers really believe in this 'ready, fire, aim' stuff and are extraordinarily nonreflective. In the practice field you create an environment where people can slow down. If there is a problem they can actually start talking about what might be causing it. We can also give people the tools and methods to help them understand it.

"In the practice field, there is also a chance for people to learn to use these tools without fear of making mistakes. As people become used to being reflective and to using the various tools and methods, they start to see that a lot of the problems have to do with their own thinking and reasoning processes."

According to Senge, "I like the metaphor of the practice field because both in the practice field and rehearsal hall what you do is slow things down. In a real performance there is a certain pace to things, often a certain frenzy to it, but in the practice field you stop, you try it, you try it a different way. At the same time, you see it from different angles. This creates a much more reflective environment."

Designing Practice Fields

The practice field is often a place where the coach has superior knowledge to the coachees. Yet, the coach has to treat the coachees with dignity and respect while being unyielding on the reality of what it takes to learn. The coach is in the position to expose the coachees to their own discomfort while "unfreezing," revising, and "refreezing" their points of view. The coach can also unknowingly subject the learners to embarrassment or threat as people try to break the grip of their skilled incompetence. Or the coach may expose people to their own ignorance or awkwardness in learning new skills.

One of the things that the coach can do to give people an experience of dignity is to keep certain ground rules in mind when designing practice fields. These rules get back to our governing values. First, the group members set their own stretch goals that require learning. Secondly, the learning agenda and practice field are determined by the group members or are based on what they consider important. Thirdly, the practice field experience is something that should not only encourage study and practice, but should be fun. If practice isn't fun, people won't want to practice. The fourth point is that people should have some way to measure their own progress in the practice field.

Practice Field Assignments

The following exercises can be used in the practice field. The exercises have been divided into two parts: the first part is on leadership transformation and reinvention and the second is on group transformation and reinvention.

I. Leadership Transformation and Reinvention

What is my group trying to create? Who do I need to be in the matter? How do I need to change? Oftentimes, in trying to realize a vision, goal, or ideas, executives or project leaders forget that this means that they themselves have to learn powerful lessons in personal change. In other words, reinventing ourselves is inseparable from reinventing the organization. According to Tracy Goss, "This is inquiry into the context from which an executive makes decisions, not a psychological process to fix what's wrong." People's inner context is otherwise often not revealed.

To paraphrase Goss from a *Harvard Business Review* article, "The Reinvention Roller Coaster," an executive wanted to increase his company's business from $80 million to $200 million in five years. He had been working hard toward the goal and was discouraged with the slow progress. Yet when anyone proposed expansion plans, like adding a new product line or reinventing an old market, he would resist, saying that all he could see were incredible problems. If you asked the executive what he did all day long, he would say he worked hard on the growth of his company. But when he finally stopped to examine what was going wrong, he realized he was operating from a context of avoiding conflict, which was not consistent with his company's commitment to real growth. He then understood why the things he was doing to produce real growth weren't working.[8]

Exercise 1. Ask people to reflect on where preaching one thing and practicing another impedes shared vision and goals. People are often quite unaware of the inconsistencies between their espoused theories and their theories-in-use and this creates consequences that they do not intend. Ask people to look at their espoused theories versus their theories-in-use and the unintended results. As people's colleagues often have more insight into where people have discrepancies between their espoused theories and their theories-in-use, have people do this exercise in pairs or in small groups of three or four. Then have a special coaching session with the coachee and examine whether the inconsistency is due to not understanding the new theory, to the old theory in his or her head, or to the inability to learn new skills and unlearn old ones. Then, jointly design ways to help the person shift his or her viewpoint or to learn new skills and techniques.

Exercise 2. Videotape a meeting to show the group leader how his or her way of speaking and listening contributes to the group's problems. I was told a story about a manager who observed that his people agreed in meetings but did not seem to act according to the agreement outside the meetings. As the manager investigated this with the help of a coach, he discovered that people never really agreed in the first place. What happened was the people believed that they had to agree publicly with what the boss said. When the manager found this out, he told the people, in no uncertain terms, that he expected them to challenge him and one another when they disagreed.

The coach then taped some of these meetings, and it turned out that every time people disagreed, the boss would say things like "Damn it! I can't seem to get the point across to you guys" or "Hell, you guys are driving me up the wall." When the manager was shown the videos, he was shocked to see the difference between what he practiced and what he preached.

Once you have made a videotape, use it to observe and make assessments about the behaviors of the leader and group. Illustrate your assessments in a feedback session by playing back selected passages of the videotape. Once you give people these examples, rather than confront them, it's better to ask some questions that allow them to gain insight into what is going on: "What's your take on this? What do you think led people to this conclusion? What's in your thinking that might cause you to say one thing and do something else?"

Exercise 3. Dealing with dilemmas. What usually happens when people are faced with a dilemma where the solution is not obvious is that people avoid the dilemma because it makes them too uncomfortable or else they come up with simplistic solutions that fall short in implementation. It is important to stay centered in the face of a dilemma while you spend time mulling on it or taking experimental action to test for solutions. The following exercise gives people an experience of staying centered.

Three people work together in this exercise. Two people hold on to the arms of a third person and pull down. The person in the middle responds in three different ways. First, the person resists as much as he or she can. Second, the person does not resist at all. And third, the person thinks of an image that represents being centered and gently keeps his or her focus on that image, breathing in an easy and regular way.

Next, the person thinks of a dilemma that he or she is facing and briefly tells the others what it is. Each person then takes one side of the dilemma and, while again pulling down on the person's arm, makes a simple statement that represents the dilemma. The person in the middle again focuses on his or her centering image, staying centered in the face of the dilemma. Centering yourself and holding the tension of the dilemma moves from being a good idea to something that is viscerally felt. This may be very confronting to people or very liberating.[9]

Exercise 4. Study and practice one skill for one week in the context of getting the job done. Practice is a form of inquiry in making distinctions that leads to deep learning and allows people to embody new skills and capabilities. Like in a ski, golf, or tennis lesson, one way to help people learn new skills is to focus on one skill at a time for a week or so. This is distinctly different from bombarding people with information that they cannot use. For example, in teaching people leadership, one key skill is "taking a stand." This starts with saying what you really want to say, consistent with your commitments, rather than altering what you want to say to protect yourself or others. Have people notice where they need to take a stand and focus on doing so for a period of time. Have periodic conversations to help them be successful in their actions and have them continue practicing until they gain some mastery. Then move on to another leadership attribute.

Exercise 5. Keep a journal as a way to further reflection. Have people keep a journal of the reflections and learnings they develop over time on the most important question they are facing in their lives right now: for example, "How do I transform a stuck team? How do I break out of an old pattern like being too nice (or being too tough)." Set ten or fifteen minutes aside in the practice field sessions for people to reflect and write. Appropriate music in the background can help stimulate the creative parts of people's minds.

6. Recommend articles and books to further people's learning. Some that we recommend are the following:

Books

★ *Theory in Practice* by Chris Argyris & D.A. Schön

★ *Overcoming Organizational Defenses* by Chris Argyris

★ *Knowledge for Action* by Chris Argyris

★ *The Skilled Facilitator* by Roger Schwarz

★ *The Fifth Discipline* by Peter M. Senge

★ *The Fifth Discipline Fieldbook* by P. Senge, C. Roberts, R. Ross, B. Smith, & A. Kleiner

★ *The Unwritten Rules of the Game* by Peter Scott-Morgan

★ *The Breakthrough Strategy* by Robert Schaffer

Articles

★ "Good Communication that Blocks Learning," by C. Argyris, *Harvard Business Review*, July-August 1994

★ "The Reinvention Roller Coaster," by Tracy Goss, Richard Pascale, & Anthony Athos, *Harvard Business Review*, November-December 1993

★ "Strategy as Stretch and Leverage," by Gary Hamel & C.K. Prahalad, *Harvard Business Review*, March-April 1993

II. Group Transformation and Reinvention

Today, organizations are committed to change. However, they often do not recognize the importance of being committed to learning. The result is that the best laid plans often go astray. As an increasing number of businesses are striving to create learning organizations, they are finding out that the generative point for doing so is often a small group that must develop new learning disciplines to get the job done: for example, building a shared vision, engaging in collaborative conversations where people are mindful of their beliefs and assumptions, or taking concerted action with a view to how work flows in a complex system.

As we mentioned earlier, change and team learning can best be achieved by having teams move continuously back and forth between the performance and practice fields. To use a metaphor, imagine a basketball team. The coach observes and then steps into the game to make adjustments on the performance field. He then takes the team to the practice field and reviews the video so that the team can learn from successes and failures. He and the team then create the game plan for the next event and further practice fields for the team to practice the fundamentals.

This had never happened in business because the level of competition, the pace of change, and the complexity wasn't high enough to demand it. That was then. Today, making use of both performance and practice fields has become essential to being able to achieve high performance and realize change. The following exercises provide some examples for how to develop practice fields for a group to learn the skills necessary for business transformation.

Exercise 1. Have people write a case study and discuss it with colleagues. An approach to helping people in groups become more aware of any discrepancy between their espoused theory and theory-in-use is to have each person in the group write an honest, one-page case study of what he or she sees as the issues in the group. Then call people together to discuss the case studies. Writing the case study allows people to look at what is going on and, at the same time, disengage from the situation emotionally. It also allows people to have a frank and open discussion about the situation and the feelings people have about it.

Case Study Format

1. What results do you or your group intend to produce?
2. How do you and your team think you act?
3. What is the feedback gathered about your actual behavior?
4. What unintended results are occurring?
5. What are the thinking patterns or actions that produce your behavior?

Exercise 2. Use protocols that help with team reflection and inquiry. The following protocols were developed by some colleagues and friends at Innovation Associates. They are useful in helping groups move from an unproductive discussion to a real quality of dialogue and for encouraging teams to self-intervene in their own conversations. When talking about a business topic, such as strategic operation issues, quality and service issues, or team learning issues, post the following questions to serve as guides. Appoint a facilitator to hold the space of balancing inquiry and advocacy by bringing the group back to the questions from time to time. After a while, the group members will get the hang of it and do it themselves. (See diagram 6.6.)

Exercise 3. Community building. This process is one that we have done at Transformational Learning Inc. in a program called "The Next Step." It is an amazingly powerful exercise, but it takes careful facilitation and at least one day before people move through bewilderment and frustration and begin to experience the benefits. It is designed to help people draw their identity not only from their individuality, but from the group as a community of inquiry or practice. It also is very

---

Questions for Team Learners

1. Am I willing to be influenced? Am I open to learning?

2. When advocating a position:

   - Do I reveal my thinking/my mental models?

   - Do I explain my assumptions?

   - Do I share the observable data from which I drew my conclusions?

   - Do I encourage others to explore my model/my assumptions/the data?

   - Do I listen to really hear?

   - Do I stay open?

3. When faced with another's view with which I disagree:

   - Do I ask "What leads you to that view?"

   - Do I seek to truly understand the view?

   - Do I explore, listen, and offer my own views in an open way?

   - Do I listen for the larger meaning that may emerge out of honest, open sharing of alternative models?

Diagram 6.6

powerful in eliminating the blocked mental models and defensive routines that keep groups from collaborating effectively.

The group sits in a circle of ten or twelve people with a task written on a flip chart: "Your task is to observe your own thinking and behavior, in the here and now, as an individual and a group with respect to authentic power, responsibility, and real communication." The group stays in the circle for ninety-minute sessions. There is a consultant to the group whose job is to further the learning of the group. At first, the group tries to ignore the task, destroy the task, or change the task, and the consultant's job is to keep the group on track. Keeping the reflection in the here and now allows people to slow their thinking process down so they can observe their own opinions and assumptions, as well as learn to reflect rather than react.

The consultant only addresses the group as a whole, not individuals. This helps to build the experience of community identity and also helps to ensure that people do not take what is said personally. The consultant speaks more in metaphors to provoke the group or stimulate reflection and learning. For example, the consultant might say "Where is the wolf in sheep's clothing?" or "This group is like a mother hen with her chicks." The process can be transformational for both individuals and the group.

Exercise 4. Completing relationships. Often relationship problems are at the source of many of the problems people face in implementing a strategy or, for that matter, in getting anything done. As people tend to be sensitive and to take things personally, it is quite common for relationships to break down. Many people do not have the practice of completing relationships. In many cases, people rationalize that they will not be able to get through to the other person, that it would not make a difference, or that talking to him or her about what is really on their minds would lead to a blowup. What follows is that people avoid others at all costs.

Providing some structure to completing relationships has proven successful. This exercise starts with two people who need to get complete with each other sitting down together. One person has a pen, which we call the "talking stick." The person with the talking stick starts and says everything he or she needs to say to feel complete. When someone has the talking stick, the other person cannot speak, only listen. When the first person is finished, he or she gives the pen to the other person. Then that person speaks until he or she is complete. This goes on until no one needs to pick up the talking stick and speak any more. It is important at this point for each person to acknowledge that he or she is complete. We have noticed that after doing this exercise with an intact group, the efficiency of the group improves dramatically.

Exercise 5. Recognizing and dispersing defensive routines. Ask the group members to reflect on and discuss the ways they avoid, accommodate, or act heavy-handed. Have people look at how their behavior is contributing to problems in the group and the results the group is getting. Ask people to give specific examples.

Exercise 6. The Hot Seat Exercise. This group feedback exercise is a very powerful, yet delicate exercise that, if managed well, can have a big impact on both the individual and the group. Seat the members of the group theater-style; then place one chair in the front and center—the Hot Seat. Provide some general guidelines about giving and getting feedback.

When giving feedback:

★ Talk straight; don't sugar coat.

★ Speak with the intent to make a difference.

★ Focus on changeable behavior, not personality.

★ Use intellect and intuition.

When receiving feedback:

★ Sit with arms and legs uncrossed.

★ Listen whether you agree or disagree.

★ Listen with the intent to learn something new.

★ When everyone is done, take a minute to acknowledge that you got the feedback.

Then one person goes to the hot seat and each person in the group gives him or her feedback based on the following:

1. "One thing I appreciate about you is..."

2. "One thing I have difficulty with is..." or "A next step for you might be..."

3. "One thing I want to create with you is..."

It's vital for people to have generosity of spirit, both in giving feedback on strengths as well as on areas that need improvement.

The person in the hot seat is asked not to speak so that he or she can receive the feedback rather then have a knee-jerk reaction to it. As more and more people in the group speak, there starts to be a common thread to all the feedback the person receives. This feedback is enriched by different people's personal experiences of the person—their wisdom, insights, and intuition, as well as their unique form of self-expression. When everyone is finished, the person is asked to say something about what he or she learned in acknowledgment of the feedback. One of the first things people often do is wipe their brow and say "Wow! It really is hot up here." In a group of six to eight people, allow fifteen to twenty minutes per person.

CHAPTER SEVEN

Observing and Giving Feedback

You see, but you do not observe.

Sir Arthur Conan Doyle

In the performing arts, sports, science, and other fields there is a long tradition of observation. Seiji Ozawa, maestro of the Boston symphony orchestra, listens carefully and taps his baton on his music stand whenever he hears an off note or two sections of the orchestra out of harmony. College basketball coach Bobby Knight's head moves back and forth like a metronome as he watches the movements of the players on the court. These observations become the basis of the assessments a coach makes and ultimately for the feedback he or she gives.

Whether the game is golf, tennis, or growing a business, the ability to observe breakdowns and intervene in them is an essential aspect of coaching. A breakdown indicates that progress toward the stretch goal has been interrupted, either because of people's thinking or their habits. Coaching starts with observing the breakdown places, growth spots, and learning edges with people and groups. A coach must have the honesty not only to observe, but to acknowledge all breakdowns, as painful as this may be. This means helping people see mistakes as an opportunity to learn rather than as a threat.

147

When coaching an individual or a group, it is important to recognize that most people have a strategy or mental model from which they operate and design their actions. Oftentimes, people's strategy or way of doing things works up to a certain point but then begins to break down, causing people to be stuck or ineffective. For example, you may observe that being confrontational works to get people's attention but then backfires when people "turn you off." Or you may see that being diplomatic can help you create what you want, but at a certain point ceases to be an effective strategy because it leads to making certain issues undiscussable. The coach's role is to anticipate breakdowns, sniff them out when they are being covered up, and eliminate them.

> *Observation is critical as people move from theory to practice.*

Help People to Become Aware

There are two phases of any coaching cycle. The first involves diagnosing or carefully observing people's breakdown places and making assessments about fundamental causes and solutions. The second phase involves intervening. This is when the coach, through his or her feedback, enters and becomes part of the person's or group's learning system with the intent of improving it. The intervening stage involves providing people with ideas, methods, and tools that expand their ability to take successful action. This entails furthering people's learning by helping them see error and eliminate it.

Observation is critical as people move from theory to practice because people cannot see the discrepancy between what they think they are doing and what they are actually doing. In the same sense, people often do not have the capacity to see themselves as others see them or detect their own errors and eliminate them. Because most people have self-protective strategies, they sometimes use defensive reasoning to bypass and cover up errors. The result is that they often wind up blinded to their own ignorance and incompetence on many different levels.

A coach or grounded observer is someone who (1) sees what others may not see through the high quality of his or her attention and listening, (2) is in the position to step back (or invite participants to step back) from the situation so that they have enough distance from it to get some perspective, (3) helps people see the difference between their intentions and their thinking or actions, and (4) helps people cut through patterns of collective illusion and self-deceptions caused by defensive thinking and behavior.

Develop Discriminating Awareness

Edward Johnson 2nd, founder of Fidelity Investments, took courses in the 1920s at the Pelman Institute. The Institute was dedicated to teaching students how to become original thinkers by strengthening their powers of mind and, especially, their powers of observation. One of the exercises was to observe a clothes iron for over an hour, noting down what was observed in a journal. Another exercise was a similar one with a rose bush. Johnson was later renowned for his keen powers of observation of the stock market as well as of people.

> *A masterful coach is someone who can walk into a situation and see things that others do not see, giving him or her penetrating insight into the situation.*

Most people are neither absorbed enough in the situation to observe what's happening nor inclined to use wisdom, intuition, and rigorous reasoning to make accurate assessments about it.

The ability to observe starts with obtaining a sense of awareness or what the Buddhists call "mindfulness." It is like learning to take a proper walk in the forest. At first, you might have to develop awareness of just one thing, then develop the awareness of two things, then three, four, five, and six. But if you are totally awake as you walk through the forest, you start to become aware of the whole situation—the weather, the terrain, the animal life, and the vegetable life. In order to do this, you can't just be preoccupied with one thing, you have to become aware of everything. The more you walk through the forest in this state of awareness, the more you detach yourself from your own preoccupations and become open to what you see.

Similarly, coaches have to allow themselves to become open to what is going on, to become absorbed in something outside of themselves, to become aware. The practice of walking into a room and noticing one thing about the people in the group, then another, then another, is very effective. To observe accurately, we have to observe as openly, patiently, and precisely as possible. In this stage, we are observing without making assessments. This requires emptying ourselves of our subjective opinions, judgments, and projections.

However, to be good coaches, we need to go beyond the first state of awareness—being aware and seeing things as they are—and begin to develop "discriminating awareness" so we can make accurate assessments. In this stage, we have to bring our wisdom, insight, and rigorous reasoning to bear on our observations. In other words, we can't walk into a room and just notice there is a problem, like that people are stuck or ineffective. We have to start to make inferences as to fundamental causes and solutions.

Questioning and listening strategies for effective observation. It's useful to have some strategies for asking questions and listening.

1. *Use empathic listening* to draw people out. "What's on your mind? I'm available to hear all that you have to say."

2. *Ask questions to re-create what happened.* Elicit people's stories about what is going on. Listen not only to their stories, but also their frames (governing values). "Why don't you just tell your side of the story with regard to what's happened since you set your breakthrough goal?"

3. *Ask for specific examples* to test all assumptions in people's stories. "You said Frank doesn't own it. Could you give me

an example?" This will give you clues as to where people's inferences have been arbitrary or biased.

4. *Use diagnostic probes* to get to the heart of the problem (or solution). "Could the problem you are facing be this?"

5. *Test your own assumptions as you listen.* It is impossible for the coach to listen without making assessments, but it is important to verify these assessments so as not to go off track. For example, a coach might say "I am assuming that everyone in the group is committed to this breakthrough goal. Is that correct?"

Separate observations from assessments. Edgar Schein provides a very good model that shows the interrelationship between results, observation, and feedback. The model starts with observing what is happening with a person or group, and then noticing one's own emotional reaction to that situation. Oftentimes, these emotional reactions, if acted on, lead to improper assessments or bad advice. Once you filter through your preconceptions and emotional reactions, the next step is to use both your intuition and powers of judgment to make an assessment of fundamental causes and solutions. This provides the basis of giving feedback that can make a difference.[1] (See diagram 7.1.)

Observe and Interview Group Members

The focus of this section is on people thinking and interacting in a small-group setting. Observing groups tends to be much more complicated than observing individuals. All too often, people who seem bright, intelligent, and committed to learning as individuals wind up in a group whose collective intelligence seems less than that of the individual and where defensive routines and antilearning patterns take over. The results can be frustrating, strange, and even bizarre. A coach or facilitator is highly useful in situations where group dynamics take over because in these situations a group rarely has the ability to observe itself.

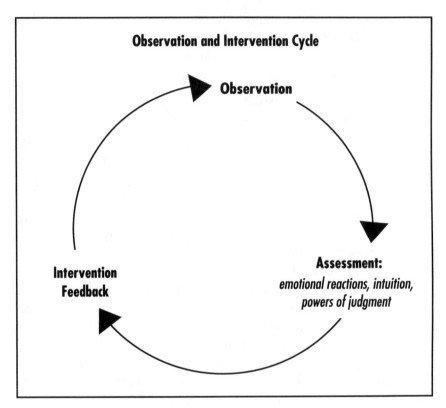

Diagram 7.1

When coaching a group it is necessary to get a sense of the big picture, as well as the small. One way to do this, whether you are group leader or outside coach, is to interview and observe the key players, asking them for their views about what is happening in the group. Doing the interviews tells you a lot about the underlying patterns that define the group situation and allows you to make observations about the individuals.

As it is important to establish a foundation for working with a group, first meet with the group leader and then later with the group members to tell them the purpose of the interviews. This is a good way to judge whether or not the group members have a commitment to change and improvement.

This is critical, as coaching for transformational learning will ultimately involve the members having to face such issues as their personal roadblocks and paradigm paralysis about technical or business issues. It will also involve people facing situations and behaviors that are potentially embarrassing or threatening. This requires a personal commitment by the individual group members, a willingness to participate in a team learning process and, above all, patience.

Ask questions to frame the group situation, obtain useful information, and gain insight. When interviewing people in the group, it is important to have some basic questions in mind.

★ Do the group members have a shared vision of what they are creating together? What is your personal vision for the group or organization? What type of team, organization, or community do you want to develop?

★ How would you describe how the group members think and interact when they meet? What, if any, breakdowns do you see?

★ What are people's relationships like outside of meetings? What's working and not working?

Pay attention to the nature of people's responses to gain insight into them as individuals. As you listen to people tell their stories about what is going on, you will have the opportunity to frame the situations, find examples, and gain insights into the personalities of the individuals. Listen for the frames people are working within, such as the demands and constraints of the group and the mental models for dealing with them. As you listen, ask questions that determine the governing values that the group preaches and that help you find out where behavior is inconsistent with these values. Inquire with openness and candor about counterproductive behavior.

★ What is your view of the governing ideas or values that people talk about?

★ What inconsistencies do you see between what people say and what they do?

★ Where do you see behavior going on that is counterproductive? How is this a matter of group dynamics? How is it a matter of individual behavior?

As you listen, you will discover that people generally fall into two categories. The first category are those who are focused on what they and the group want to create. They tend to be learning oriented and reflective. They will use the interview as an opportunity to inquire about and reflect on the issues that they and the group are facing. They also tend to look at things from the viewpoint of responsibility: "How am I a cause in the matter?" The second category, which is more common, consists of people who are self-protective, reactive, and resistant to learning. People in this category will tend to use the interview as an opportunity to grind their axes, blame others, or justify counterproductive behavior.

Recognizing which category people fall into is important, as one of the main purposes of any intervention is to transform the critical mass of people from an orientation of posturing and defensiveness to one of learning. Once this happens, individuals and groups become capable of self-correction.

Creating Action Maps for Groups

Most group situations are a complex tangle. For example, the group members may have a vision that they do not know how to achieve. On top of this, they may be loaded with defensive routines. They may be saying one thing and doing another due to the unwritten rules of the game. Creating an action map that diagrams the complexity of the situation is a good way to untangle what is going on.[2]

There are basically three ways in which an action map can be employed:

1. It can be used privately by the coach if he or she is just trying to facilitate the group to get a particular result and wants to avoid stepping on a land mine of hot issues.

2. The action map can be prepared privately by the coach and then presented to the group for discussion in order to further team learning.

3. The group and coach can make the action map together.

It is important to point out that the action maps may touch on hot issues like paradigm paralysis in dealing with complex dilemmas and defensive routines. When working with a group, the coach must be prepared to deal with these issues as they arise.

A simple example of an action map might be the illustration of the dynamics between a team and a team leader. For example, in doing the interviews, you might hear people say that the leader is saying one thing and doing another. You may hear from the leader that the team is not taking responsibility. On top of this, you may hear people attribute nasty motives as to the cause of this. This can easily become a vicious circle. Let's say that the leader asks the team to take more responsibility. The group thinks that he doesn't mean it because he often takes over. The result is that people act like they are taking responsibility, but later back off from making decisions, expecting the leader to decide. This reinforces the leader's view of the team and the team's view of the leader. (See diagram 7.2.)

CASE STUDY:
Action Maps Surface Dilemmas

What follows is an action map that a coach can use to sort out complex dilemmas, puzzles, and problems that occur in many work groups. It consists of five categories: (1) context or background, (2) frames and governing variables, (3) dilemmas and puzzles, (4) action strategies, and (5) unintended results. Let's look at each one.

What is the context or background of the group or organization? Observe the background conditions that affect the group. For

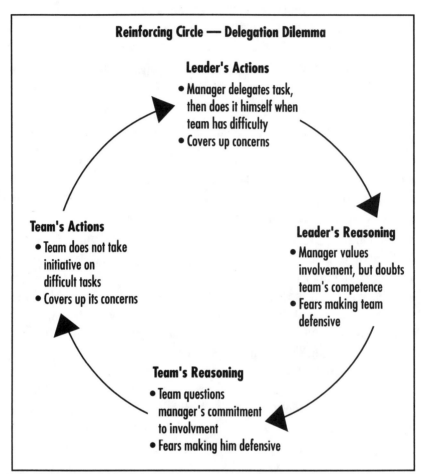

Diagram 7.2

example, what are the market conditions and demands, major changes in the industry, formal policies of the organization, and the unwritten rules of behavior?

What are the frames that shape, limit, and define the group and its situation? It is important for the coach to understand the frames that the group is operating from. These include the vision, goals, governing values, demands, and constraints. For example, I coached a group of executives from a computer firm in the Far East. They saw themselves as a high-tech manufacturing firm. Their *vision and goal* was to sell products outside their home market and have a marketing breakthrough. Their *governing value* (mental model) was one of design and engineering excellence. The *demands and constraints* involved having to make the marketing breakthrough within a year or be sold to a bigger company. Another constraint was that the organization structure consisted of separate product divisions that were being run like separate fiefdoms. There was no structure for collaboration or a team approach to dealing with complex problems.

What dilemmas or puzzles is the group facing? Most groups have tame problems that the group enjoys solving and wild and woolly ones where the search for the solution is bewildering, frustrating, and elusive. It is important for the coach to observe these.

Continuing with our example, the computer group had three sets of dilemmas. On one level, the group was at an impasse in trying to solve certain strategic and operation problems for which there were no obvious solutions, like expanding manufacturing capacity and breaking into new markets.

The group also had dilemmas that involved being polarized around two opposing views. The leader of the group, Tom, wanted to shift to a team-oriented management style to increase sales, yet the fiercely entrepreneurial group members felt this would wreck the existing business, which was based on separate product divisions. Tom and the group members also had uncertainty as to how to handle embarrassing or threatening situations that arose from this. Tom didn't know how to confront the others with how strongly he felt about his approach or his doubts about them. The group members did not want to give up control of their areas, yet wanted to appear to be team players.

What action strategies is the group using to deal with the dilemmas? Action strategies are the coping mechanisms that the leader and the group engage in to deal with the dilemmas. These strategies are generic in nature and usually have to do with bypassing and covering up dilemmas. Let's look again at our example.

Leader's strategies: Tom went back and forth between using defensive reasoning and using creative reasoning to design a new future. He tried to handle the marketing issues by making a unilateral decision to hire a new marketing chief and tried to solve manufacturing issues by doing a study, hoping it would build commitment to reinvent the processes. He avoided confronting group members who disagreed with his new "team approach," as this represented threat or embarrassment: "I don't want to have a blowup," especially with Joseph, a particular division manager. He used a cover-up and bypass strategy to take hot issues off the agenda, rather than engage in public inquiry into the dilemmas. He justified his actions with more defensive reasoning—"the group isn't ready for it" or "the board wouldn't like it"—but did not test his assumptions with the board or publicly with the group.

Group's strategies: The division managers, especially Joseph, also crafted defensive action strategies. For example, Joseph loudly made unilateral statements like "a team organization will never work" and left no opening for his assumptions to be tested. He and others began suppressing the dilemmas in order to protect their turf by saying that moving beyond the home market was not that important or saying they were already doing it, although their sales were low. They blocked the new marketing manager and insisted on having their own sales offices and shot down the manufacturing study. The marketing manager responded to being blocked by going off on his own, building up his own team, and in effect starting his own company in a marginal product area within the company.

To make sure that they wouldn't be challenged or questioned, the product division managers worked very hard at making results look good in their own areas. Their theory was "If something works, don't fix it." Unfortunately, to support their theory, they began bypassing problems in their areas and camouflaging mistakes. They also secretly collaborated against the leader in order to maintain a united front even though they were hostile toward and distrustful of one another.

To preserve the feeling that they were acting in an honest and ethical way, group members covered up these cover-up efforts by using defensive reasoning to justify their actions: "Our business has

MASTERFUL COACHING

increased." "Prove to us we are doing a bad job and then maybe we'll change." "Our products are too specialized to have third parties sell them." The leader and everyone else knew they covered up issues by making them undiscussable at meetings: "Let's stick to facts and figures." "We don't want to have a blowup."

Describe the unintended results or breakdowns. The last part of the action map shows the unintended results that are being produced from the action strategies. Back to our example: The leader wanted to create a breakthrough but wound up getting caught in the defensive strategy of not rocking the boat. His defensive strategy resulted in losing precious time in turning the company around. The rest of the group members had stopped focusing on what they wanted to create and had started focusing on protecting themselves. Their defensive reasoning led to skilled incompetence and unintended consequences.

The first level of breakdown was that everyone felt bewildered, frustrated, and like they were in the wrong place, assuming others had nasty motives. There was a lot of crazy behavior due to the pressure of the dilemmas. The second level of breakdown was that the group became dysfunctional due to the group members' self-protective, antilearning attitudes and the large number of undiscussables. Group members might have used the strategic impasses to do some breakthrough thinking, but couldn't without raising undiscussables. Also, their logic on issues tended to be self-sealing, due to the fact that they wouldn't allow their assumptions to be explored or tested. This made it impossible either to build shared understanding or to come up with anything new.

The third level of breakdown was that the organization started to become unmanageable. There was a piecemeal or fragmented approach to new product development and marketing rather than a holistic one. This led to being shut out of several key opportunities. The unmanageability was also due to the group members camouflaging operational issues in their areas. The dysfunctionality of the group led to a number of crises and to the group members' overdependence on the leader to do all their thinking for them. (See diagram 7.3.)

Action Map

Context / Background

- Increased market pressure
- Company not integrated, run like small businesses
- Main customer becoming competitor
- Loss of money for past three years

Frames

Demands:	Constraints:	Mental Models:
• A marketing breakthrough • Design and engineering excellence • Collaboration—functional structure	• One year to do it or be sold to bigger company • Separate product divisions • Increasingly complex problems in market	• Engineering, manufacturing mentality • Entrepreneur vs. team • Local vs. global

Dilemmas or Puzzles

No obvious solutions	Polarized views	Embarrassing / threatening situations
• How do we expand manufacturing? • How do we break into new markets?	• We should uses a team approach to increase sales. • We should keep separate product divisions and not hurt business.	• If I confront division heads, they will blow up; if I don't, we can't solve problems. • If I become a team player, I will lose control of my area; if I don't, I might lose my job.

Action Strategies

- Cover-up and bypass hot issues
- Make unilateral decisions
- Keep thinking private; no public inquiry into dilemmas
- Don't rock the boat
- Make results look good even if they're not
- Camouflage mistakes
- Make attributions; do not test them
- Secretly collaborate against leader

The first order of breakdown

- People feel bewildered, frustrated, and in the wrong place
- People assume others had nasty motives
- Crazy behavior from pressure of dilemmas

The second order of breakdown

- Issues made undiscussable; no shared understanding
- Group becomes dysfunctional; adopts self-protecting and antilearning attitude
- No questioning of self-sealing logic or assumptions, no new possibilities

The third order of breakdown

- Organization unmanageable due to camouflaged operational issues
- A piecemeal, fragmented approach to new product development and marketing
- Key opportunities missed; lose time in turnaround
- Crises and over-dependence on the leader

Diagram 7.3

Crafting an Intervention

Once you create the map, you are in a position to start to craft the kind of coaching intervention you can use to eliminate unintended results. It is important at this point to not focus on what's wrong, which could be overwhelming, but on *what's missing that could make a difference*. This requires creative and critical thinking. As you are faced with certain dilemmas here, it is best not to try to force the solution.

David Ogilvy, an advertising man, once described the process of coming up with a great campaign theme. "Big ideas come from the unconscious. But your unconscious has to be well-informed or your idea will be irrelevant. Stuff your conscious mind with information and sound analysis. Then unhook your rational thought process. You can help this process by going for a long walk, taking a hot bath, or drinking half a pint of claret. Suddenly, if the telephone line from your unconscious is open, a big idea wells up within you."[3] There are certain key tactics that can help.

1. *Ask "What's missing that could make a difference?"* Focus on small, high-leverage actions, if possible. Think in terms of root causes and solutions. For example, set up a conversation between Tom and Joseph.

2. *Keep it simple.* What is the most simple, straightforward, and logical thing to do that does not require any complex theories and whose need can be demonstrated with factual examples? "Tom, if you and Joe handled your undiscussables on issues (XYZ), it would create an opening for the group to move forward. I would be happy to facilitate that conversation and I think we could transform some of the defensiveness into learning."

3. *Build preventions into the intervention based on what could go wrong.* For example, Tom might say that there could be a blowup in such a conversation. "Tom I would be happy to role play the conversation with you in advance, if you

want, so that you can come to it with some skill and confidence."

We will look further at the nature of the intervention that was crafted with this case study later in the chapter.

Giving Feedback That Makes a Difference

The most intolerable state is the absence of acknowledgment.

William James

Feedback is essential for learning at the individual, group, or organizational level. It is feedback that can help people see the discrepancy between what they think they are doing and what they are actually doing. It is feedback that can interrupt the defensive reasoning or routines that happen with individuals and groups. It is feedback that allows people to recognize and eliminate error and thus allows learning to occur. It can show people where new skills and capabilities need to be developed and lead to insights into ways to improve work processes.

It is important to consider the context in which feedback is given. In the command and control model, feedback often becomes a way to gct people to achieve goals and learn to do things that they do not necessarily want to do. The coercion is often disguised in the form of management by objectives and usually includes performance appraisals, a reward and recognition system, personnel planning, and so on.

In the stewardship or internal commitment model, feedback is a means for individuals or the group to realize their potential. It is based on finding out what people care passionately about and have an internal commitment to, rather than on command and control. Providing feedback in this context involves releasing collective aspirations and helping individuals realize their potential as human beings. It is directed toward helping people discover who they are and what they are magnificently capable of. It involves helping people discover their natural group and finding out what it is they can do to make a real contribution to the group. It is based on people setting their own goals and learning strategies to achieve them. It involves sharing observations that assist with both transformational and incremental learning.

This kind of feedback can be tough-minded. People are made aware of what the vision and goals of the organization are so that they can make a free and informed choice about whether or not they want to participate. If they elect not to participate, they are not regarded as bad people. They are assisted in finding another area in which they can make a genuine commitment.

High-Quality Feedback Requires Generosity of Spirit

Giving high-quality feedback doesn't have to do with a skill or technique; it has to do with caring enough about people to tell it like it is. There are two sides to this. On the one hand, it involves having the generosity of spirit to acknowledge people for who they are and what they are capable of. As Ranganath Nayak, a director at Arthur D. Little consulting company, says, "In my experience, people are starved for praise; not just praise of their accomplishments but for who they are as human beings." On the other hand, generosity of spirit includes being willing to have the tough conversations with people. This requires a degree of trust in people's desire for self-improvement and their capacity for inquiry and self-reflection. Remember to praise publicly and criticize privately.

Most Olympic athletes get coaching feedback for hours a day for years. In most work groups, however, managers will tell you that feedback is the exception to the rule. There are several reasons for this. First the bar of excellence is not high enough to expose people's ignorance and incompetence and thereby create a need for coaching. Secondly, managers are often afraid to step on other people's toes or to say something that might be threatening or embarrassing or that they believe competent professionals should know for themselves. Thirdly, many managers are predominantly left-brain people—

accountants, MBAs, engineers. It has been my observation that predominantly left-brain people are often reluctant to give praise, even though they may desperately be in need of it themselves.

One of the signs of an effective coach is that he or she provides close observation and feedback on a regular basis in light of shared goals.

In so doing, a coach is able to watch people make committed attempts to perform and give them feedback that allows them to adjust their actions and eliminate error. This feedback may have to do with helping them develop new ways of being or altering their thinking and behavior. It may involve providing guiding ideas or fundamentals during practice sessions, as well as extending a keen eye and helping hand with regard to unlearning old habits and learning new ones. The idea is that the coach consistently observes and gives feedback in a way that allows individuals or groups to alter their approach and achieve desired results. Giving feedback only one or twice a year generally has no impact on performance and is only evaluative in nature.

Guiding Ideas for Giving Feedback

Oftentimes, the feedback given to individuals and groups is not particularly meaningful. One reason for this is, as we have said, that feedback is not given in a context of one's internal commitment to goals and a self-directed learning strategy but as an extension of control systems. Another reason is that feedback is often just based on arbitrary opinions and assumptions and is not grounded in examples that the person can learn something from. Finally, feedback is often given in a quasi-dictatorial way. The message is "Do what I say, according to my governing values, or else." As people are not given a free and informed choice, they may resist the feedback.

The following guidelines help to ensure that feedback is meaningful:

★ **Speak with honesty, integrity, and good intent.** In general, the things to give a person feedback on are (1) future potential, (2) general and specific performance, (3) attitude and behavior, and (4) patterns of self-deception. A good principle to follow is to speak with good intent. At the same time, talk straight without avoiding or sugar coating your message. First take a moment to focus on the person before speaking. When you give feedback, speak slowly. This gives you time to integrate your intuition and intellect in saying things in a way that will make a difference.

★ **Link feedback to what the individual or group cares deeply about.** In many cases, groups have visions or goals that they don't care about that much or do not have much at stake in. It is important for the facilitator to distinguish between these and the things people do care about, like their deep beliefs and values.

It is better to motivate with inspiration than fear: "In order to create the desired future, we need to create a culture of transformation and learning."

Sometimes introducing anxiety is necessary to get people's attention: "If we do not change, we may not realize the desired future and may not even survive."

The same applies to the individual: "I know that you want to make a difference on the team. Here is what I see you doing that is getting in the way."

★ **Show where there is a problem and connect it to the way people think and interact.** One of the messages I often give leaders and groups is that the problems that they are facing are usually directly related to their thinking and behavior, rather than something in the organization. Typical feedback to a leader might be "I know you have a sincere and honest intention to realize the vision. However, it isn't being realized and there may be a few ways that you are contributing to this. My sense is that you are depending too much on someone or something external to yourself to make things happen." I then illustrate this with some examples. I might also point out where others are role modeling the leader's behavior, again providing examples.

★ **Make assessments and provide specific examples.** People will be much more ready to entertain feedback if they see that what you are telling them is not based on subjective opinions or value judgments, but on witnessable events and valid information. Praising individuals or a group by saying "You did a really great job" without telling them what they did that was great might leave people feeling manipulated. Instead you might say "You each made an all-out effort. As a result, the team finished the project ahead of schedule and under budget. We are all proud of you." The same applies to giving criticism. Connect all assessments to observable data, using specific examples. It is a good idea to ask people to confirm whether they agree with the assessments you made and the examples you based them on. Perhaps they have different assessments, with different examples.

★ **Show inconsistencies between what people say and what they do.** As already mentioned, people form action strategies based on creative and productive reasoning and then change those strategies midstream to protect themselves, using defensive reasoning. (They are usually unaware of this.) It is important to highlight the discrepancy between what people say and what they do, as well as the unintended results produced. For example, most people have had the experience of going to a big meeting intending to take a stand for real change, but then caving in to get approval from someone else in the group. In a case like this, I might give feedback to empower the person to take a stand: "And now I am going to be provocative. If you compromise half of what you want today and half again tomorrow, you will have nothing left of what you believe in by next week." By announcing that you are going to be provocative, people get the message but tend not to take it personally or resent you for it.

★ **Provide feedback that allows for both transformational and incremental learning.** Both transformational (double-loop) learning and incremental (single-loop) learning are often needed to help people eliminate error. A good coach makes observations and assessments about people's thinking and actions with this in mind. For example, when a good coach sees a person make repeated mistakes in spite of instruction, he or she will ask the coachee "What is the theory you have in your head?" At the same time, once a coach has helped a person find the right theory of action, the coach can help the person to adjust his or her actions on an incremental basis to get the desired results.

★ **Provide feedback with the intent of penetrating collective illusions and patterns of self-deception.** Many people are not aware of their own possibilities and potentials and unknowingly make themselves small. I once did a coaching program for a German company, Adidas, whose sourcing office was in Hong Kong. The seminar included expatriate managers ("expats") and local Hong Kong Chinese. I noticed that the expats adopted a paternalistic attitude toward the locals, excusing their shortcomings. I also noticed that the locals frequently referred to themselves as "just small potatoes." I told them "even a small potato can make a difference." I also told them that their "small potato" act was a way to avoid having to take responsibility. The group resisted the feedback at first, but it later led to a groundbreaking discussion with the expat managers, who had reinforced the locals small potato self-image while blaming them at the same time.

★ **Focus on what's missing, not what's wrong.** Almost anyone can walk up to any person or group and say what's wrong or what is at fault. The most difficult thing is to give feedback in a way that will impact people's ability to perform in the future. Figuring out what's missing usually involves observing breakdowns, separating causes from effects, and then pondering for a while until a creative idea comes to mind. Pat Riley, while coach of the Los Angeles Lakers, was in a championship playoff game with the Boston Celtics. His players felt intimidated by the legendary Celtic's general manager, Red Auerbach, who was famous for tricks such as turning off the air conditioning in the visiting team's locker room, as well as by the fact that they were in a strange and hostile town. Riley knew his team could win if he could make them feel at home. He went out to a store and bought every member of the team huge pastel towels. He reasoned that you only get pastel towels at home. The Lakers swept the series and won the championship.[4]

★ **Praise people for who they are, not just for their accomplishments.** You can have the biggest impact with people by acknowledging them for who they are and their unique qualities of excellence. The clues to who people are, however, often reveal themselves in the things that people do. To acknowledge someone, a coach might say "I want to acknowledge you, not only for the work you put into that great presentation, but also for your personal commitment to excellence. Here are some specific examples...."

★ **Present feedback so it is perceived as an opportunity, not a threat.** It is important to make sure that you present your comments as an opening or opportunity to learn and grow rather than as a scolding. If you are in a situation and are struggling with how to do this, get up from your chair, walk to the window, and think about it. Ask yourself "How can I say this so that the person really gets some value out of it, rather than in a way that makes them react and take it personally?" Sometimes people are uninterested in or indifferent to your feedback, denying that the issue you are raising is really a problem. By understanding the source of their resistance, you put yourself in a position to learn how to deal with it. For example, you might say "I don't feel that I have been successful in getting my message across and I feel that we are not making the progress I would like. What is really bothering you about this?" (See diagram 7.4.)

Feedback Guidelines

1. Speak with honesty, integrity, and good intent.
2. Link feedback to what the individual or group deeply cares about.
3. Show where there is a problem and connect it to the way people think and interact.
4. Make assessments, then tell people witnessable events.
5. Show inconsistencies between what people say and what they do.
6. Provide feedback that allows for both transformational and incremental learning.
7. Provide feedback with the intent of penetrating collective illusions and patterns of self-deception.
8. Focus on what's missing that will make a difference, not what's wrong.
9. Praise people for who they are, not just for their accomplishments.
10. Present feedback so it is perceived as an opportunity, not a threat.

Diagram 7.4

Designing Group Feedback

One of the difficulties in giving feedback to a group is that the situation often contains many different layers of complexity. The tendency is to oversimplify things or use a pet theory: "There is no shared vision." "We're too pie in the sky." "The group is a plane without a pilot." "Everyone has crawled into their bunkers." While this kind of figurative language might be useful, it usually doesn't do much except aggravate people or pass for office gossip. In many cases, these comments are based on untested assumptions. I have found action maps useful in giving feedback to groups. As a coach, you have to adapt the presentation of the action map according to your situation. Are you an insider or outsider? If you are an outside coach, as I am, you might want to present your findings to the leader of the group.

Feedback to the leader. Let's return to our example of the computer company. I summarized my findings and presented them to the leader of the group using the action map. The key in giving him feedback was to help him to see that, while he had a sincere and honest intention to do a good job, he was in large part contributing to the problems of the group. I tried to show him with specific examples where his behavior was leading to unintended results.

I suggested that one thing that was missing that could make a difference was a shared vision or something to rally around that would give people a sense of urgency. Group members felt that he arbitrarily decided to push for a marketing breakthrough and radically transform the organization without consulting them. Therefore, they did not really have an internal commitment to his plans or anything else. I pointed out that group synergy was negatively affected by his saying that he wanted to have more of a team approach, but then making arbitrary decisions in hiring a marketing manager and doing a manufacturing study.

I also hit hard the point that, when embarrassing or threatening issues arose, his tendency was to avoid confrontation by covering up problems and making them undiscussable. I showed, with examples, how he had justified his behavior by blaming the other people, saying they weren't capable of learning or that they would become angry. I then asked Tom how he felt about the feedback and if he wanted to make a change. I also said that I would be available to coach him.

Tom was gracious in accepting the feedback. He said he wanted to change and that he wanted my help. We looked at the next steps and he agreed, first of all, to having a conversation with Joseph where he would raise previously undiscussable issues. The two men did converse and it was obvious at the next group meeting that some of the weight was taken off people's shoulders. The other people sensed the difference and asked for a general meeting to discuss the findings of the action map. I said that this would be fine if they were willing to put their issues on the table as well, as opposed to just having me make a report. They agreed.

Feedback to the group. At the feedback meeting, the leader started out by saying "It is obvious there are things we have not talked about and we have to start doing that now." He acknowledged that he was faced with a tough dilemma. He characterized this dilemma as trying to change a tire on a moving car: "How do you create a new future for the business fast enough, while at the same time not destabilize the existing business?" He revealed that his attempts to deal with this dilemma had been inconsistent, involving both dominating actions and team-building actions. He acknowledged that the group needed to build a shared vision that created a new future and provided stabilization for the business today.

The leader then ask me to present my coaching comments. I advised the group that some of the information might be potentially embarrassing or threatening and requested that they adopt an attitude of learning rather than automatically reacting and becoming defensive. Of course, they agreed. I then went through the action map, illustrating it with as many examples as possible. I hit hard the point about the undiscussables, as well as the bypass and camouflage tactics. I asked people "Where do you agree and where do you disagree with what I have said?" At this point, people in the group started to attack my position as the coach, as well as my thinking, assumptions, data, and so on.

Tom, the leader, urged the group members to see what they could learn from the comments, rather than to try to protect themselves. This led to a discussion about what was right and what was not right on the action map. At one point, Joseph said "Enough! We are chasing the rabbit down the wrong hole. The action map and our comments here today show that there is a fundamentally defensive pattern operating in the group. We can either choose that and have it be the norm for us as a group or we can choose here today to change it and become more of a learning organization." This was a breath of fresh air. The group decided to become a learning organization and began to look at how they were responsible for some of the things in the action map, whether they entirely agreed with it or not.

Other suggestions to the group. I provided other recommendations to the group aimed at providing what was missing that would make a difference.

1. Have a session, as soon as possible, to clarify that the vision is based on a strong business case as well as what matters to people.

2. Because of the complex business dilemmas, learn to use impasses as opportunities for breakthrough thinking. This requires rigorous inquiry and dialogue to both come up with solutions and to build a shared approach. (See Chapter 9, "Trigger Breakthrough Thinking" and Chapter 10, "Build Shared Understanding.")

3. Do more work in overcoming defensive routines, starting with all the things made undiscussable. Do a left-hand column exercise to help people speak with more openness and candor. (See Chapter 11, pages 249-250.)

CHAPTEREIGHT

Teaching New Skills and Capabilities

Knowing "what" is different than knowing "how."

William Isaacs

What's Missing: The Ability to Think and Work Together

Today, companies have to reach new levels of performance, introduce constant change, and bring out the best in people. Our observation is that the basic tool chest of skills and capabilities that most managers have at their disposal—budgeting, planning, marketing, and so on—does not provide them the necessary wherewithal to accomplish these goals. More recently, managers have begun focusing on developing the ideas and analytical techniques offered in total quality programs and "process redesign" efforts. Yet, something is still missing from the tool chest.

Again and again, managers tell us that the skills they need are those that have to do with expanding people's capacity to think and work together.

The purpose of this chapter is to introduce a radical new method of coaching and teaching people new skills and capabilities. It is grounded in transformational learning. It has to do with altering people's frames of reference or mental models so as to produce profound shifts in their perceptions, ways of being, thinking processes, and behavior. This then becomes the base for reliably altering their daily practices. The intent here is to apply this methodology to helping people develop those skills and capabilities that are essential to expanding their capacity to think and interact. This involves coaching people to develop the skills and capabilities that will allow them to transform conversational patterns and collective thinking that lead to unintended results. It consists of helping groups develop a collective intelligence and the ability to take effective actions that are greater than those of the individual members.

This is the essence of what Peter Senge has called "the art and practice of a learning organization." In a learning organization, people develop the capacity to create a new future and reflect on critical and hidden assumptions and patterns of behavior, both individually and as a group. Building these new skills and capabilities is easier said than done, as many people in today's organizations think in a highly reactive way in response to crises and key events and are highly nonreflective. Even conversations often turn into sword fights where the goal is to win by advocating one's views, rather than to listen deeply to other people.

When people learn to think and interact better together, they suddenly see things in a whole new way and act in a new way. Instead of individuals seeing themselves as isolated entities or cogs in the wheel, they see themselves as part of a whole community of practice and act as if what they say and do matters. Rather than seeing that sales are down, they see assumptions and practices that have been taken for granted and need to be examined. Rather than seeing people in other departments as uncooperative, they see that people have different mental maps or ways of thinking. They seek to explore these mental maps in order to build shared understanding. Instead of doing the same thing harder and getting similar results, they see that the old instructions no longer work and need to be reconsidered.

Five Essential Skills

The following five skills and capabilities are essential to helping groups think and interact better together. They are similar to those Peter Senge has written about in *The Fifth Discipline: The Art and Practice of the Learning Organization.* Many of these skills are not new. What is new is how they fit together to make a whole package of what makes team learning possible.

Leadership Commitment. *Leadership is missing when* there is a lack of excitement about the future, when people vacillate about a situation rather than take a stand, when people are not taking risks or initiative. *What is leadership?* Leadership involves shaping an organization's vision

> **N**othing happens in most organizations until someone takes a stand for something different, even if it is controversial or unpopular.

and values so as to bring out the best in people and to generate a conversation for action that makes something happen and that results in things being different. Leadership of the team and personal mastery go hand in hand because the leader must be able to link the organization's goals with his or her own personal goals and aspirations. *Why is it important?* In reality, nothing happens in most organizations until someone takes a stand for something different, even if it is controversial or unpopular.

Reflecting on Mental Models. *Reflecting on mental models is missing when* intelligent and hardworking people and groups are not succeeding. The blocked mental models often result in personal problems, lack of shared understanding, or doing the same thing harder without getting different results. *What are mental models?* Mental models are internal pictures or critical and hidden assumptions about the way the world works. These mental models, though largely transparent, shape the way people think and interact. The discipline of reflecting on mental models involves helping people and groups surface, test, and improve their mental models. This can result in profound shifts in thinking and behavior. *Why is it important?* People often assume that what they believe about colleagues or customers or their approach is true, even though these assumptions are untested. Creating a more insightful and accurate view of reality is essential to producing desired results. Creating a shared mental model is essential to building and implementing a shared vision.

Shared Vision. *A shared vision is missing when* leaders and managers live from day to day and do not have a point of view about the future. Instead of casting their lines to the stars with boldness, daring, and imagination, people spend most of their time trying to fix, help, or solve today's problems. They do not understand the way others think or operate and find it difficult to coordinate even the most mundane activities. *What is shared vision?* Building a shared vision involves people in a group asking "What do we want to create together?" Answering this question requires constructing a shared mental model of the desired future and how it will be realized. *Why is it important?* Shared vision is really an opportunity to create a new future that gives everyone in the organization the chance to be a part of something larger than themselves, as well as to experience being the authors of their own destiny. Unless the vision is shared and means something to the individuals, it will never be implemented.

Dialogue and Conflict Resolution. *Dialogue is missing when* the person with the biggest stick tries to dominate other people while manipulating them to make sure they don't become upset. Disagreement is avoided by all team members because it is potentially threatening or embarrassing. *What is dialogue?* A dialogue is a conversation where there is a free flow of meaning in a group and diverse views and perspectives are encouraged. The key to engaging people in a real quality of dialogue is to make disagreement acceptable so that people focus on what they can learn in the conversation rather than on winning or avoiding losing. Encouraging diverse views and perspectives often leads to shared understanding as well as to discovering something new. *Why is dialogue important?* It is the primary way by which groups think and interact. Lack of dialogue leads to poor decisions, lack of team learning, and a general deterioration of the group.

Systems Thinking. *Systems thinking is missing when* people get stuck in the view that "I am my position" and in their functional stove pipes, which leads to organization fragmentation and profound feelings of isolation. Business processes may change, but the barriers to thinking and working together remain. People may also react to problems in isolation, not seeing how these may be caused by slow, gradual processes. *What is systems thinking?* This involves a shift in viewpoint from seeing ourselves as separate to seeing ourselves in unity with other people and things. In practical terms, it involves thinking in terms of balancing the big picture and the small picture, the long-term view and the short-term view, and making sure that all the different pieces of the organization fit together to make a whole. *Why is systems thinking important?* For one thing, it's the key to dealing with the issues of cooperation, as well as to managing change and complexity.

The development of new skills or capabilities, like those mentioned above, involves people learning to see things in a new way. But learning to see and do things differently is only half the battle. The other side of it has to do with unlearning old ways of seeing and doing things.

A Methodology for Building New Skills and Capabilities

Now let's look at a methodology for teaching people new skills and capabilities that is based on transformational learning. (See diagrams 8.1 and 8.2.)

1. Label the skills that are missing and tell people why they are important.

2. Give people guiding ideas concerning the new skills that help them to establish a new frame of reference and begin to build new practices.

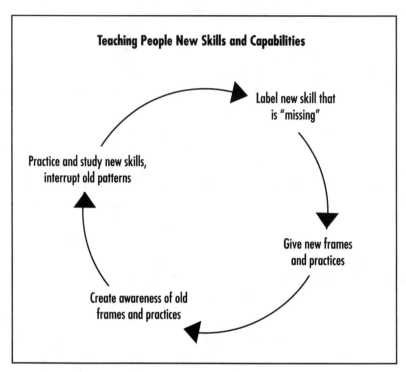

Teaching People New Skills and Capabilities

Label new skill that is "missing"

Give new frames and practices

Create awareness of old frames and practices

Practice and study new skills, interrupt old patterns

Diagram 8.1

3. Help people become aware of old frames of reference and practices that are counterproductive and inhibit learning the new skills.

4. Coach people in action, interrupting old patterns, until they gain competence.

Let's look at each step.

1. Label the Missing Skills

One of the most important phases in the process of coaching people to develop new skills is labeling the missing skills. Until people can distinguish these missing skills by putting them into words, they will not be able to act effectively. For example, today the skill of dreaming

MASTERFUL COACHING

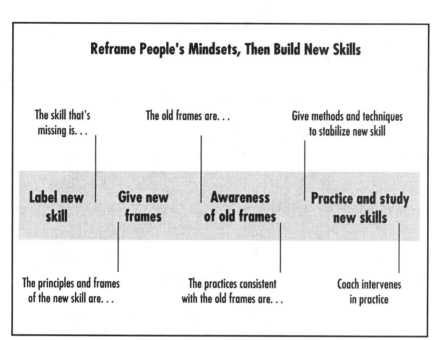

Reframe People's Mindsets, Then Build New Skills

The skill that's missing is. . .

The old frames are. . .

Give methods and techniques to stabilize new skill

| Label new skill | Give new frames | Awareness of old frames | Practice and study new skills |

The principles and frames of the new skill are. . .

The practices consistent with the old frames are. . .

Coach intervenes in practice

Diagram 8.2

about the future and using creative and critical thinking to regenerate industries and come up with fundamentally new products and services is beginning to be labeled. For the last ten years or so, this skill was, for the most part, felt but unspoken in management circles where the emphasis was on skills that involved finding ever better ways to cut costs, like restructuring, reengineering, and total quality.

The act of putting an idea into language has real generative power. To begin with, it announces a new domain of practice that is different from everything else that people are doing. Also, if the idea is expressed powerfully and precisely, it helps refocus people's actions. For instance, my friend Bob Fritz makes the distinction between "being creative" and "creativity." Being creative leads to creating something that never existed before, such as a new industry or a new product or service. Creativity is more about creative or artistic expression. Once people know what it means to "be creative," they can begin to learn about the behavior that will allow them to create something new.[1]

Once the coach labels the new skill, the next step is to make sure people understand why it is important. This is especially vital if the new skill or capability does not fit into the prevailing context of the organization. To introduce the idea of "creative thinking" in the cost-cutting context that we have described might lead someone to say "Yes we need creative thinking, but first of all we need not to lose money in this project." To make sure people understand the importance of the skill, you have to put it out to them so they can see it and accept it. "We can cut all day long, but if we don't come up with some innovative product ideas in this development process, we may miss the turnoff to the future and our customers will go somewhere else."

2. Distinguish New Frames and Practices

What is the source of skill? If you look at the people you know who are masterful at something, and look behind what's easy to see, you start to observe that a high level of skill development is a complex phenomenon. First of all, people who are highly skillful in a particular domain possess and strongly identify with guiding ideas, beliefs, and values that are pertinent to that domain. These ideas, beliefs, and values become a frame of reference that shape their perceptions and whole way of being. When people are highly skillful at something, it seems to be an expression of their personal essence. Along with this, they have a particular way of thinking about things that shapes their actions. Over time, this whole orientation leads to the development of certain practices that are deeply grounded in action.

New frames of reference touch people with new possibilities and choices and lead to new skills and capabilities.

The question is how to help people develop new skills and capabilities when it actually involves new ways of being, new ways of thinking, and new practices. My observation is that the area of highest leverage is in producing an alteration in people's governing ideas, beliefs, and values. When people see things differently, they act differently. This alteration in people's frames of reference is the trigger of transformation. The idea is not to replace one guiding idea or belief system with another that is superior. It is to distinguish new frames of reference that touch people with new possibilities and choices and that lead to new skills and capabilities.

CASE STUDY:
Swissair: Giving People the Right Frames

Most of us live under the massive illusion of separation. We feel separate from our feelings, separate from others, separate from the universe. In personal relationships, this leads to fear, anger, or intolerance of others. In organizations, it leads to increasing fragmentation, rigidity, and deterioration. (See diagram 8.3.)

Two Fundamental Frames

Separate	Related
• Seeing parts—fragmented	• Seeing whole—systemic
• I am separate • Fear • Ego-centered	• I am related • Caring • Cooperative
• How do I maximize winning and avoid losing?	• How do I (we) learn to create what I (we) need?
• Seek approval • Be nice; manage impressions	• Be authentic • Forward purposeful action
• Convince; avoid disagreements and upsetting people	• Question assumptions and see disagreements as an opportunity
• Monopolize air time • Protect turf • Competition	• Build shared meaning • Build bridges • Cooperation

Diagram 8.3

Heady stuff but, nonetheless, true. How do you overcome this if you are running a business? "To start, you have to hire people who like people," says Philippe Chéhab, division manager of Swissair, "and they have to like them enough to be able to embrace their idiosyncrasies rather than be intolerant and judge them."[2]

"Our commitment is to offering world-class service on our flights. We have special orientation programs for all our flight crews that help people break down the walls that usually separate them from other people and lead to premature judgments and emotional reactions." Chéhab continued, "Besides hiring people who like people, we try to give them the right mind-map. Our mind-maps shape our behavior. We tell people that Swissair is about being of service and ask them to identify with that and to put themselves in the customer's shoes. If our flight attendants like people, identify with being of service, and have the right mind-map so they can see things from the customer's perspective, the rest takes care of itself. We don't have to tell them how to behave. We no longer have to tell them to put the fork here or there. That's our strategic edge."

The next phase of the Swissair staff-development program teaches people that they are part of a living organization rather than just isolated individuals doing a job. Most people are like ants crawling on Picasso's "Guernica." They can sense their place and the procession of changes, but they cannot see the whole painting. According to Chéhab, "Getting people to see the importance of their job position in the airline and, at the same time, to have a sense of the whole is something we have been working on at Swissair for the last fifteen years."

Chéhab, a former geographer who studied the work of Frederick Vester, a German who wrote about systems dynamics in 1924, seems to embody these principles. It is clear from his entire presence that looking at things from the systems thinking perspective has profoundly altered what he sees, along with his sense of self. While he honors his individual identity, he also identifies with "the whole community" and it comes across as a profound sense of connectedness, caring, and sensitivity to wisps of information or feedback that might seem only distantly relevant to others.

To help people expand their outlook from an "I am my position" perspective to a "systems thinking" perspective, Chéhab and his group give people a "helicopter ride" of the business, using some loop diagrams that allow people to see the business from a holistic perspective. These show how the different parts of the airline system interact in a dynamic, holistic way and how seemingly random decisions and actions can have an impact. (See diagram 8.4.) This not only helps people to see the business differently, but to feel a new sense of responsibility.

"If there is a problem, it's part of our culture to find the trigger point for the problem in the system even if it is many steps removed from you, not just to blame someone who seems to be the apparent cause of the problem. The apparent cause of the problem is often different from the real cause," according to Chéhab. "For example, if someone asks for an aisle seat on a plane and doesn't get it, this error could be a problem with ticketing, with flight scheduling, with the travel agent, or with how many hours people have slept and,

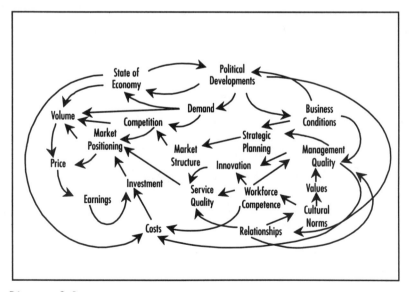

Diagram 8.4

therefore, how attentive they are. When we get information about a problem, we try to find the systemic cause."

"People need to see that they are part of a whole system and that their individual actions can set in motion processes that impact the whole system. At the same time, they need to see how individuals far removed from them can take actions that directly affect their part of the business," says Chéhab. At Swissair, people are expected not only to notice things and make improvements in their areas, but to take responsibility for noticing things and suggesting improvements in other areas that might have consequence on a system level. "We show them the consequence of noticing something that doesn't work and saying something or not saying something about it."

"Seeing things from a relationships point of view, from a systems point of view, or from a view of being responsible for the whole, not just your area," says Chéhab, "starts out as being an interesting idea for people and is something they have to get used to. But in time, it becomes part of a whole new identity structure for them. What we are looking to do is to find ways to accelerate this process." The combination of reframing, plus the reinforcement over time, results in a real spirit of cooperation that probably would never have happened if you had just told people to cooperate. According to Chéhab, "It leads to a feeling of community, of being part of a network that extends to people around the world."

3. Help People to Become Aware of Old Frames and Practices That Inhibit Learning

When you are teaching people new skills, it is not as if you are projecting these onto a blank screen. People already have frames within which they are highly skillful and which may be counterproductive to getting the results they want. They are also highly skillful in the ways of being and acting that go along with these old frames. This may have a huge impact on people's ability to incorporate the new skills and capabilities that you are trying to teach them. This applies to all of the skills we have been talking about here: leadership, mental models, shared vision, dialogue and shared understanding, and systems thinking. (See diagram 8.5.)

For example, we were once teaching a local manager about leadership. The manager had learned some of the juicy vocabulary of leadership like "taking a stand" and went around talking about it all the time. Yet, he got himself into trouble because he was so highly skilled at "trying to please others" and at altering what he stood for according to the political situation. The hardest thing for him to do was to take a stand. He took one stand one day, another

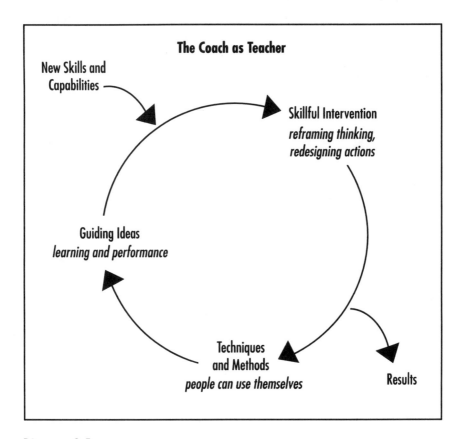

The Coach as Teacher

New Skills and Capabilities

Skillful Intervention
reframing thinking, redesigning actions

Guiding Ideas
learning and performance

Techniques and Methods
people can use themselves

Results

Diagram 8.5

stand the next, and then convinced himself that he was standing for the same thing. As the manager's inability to take a stand was based on behavior that he was highly skillful in, we might call it "skilled incompetence." The interesting thing was that the manager was totally unaware of the skills that caused him to try to be liked or to vacillate from one day to the next. Chris Argyris calls this "skilled unawareness."

Thus, it is the role of the coach to help people break the grip of and excel beyond those frames that have become counterproductive. This means helping people surface, test, and revise their underlying assumptions. If people have a lot at stake in their old frames, just mentioning the new ones—like operating in the domain of risk, taking a stand, seeing things from a systems perspective—and engaging people in a dialogue about them will be a provocation. In this stage of the coaching process, people are likely to have one of the following reactions:

1. People superficially agree with what you are telling them because they are looking for advice, but do not really question their own underlying thinking processes.

2. People become confused and do not really seem to understand what you are talking about. This is generally a sign that you are presenting them a frame that is inconsistent with the one in their heads.

3. People may become sad, angry, or even afraid because they have a lot invested in their old frames.

Do not take these reactions personally. These reactions are all part of the transformational learning process.

The role of the coach is to use whatever people say or do as an opportunity to help them reflect more deeply, listening for opinions, assumptions, and meanings. Often, the things that people say will be in disagreement with what you're trying to teach them. For example, people might say "You tell me I should care, but if I allow myself to care, I may get disappointed later on," "Why take a stand and get my head chopped off?" or "The message that comes across is that we should work as a team and see things from a systemic point of view. Let me ask you something. What's in it for me? I won't get paid for it." When these kinds of responses come up in a group you are coaching, it is important to understand that what people say makes logical sense to them given their way of seeing and thinking about things.

To help people gain more awareness of how they are thinking about things, ask questions that take the reflection deeper: "What leads you to say that? What is the thinking behind that?" or "What are the results that you are producing based on looking at things in that way? Are they the results that you intended?" Or make a provocation: "I hear resignation. What happened to cause you to think this way? How do you feel about that?" or "It sounds to me like you are protecting yourself. Why do you feel like you have to do that?"

> *Gaining awareness of previously unrecognized frames is a vital link in the process of learning new skills and practices.*

As we have said, people have emotions that are tied to their frames—anger may go with blaming, sadness may accompany avoiding loss, or fear may be tied in with a competitive frame. These emotions are usually a result of incidents that have happened in the past that caused people to create the frames to begin with. I have found that when people get in touch with the emotional side, they can then begin to have clarity about the frames they have created. Asking people about the feelings around their frames, or what they are feeling as they talk about them, is often very critical. Although it may not be easy for people to get in touch with the emotions or share their vulnerability, the coach can make it easier by saying something like "I am available to hear all that you have to say about what you think and feel in regard to this. Any emotions you are feeling are okay with me and I encourage you to recognize and express them."

Remember, old frames have power because people are unaware of them. It is this lack of awareness that often keeps people trapped in seeing things or thinking about things in a way that leads to unintended results. Gaining awareness of previously unrecognized frames is a vital link in the process of learning new skills and practices.

There is a good three-step technique for reframing. You can either take people through this process by asking a carefully designed series of questions or you can present it as a team exercise so that people can do it themselves.[3]

I. Surface the old frame: Look for critical and hidden assumptions

★ If people superficially agree with the new frame, take the reflection deeper by asking them where their behavior is inconsistent with it.

★ Invite people to use disagreement with new frames as a way to surface old frames.

★ If people are confused, tell them that is part of the reframing process and to take the reflection deeper.

II. Suspend frames: Test for validity and usefulness

★ Ask people to suspend their frames by observing them and becoming aware of their unintended consequences rather than just defending them.

★ Ask "Is that frame of reference valid based on what really happened?"

★ Once a belief or assumption surfaces, ask "Is it useful?"

III. Revise the frame: Find a better way to look at it

★ Ask for alternative ways of looking at things or thinking about things.

★ Restate governing principles of new frames.

★ Begin to provide operating principles.

When the frame of reference that shapes people's actions shifts, an alteration occurs. What shows up is a whole new way of being, a whole new dynamic mindset, and a sudden and visible change both in people's attitudes and behavior. This creates the opportunity for people to become skillful in new ways and to incorporate principles and techniques that before would have just seemed like bullets on an overhead slide in a training program.

4. Practice and Study Until People Embody the New Skills

To review, a new skill or capability has been labeled, as have the frame or guiding ideas behind it. At the same time, people have had an opportunity to reflect on and become aware of the frames and behavior that might be counterproductive. At this point, there is a danger that people will take the "new" good advice as gospel and go around talking about it, yet wind up looking insincere or incompetent when they try to practice it. The reason for this is that people are experts in the old frames and old practices, while just novices in the new frames and practices. Thus, when they try to show leadership or team learning skills, they wind up blundering and then reverting to their old ways under stress and pressure. The new frames and practices are not stabilized.

If a person's basic strategy toward life has been to dominate others by lecturing at them, it's easy for that person to bounce back to old ways when he or she feels threatened or doesn't know how to handle a situation. And the person may not even be aware that he or she is doing so. This is because when people are "experts" at something, they know those skills and behaviors in a tacit way and do them automatically.

To demonstrate what we mean by this, let's do a quick test. Imagine that you are riding a bike and you start to fall to the left. Which way do you turn the wheel, left or right? You may not be able to immediately answer the question, but you probably moved your body or thought about the movements of your body to find the answer. The knowledge is tacit, in the muscles. If you were on a bike, you would do it without even thinking about it. The same goes for all of the things people are skillful in, whether these skills are allowing them to get the desired results or not. Again, to learn new skills, people need to unlearn old skills and to practice and study over time to develop the new ones.

One powerful method for coaching people to integrate new skills and capabilities is to help them find a role model who embodies those skills in a similar context. If a project manager in a big firm wants to learn how to create a real team, he or she might find project managers in the same category. A key is not just to focus on one role model, but to scan the horizon for many different role models. This is helpful in incorporating the skills or capabilities into one's personal style.

It is important that the coach interact with people as they make committed attempts to perform the new skills. This might involve setting up regular coaching conversations, over a period of time, to look at the places where people have been stuck or ineffective in practicing the new skill. (See Chapter 3 for methodology.) Or it may involve creating a practice field apart from the day-to-day grind where you go through various exercises, allowing people to incorporate the new practices, while observing their old behavior. In a process like this, people can see how ingrained the old ways are. The important part of doing exercises on the practice field is that people can make mistakes, get feedback, and learn without having their learning experience affect the business results. Again, the practice field is an opportunity to slow everything down.

At one company, over a period of a year, we coached members of a team who were in charge of a project designed to decrease costs and speed up deliveries in a complex supply chain. The success of this project involved significant organizational changes, not only in technical aspects, but also in company mindset and behavior. To empower the group we created a managerial practice field that met on a monthly basis to develop a variety of skills and capabilities that were missing. The members would study skills like leadership, dialogue, and systems thinking and then go back and look at how they could directly apply these to the task at hand. They also used the breakthrough technique to forward the project through a widening circle of short-term successes. (See Chapter 12.)

Learning new skills while trying to achieve real-world results can be powerful. When it works, everyone becomes engaged in the same learning process and people have a common frame of reference and language. You will also have the pleasure of watching your group or organization reach new levels of performance.

Part III

The Secrets of Masterful Coaches

This section of the book provides people on the journey to becoming masterful coaches the ideas, tools, and methods they need to succeed in specific situations that might otherwise be baffling, confusing, or frustrating. For example, what do you do when you are coaching a leader who has set a personal stretch goal or defined a problem but seems to have exhausted all known possibilities? What do you do when you are facilitating a team decision and there is no shared view, defensive behaviors are rife, and people are ready to throw in the towel? What approach do you take when you are leading a complex project where people are making lots of plans and preparations but not producing any tangible results? These are questions that anyone who takes coaching seriously will eventually face.

Each chapter of this section is based on a secret or guiding principle that will help the reader deal with these questions. In most cases, the guiding principle is widely known but its importance is overlooked. In other cases, people do not know the tools and methods for putting the principle to work in their businesses with different stakeholders and factions, amidst change and complexity. It is important to point out that the only way to master these principles, ideas, and methods is to practice them until you actually embody them. Just knowing about them isn't enough, as you will see the first time you try them out.

The following chapters will help you discover your own ability to help other people and groups transform impasses into opportunities for breakthrough thinking. You will learn how to facilitate collaborative conversations that result in a shared vision and shared approach, as well as how to recognize and disperse defensive routines. You will learn how to help a group take a large project that was stalled and produce measurable, bottom-line results in weeks, not months. And you will learn how to create a climate or environment where people add value by design.

CHAPTER NINE

Trigger Breakthrough Thinking

At the boundaries, life blossoms.

Gleick, *Chaos*

From Archimedes to Plato, from Mozart to Madame Curie, from Edison to Einstein, and from Freud to Maslow, all the greatest artists, thinkers, and innovators in the world have had one thing in common: the ability to put to use the one durable resource they had—their minds. They had the ability to think more powerfully and more flexibly. The result was new possibilities and opportunities. For Einstein, it was $e = mc^2$. For Edison, it was the electric light and phonograph. For Freud, it was the subconscious. For Madame Curie, it was the x-ray. What does this have to do with creating new value, coaching, and outrageous goals? Lots!

The reason why most managers never produce a breakthrough is that they often do not distinguish between thinking and action.

If people aren't doing something, we assume they are doing nothing. It is said that Socrates' wife used to yell at him when he was looking out the window, assuming he was just daydreaming. In reality, he was hard at work. There are a lot of people like Socrates' wife in today's organizations. People are expected to be doing something all the time, so they seldom have time to think or to really ponder things, let alone exercise breakthrough thinking. Also, when they do try to think, they are often interrupted, as if what they are doing is not important. On the one hand, this is very sad. On the other hand, it represents a hidden reserve of talent, ability, and energy that is available in many organizations. This chapter presents the opportunity that you have as leader, manager, and coach to tap that hidden reserve, as well as to invite people to explore the passions of the mind.

> **B**reakthrough thinking is when we conjure up possibilities that result in creating something that never existed before that alters our environment.

What do we mean by breakthrough thinking? First of all, by thinking we mean the mental processes by which an individual learns to meet basic needs, solve basic problems, and adapt to one's surroundings. A fancy word for this adaptive kind of thinking is cognition. For example, when it is cold you think of putting on a coat. This kind of thinking is essential but it is not creative or generative. Breakthrough thinking is when we conjure up possibilities that result in creating something that never existed before that alters our environment. It can also lead to a sudden and visible change in human behavior. Breakthrough thinking can be applied to setting outrageous stretch goals—inventing new products, redesigning processes, managing information, or exploring new ways for people to think and interact. It can also be used to get past the detours, halts, stuck places, and human predicaments that arise while trying to realize a breakthrough goal.

Think, Plan, and Act From a Breakthrough Perspective

In the normal course of events, people think, plan, and act from their current perspectives. They tend to create a vision of the future that is an extension of the same old story. They set predictable goals that are easily planned right up through the last steps. These goals allow people to stay within their existing skill-set, almost guaranteeing effective action. If you dig deep down into the source of this behavior, what you see is incremental thinking, fear of taking a risk, and a willingness to have life creep along at the same petty pace. It is my observation that seven out of ten people in most organizations operate this way. The only time they don't is in a crisis when they are forced to go beyond their definition of what is "reasonable." The result is often crisis-generated miracles. The question is "How do you make miracles routine?"

Breakthrough thinking is not just a creative thinking technique, it is an entirely different approach to life and work. It is based on being able to think, plan, and act from what will produce a breakthrough. This leads to using your knowledge of the environment, your company's core competencies, along with your creativity and imagination to create a point of view about the future. It leads to formulating a vision based on a new future and to setting outrageous goals that are not predictable or likely; furthermore, the steps needed to reach these goals cannot be planned. It leads to having to develop new knowledge and skills and "out-of-the-box" solutions. At the same time, breakthrough thinking involves a particular set of ideas, methods, and tools for solving problems that look difficult or impossible.

It is not the intention of this book to cover the map on breakthrough thinking but to give the reader a reference point for understanding what it means, as well as some basic tools and methods that you can use in helping to coach people to achieve breakthrough goals.

A Framework for Triggering Breakthrough Thinking

1. Ask people "What's really possible and achievable?" Ask the question "What's really possible and achievable?" the next time your team is about to set goals; then let your imaginations soar. This will not only lead to breakthrough goals but to creative and effective solutions. Peter Jackson, group general manager of marketing for Royal Insurance, says "We've applied breakthrough thinking at Royal to creating our vision. We thought about where we really wanted to be in the future if there were no constraints. We then thought backward toward where we were and 'invented' what was missing. This, along with a healthy dose of ambition, pushed us well beyond what we normally think is possible and achievable."

According to Jackson, "If we tried to create our vision based on where we are now, we would not only wind up settling for less in terms of profit and growth, but fail to challenge our own thinking and behavior." A firm advocate of "thinking outside the box," Jackson was looking for a way to expand Royal's fortune in a tough market where most people don't like insurance companies. So he asked himself and his team how to reach the outrageous goals that they had set for themselves. He and his team came up with two out-of-the-box solutions; one had to do with improving the company's 24-hour hot line that provides instant service to people who are in a crisis. The other had to do with investing a big chunk of the marketing budget in anticrime programs that provided neighborhoods all over Great Britain with extra streetlights, security cameras, and youth programs.[1]

2. Make sure that the commitment to the stretch goal is nonnegotiable. Research shows that realizing stretch goals is related to making nonnegotiable commitments. Closing all escape hatches and holding people to the commitment is a powerful way to trigger breakthrough thinking. In the early days of the American auto industry, Henry Ford asked his engineers to design an automatic transmission in less than a year. They told him that it was impossible and that it would take decades for the technology to be developed. Ford was unrelenting. He got his hydromatic transmission in nine months. Today, many managers take this same approach, knowing that holding people to a nonnegotiable commitment often leads them to tap their creativity and effectiveness, even if such an approach seems unreasonable. This

MASTERFUL COACHING

doesn't mean that you never change a commitment or promise, but that you err on the side of keeping it—not breaking it.

3. Ask people to state the problem that they are trying to solve in one sentence. Once people create an outrageous objective, they are usually presented with a number of complex issues and problems. The problem must be stated in the proper way or people will find that they are looking for the solution to the wrong problem. George Lois, recognized as one of America's advertising geniuses, was once trying to create a campaign for Volkswagen in post-World War II New York. About a month after he had been given the assignment, he called the CEO, who had been wondering what had happened him. Lois said "I've got it." The CEO said "At last the solution." Lois shot back "No, the problem—how to sell a German car in a Jewish town." He had spent a month trying to state the problem in one sentence. Lois believes that if you can't define the problem in one sentence, you don't understand your subject. If you can, that "problem" can become an opportunity for truly inventive work. In Lois' case, it led to a new advertising campaign that focused on trying to make the Volkswagen something people could identify with. The campaign was called "Think Small" and "The Beetle."[2]

4. Get people to see that their current knowledge and options won't take them where they want to go. People sometimes think the difficulty they experience in reaching their goals is due to a lack of creative thinking or brainstorming. In fact, this is often not the case. The problem is that people are unaware that their attempts to come up with a home-run, out-of-the-box solution are taking place within an inaccurate or obsolete mental model. This is why Edward de Bono recommends "lateral thinking"—not going down the same ruts but cutting across them and creating new pathways.

Another issue is that people often don't like to admit that they are wrong. "Want to know my definition of insanity?" McDonald's CEO Mike Quinlan asks. "It's doing the same thing over and over again and expecting different results."[3] People tend to identify with ideas and ways of doing things that have worked well in the past, even though they may not be getting the results now. One of the things that a coach can do is to tell people "Look, we have reached a fork in the road. One road means doing the same thing harder. The other involves acknowledging that our current options won't take us where we want to go." This is a very important step in freeing up people's creativity and imagination for breakthrough thinking.

To help people break out of a rut, Joel Barker, filmmaker and author on the subject of "paradigm busting," suggests the use of "accelerator phrases." Have people gather together in a group and spend fifteen minutes or so completing these statements: "We act as if the only way to do this is...." "A standard practice for us to deal with this problem would be...."[4] Then look at whether or not those paradigms are helping or inhibiting the creative process.

> **B**reakthrough thinking seldom occurs without people engaging in questions over a significant period of time, as well as taking rigorous, experimental action in pursuing their goals.

5. Engage in a rigorous, active inquiry to reveal the possibilities that are really available. If there are more possibilities available to us than we are presently experiencing, we need a way to access them. The primary way to do this is through rigorous, active inquiry. Breakthrough thinking seldom occurs without people engaging in questions over a significant period of time, as well as taking rigorous, experimental action in pursuing their goals. As a coach, you have to get the message across that a breakthrough idea comes like a crack of lightning. The process of pondering the key questions involved in trying to realize an outrageous goal is vital. One way to get the message across is to model the process. Find a key question and spend time mulling it over with your team.

Another approach is to use examples. Nayak and Ketteringham, in their book *Breakthroughs!*, show that almost every major product and marketing breakthrough of the last thirty years was a result of people engaging in what Einstein called "the sacred art of inquiry." This includes the invention of the VCR, 3M's Post-it™ pads, the microwave oven, the CAT scanner, Nautilus weight machines, and the compact disc. Archimedes, when told to weigh the gold in a crown without melting it or separating the different metals, fretted constantly and found the problem most intrusive when he was relaxed and resting. Unable to let go of it, even in his bath, Archimedes noticed his body displacing the water in his tub and shouted "Eureka!" He had discovered the law of displacement of solids.[5]

6. Encourage people to question sacred cows. Human beings work within a limited space of possibilities. These possibilities are determined by our culture, upbringing, education, immediate environment, and by our own lens of perception. In most cases, the possibilities that we have to work with are determined more by our own mental models than they are by physical reality. For example, at the very same time that the pony express was trying to deliver the mail faster by getting speedier horses and moving stations closer together, someone else was inventing the telegraph.

Coaching people to be able to invent the telegraph, virtual reality, or better ways of thinking and working together starts with encouraging people to question sacred cows. This helps them to become more aware of how their own mental models are limiting them from seeing new possibilities. It also involves an act of faith on the part of the coach. This might consist of saying things to people like "There is a way to get this done—we just haven't discovered it yet." Examples that show how people limit their possibilities by the interpretations they make can be helpful. Here is one of my favorites. In 1902, the Daimler Benz company said that the world market for cars would never exceed a million. The limiting factor? It would never be possible to train more than that many chauffeurs.

7. Harness the knowledge in people's heads to find breakthrough solutions. One of the most powerful sources of breakthrough ideas is the tacit knowledge that is already in people's heads. This tacit knowledge is based on wisdom, subjective insights, hunches, and intuitions that people have gained from customers or workplace interactions, as well as years of experience. The coach can play a powerful role in helping people to harness this knowledge. Sometimes just asking people for their ideas and listening intently, while suspending judgment, can help.

Another good approach has to do with questions: "Ask questions, lots of questions, crazy questions," says Bob Galvin, chairman of

Motorola.[6] According to Nicolas Hayek, chairman of SMH Industries, "Too many of our institutions are like prisons—all steel and cement and rules. We kill too many ideas by rejecting them...by laughing at them." Hayek believes that miracles can be produced only if we believe "dreams" and "fantasies" and ask the same naive questions children ask all over the world: "Why does something work that way?" "What if...?" In a late-night session, Hayek asked a crazy question that led to a breakthrough: "Why can't we design a striking, low-cost, high-quality watch and build it in Switzerland?" This question led to the creation of the highly successful Swatch.[7]

8. Use metaphors, analogies, and models to create new knowledge. Ikujiro Nonaka, in an article called "The Knowledge-Creating Company," writes that Japanese companies are particularly adept at using metaphors and analogies to help link similar or dissimilar ideas in a way that results in thrilling, creative, breakthrough solutions. He also shows that finding "models" from other firms who have solved similar problems differently can be a powerful vehicle for the same.[8]

Metaphors. When the idea of "Let's Gamble" was presented to the Honda design group, the leader of the group came up with the metaphor "the theory of automobile evolution." Automobiles generally don't evolve, but asking people to think as if they did led to the idea of "man-maximum, car-minimum" in an all-night, think tank session. The designers felt that if a car was to evolve in the Tokyo environment, it would be spherical, compact, tall, and easy to park. This idea, in turn, led to the highly successful Honda City Car. This was in the 1970s when Detroit was building long, low sedans. According to the head of the project, Hiroo Watanabe, "We wanted to challenge the conventional thinking of Detroit."[9]

Analogies. Sometimes analogies can help move a project forward. At the Xerox research center in Palo Alto, California, someone asked the question of how they could build a computer without a keyboard. Then someone in the group suggested something that could be moved around on the screen like a mouse darting to and fro. The rest is history.

Models. Though managers often spend time thinking about a creative solution to a problem, they often suffer from insularity. If you look in the wrong places, you won't find what you are looking for, no matter how hard or intelligently you try. Les Wexner, chairman and founder of The Limited, who likes to think of himself as the company leader and coach, recognized the need to find other models when his company started to lose its focus and falter in the marketplace. "I looked for successful models of multidivisional businesses in retailing and I really believe there aren't any. So I saw I had to talk to people outside of retailing."[10] Wexner then looked outside retailing, spending three months visiting people like G.E. chairman Jack Welch and Pepsi chief Wayne Calloway. The models Wexner uses now come from far outside the world of retailing.

A model can be used to help solve almost any business problem—strategy or structure, marketing, or product development. For example, the idea for the Reebok® "pump" came when a shoe designer found an old pair of ski boots in his closet that used a similar bladder system. The boots were pulled out more than once for study in the process of designing the shoes. Finding or building a model also provides a way to share with other people in the company the new knowledge that is created. (See diagram 9.1.)

Breakthrough Thinking

1. In setting stretch goals, ask people "What's really possible and achievable?"

2. Make sure that the commitment to the stretch goal is nonnegotiable.

3. Have people state the problem they are trying to solve in one sentence.

4. Get people to see that their current knowledge and options won't take them where they want to go.

5. Engage in rigorous, active inquiry to find new possibilities.

6. Encourage people to question sacred cows.

7. Harness the knowledge in people's heads to find breakthrough solutions.

8. Use metaphors, analogies, and models to create new knowledge.

Diagram 9.1

Triggering Breakthrough Thinking at Engelhard Corporation

The following is an interview with Stephen Pook, a vice president of Engelhard Corporation in New Jersey. He describes how Engelhard used the power of outrageous goals and breakthrough thinking to produce dramatic results. The change process started when the CEO and the senior management of this worldwide maker of specialty chemicals got together and came up with the stretch goal of reducing manufacturing costs 20 to 33 percent in twelve months.[11]

A breakthrough is needed...

Stephen Pook: As vice president in charge of information technology, I was chosen to lead an executive task force to spearhead the company-wide effort to reinvent the way we do business. We had a vision of being the premier catalyst company in the world. We have gone through the typical things that most companies have been going through for the last five to ten years. That is, all the restructuring, reorganization, exceptional quality, etc. And while they all provided some results, they only provided incremental results. And when added up, the results were insufficient to enable us to realize our long-term vision for significantly improved financial performance. For example, the restructuring effort mostly centered around a head count reduction exercise, as opposed to really changing the way we do things. We knew that, on some level, what was needed was a breakthrough in the way we think and operate. Since the economy was growing slowly, we knew that the greatest opportunity to impact our business performance was on the cost side.

Set an outrageous goal, then take a stand and make it nonnegotiable...

Pook: The first rule of producing a breakthrough is to set an outrageous goal. Our executive committee got together with the business-unit heads and identified an "outrageous goal and objective" for the company, which was to reduce our manufacturing cost at six key sites by 20 to 33 percent within twelve months.

The second rule is "don't change the first rule." People will say "Well, you know, it's going to take a little longer" or "We have all these things to do; can we settle for less?" Our COO Don LaTorre made sure everyone understood the goal was nonnegotiable. His answer was always "No, I told you what the objectives are, and I expect you to deliver. I believe you can deliver it, and you will deliver it."

Create a case for action...

Pook: We created a "case for action" that tells people why the breakthrough goal is important. Keep in mind that, in a process like this, you are asking people to think very differently than they have ever thought before. You are asking them to commit to things that they think are difficult or even impossible, and that is not an easy thing for anybody to do. If you don't have a strong case for action up front that people believe in and can really rally around, then you are never going to get them to go through things that make them uncomfortable. After our team came up with the case for action, each business-unit team came up with one, too, and each was different. One case for action was a page and a half long, but if you read between the lines, it boiled down to one line: "In five years, we will be out of business if we don't."

Introduce people to new possibilities through breakthrough thinking...

Pook: We had to help people break out of their existing paradigms so that they could see new possibilities. For example, take the whole concept of reengineering. When we first went to the businesses and said "We're going to teach you how to take 33 percent of your manufacturing costs out of your organization," they thought we were crazy. They said "We've been through restructuring, we've been through reorganizations, an earnings-improvement program, and exceptional quality. We've already got everything out of the organization that's possible." The problem was that they didn't see any possibilities for reducing costs. So we asked people to take a "balloon ride" with us where they would start to see the organization from a process point of view rather than from the point of view of the functional silos. For the first time, they were able to see some possibilities that they didn't see before from the ground. The mindset of people began to shift from "There is no way that we can reduce costs any more or do these things any differently than we are doing them now" to "Wow, look at the possibilities" and "It's okay to change things so that we can really convert them into opportunities for reducing cost."

Generate an approach...

Pook: We created an enterprise map of each business unit, which gave us a picture of the key processes. We then looked at those key processes through various scenario exercises that helped us identify different issues and opportunities. For example, we looked at it from the customer's perspective, from a green field perspective [starting from scratch], from the technology perspective. The intent of these exercises was to learn how we might reinvent these processes, reduce costs, and add value. We were able to identify a bunch of leverage points for improving each of these processes. There were those that were quick hits, those that were two- to six-month projects, and those that were true reengineering efforts—business transformation things. The important thing was that, as soon as we identified an opportunity, we told the team not to wait until we uncovered the rest of them, but to go ahead and implement some of those things.

Early successes generate results and momentum for a breakthrough to occur...

Pook: Almost from the first meeting on, the team had an opportunity to implement ideas and suggestions as it came up with them. This helped to build the confidence level of the teams both in the process and in themselves. The more we accomplished, the more this increased. We soon began to develop some real momentum, which drove the process forward. By twelve months, we were already running significantly above 20 percent cost reduction, and by eighteen months it was closer to 33 percent.

Outrageous goals and breakthrough thinking pay off...

Pook: There was a point where the task force started to feel "this thing is going to happen." It was after the second workshop where we tried to quantify the possibilities without knowing how we were going to accomplish the goal. And the financial results of the quantification were one-and-one-half times what the objective was. At that point, we said "Holy cow, we may be able to pull this off."

I'll tell you another story. In coaching one of the business-unit teams, what we found was that they kept coming back saying "This is how much we've got." And we kept sending them back saying "But the objective is 33 percent." And every time they came back, they had an order of magnitude improvement for the business process in the way they were going to do it, but they were still short of the financial target. So we kept on sending them back and one day we had a conversation in the task force that went something like "Where do we stop?" because it seemed like they were coming back with better and better solutions in order of magnitude improvements and that there was no limit to their creativity and breakthrough thinking."

CHAPTERTEN

Build Shared Understanding

Why do some executives talk about a vision and purpose, sign off on a strategy, and make decisions at the big meeting only to find out later that nothing ever happened?

Why is it that so many project groups get stuck with people from one department canceling out the efforts of another, even though everyone is sincerely committed to cooperation?

Why do we criticize others before we even try to understand them?

Today, almost every group and organization stresses the importance of real teamwork and effective collaboration. In many cases, great efforts are made to bring people together to discuss important issues, to form a team around an important project, and to take aligned action. Yet as we can see from the questions above, the experience of real collaboration is often missing due to a lack of shared understanding.

In many organizations, people in authority make arbitrary decisions that result in a climate of resignation and anger. Executives may try to build a shared vision or common goals, only to see implementation fail because people in the group don't have a shared understanding of what certain key words mean. Project groups often wind up trying to solve problems amidst gridlocked mental models and defensive routines.

A closer inspection of these groups shows that their speaking and listening is inauthentic. Their main concern is not to say anything that is at odds with the viewpoint of the boss or the prevailing majority. If someone in the group does have the courage to disagree, he or she may be seen as a poor team player rather than as a source of insight. The result is that breakdowns appear in morale, products, and business processes and the organization becomes unmanageable.

> **Coaching a group to think and interact better together involves teaching people how to have a collaborative conversation.**

The remedy is often to get people out of their departmental stovepipes and to teach them to work as a team. While removing organizational barriers can help, the gridlocked mental models and patterns of defensive behavior remain substantive barriers to cooperation. Rarely do people grasp that the group's problems are inseparable from the way its members think and interact. In many companies, the sad fact of life is that people operate from collective illusions that do not allow them to see the cracks in their paradigms, and it's almost impossible to have a normal conversation.

Collaboration: Transforming Unproductive Discussion Into Quality Dialogue

Coaching a group to think and interact better together involves teaching people how to have a collaborative conversation. In many cases, people do not understand the nature of a collaborative conversation or the reality of what it takes to have one. Collaborative conversations are those in which people in groups seek to realize their noblest aspirations with others from divergent views and backgrounds. This involves reframing the way people think and operate as well as looking for specific implementable solutions.

Collaboration often requires transforming the underlying pattern of conversations from an unproductive discussion to a real quality of dialogue. A discussion often results in people trying to beat down one another's views rather than to achieve a shared understanding or to learn something new. Physicist David Bohm writes that conversation in most groups is incoherent because people speak and listen in such a way as to cancel one another out.[1]

In a dialogue, the intent is to generate shared understanding or shared mental models that allow people to build relationships and to think and interact in a coherent way. This is essential for effective collaboration. It involves people saying what is really on their minds and exploring diverse views and perspectives by observing rather than defending their own thinking and behavior. A real quality of dialogue is always laced with wisdom, compassion, and humor and leads to insights not attainable by an individual.

A New Way of Speaking and Listening

In "normal" business conversations, we tend to advocate our position in order to win, but try to do this in a way that does not upset others. In a collaborative conversation, by contrast, we balance advocacy with making our views available for revision. For example, instead of an executive falling into the habit of saying "I have decided this and I really don't want to discuss it," he might say "What is our current thinking about this issue and how does it need to change?" Or a member of a group might say "Here's how I see the problem. My data is.... How do you see it differently?"

The same applies to listening. Instead of trying to understand and be influenced by what another person is saying, people listen through a stream of assessments: "That's nuts," "I fully agree," "That's wrong," or "I like that." The context in which people make these assessments is one of guarding their particular perspective or holding on to their opinions and assumptions.

In collaborative conversations, people learn to listen by trying to understand what another person is saying and by having the courage to step into his or her frame of reference and be open to change. This makes it possible to detect gaps in thinking and to learn from other people.

One of the reasons that people often resist collaborating is because they do not want to be influenced or to be changed by understanding what others have to say. The idea of suspending one's opinions and assumptions and stepping into someone else's frame of reference is scary. While this is understandable, this kind of mental rigidity, egocentric thinking, and resistance can lead to a group's demise.

The Four Levels of Collaborative Conversation

★ Conversations in which the group clarifies its purpose and whether or not its members have enough at stake

★ Conversations in which the group builds a community of commitment based on authentic communication, vulnerability, and healthy respect for diversity

★ Conversations in which the group expands people's capacity to think and interact by building a shared mental map

★ Conversations in which powerful commitments are made, in which people are held to account for their word, and in which people forward action

Level I. Conversations in which the group clarifies its purpose. In today's organizations, "teamwork" is a word that often gets bandied about. It is automatically assumed that every organization should be a team and every group should work like one. In reality, the only time people will collaborate is when they have a clear and inspiring purpose in which they have a lot at stake. Therefore, the first level of collaborative effort for a group is to have a free and informed discussion about its vision, purpose, and goals. Then, the group must create a mission statement. This should be done even in the case of a group assigned to a project by top management. The questions to consider are "What are we here for? What is the purpose of being a team and collaborating?

Does it make sense in terms of the business or organization? Can we each come to it with conviction? Do we each have enough at stake in it?"

Level II. Conversations in which the group builds a community of commitment. Experience shows that when even a small group of people begin to draw their identity from a shared vision or purpose and their relationship with one another, a community of commitment is born that can generate the desired results in miraculous and unexpected ways. On one level, creating a community of commitment involves speaking to the personal visions and purposes that live in people's minds and hearts. On another level, it involves encouraging people to step back from the front lines and engage in a different kind of conversation.

The conversations that build community are those where people speak with authenticity and vulnerability about themselves, about one another, and about the problems they are faced with. This creates the opening for people to expand their personalities and to embrace others in the group who have dissimilar personalities or contrary perspectives.

Building community becomes the cornerstone for productive conversations on issues and problems and makes possible decisions, plans, and strategies that everyone can stand behind.

Level III. Conversations in which the group learns to think and interact better together. To help people learn to think and interact better together, provide them with new guiding ideas, methods, and tools. For example, people normally operate from a "cook alone" or "potluck" model of conversation: "You bring your ideas and opinions to the table and I'll bring mine." In the potluck model of conversation, all you get are finished opinions or assumptions—take them or leave them. People do not disclose the reasoning processes or data that led to their views.

Let's imagine a different model of conversation called the "cook together" model, where people share the whole thought process. In the "cook together" model of conversation, people bring their different views and backgrounds along with all the ingredients of their thinking and enter into a shared creative process. Instead of serving up finished products, people take their raw ideas, cook them together with other's thoughts, question the reasoning process, and perhaps come to a new idea or insight.

Level IV. Conversations in which powerful commitments are made. One of the things that a coach can do to further collaborative conversations is to elicit powerful commitments from people, while at the same time creating a context where people are expected to honor their word as themselves. It is important that these promises and requests be explicit. Often, when people listen, they think they hear a promise when really what they got was an "I'll try." Or they think they made a specific request when actually it was vague and fuzzy. When coaching people, it's important to help them make a distinction between a promise and an "I'll try," between a request and a complaint, and between an offer to do something and an opinion on how things should be done. If you hold people accountable to making explicit promises, requests, and offers and to living as their word, you will not only forward action, you will help people to learn and grow.[2] (See diagram 10.1.)

CASE STUDY:
Generating Collaboration

Facilitating any diverse group to collaborate is a challenging undertaking, especially when there is a lot at stake for each person, much to be achieved, and conditions of time and pressure. The path can be filled with rule-altering changes, unknown complexities, and booby traps. There is no magic formula or secret recipe, and a lot comes down to the degree of mastery of the coach or facilitator. One sterling example is Nita Kincaid of Fidelity Investments, who applied a "cooking together" approach to a huge systems replacement and redesign project.[3]

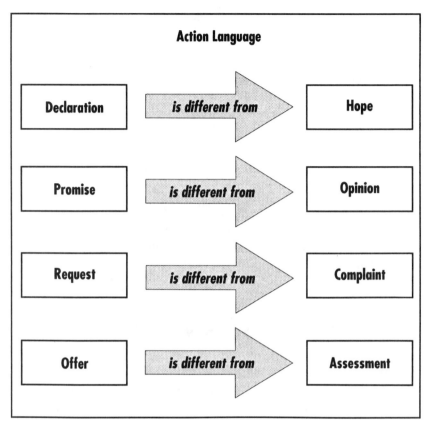

Action Language

Declaration	is different from	Hope
Promise	is different from	Opinion
Request	is different from	Complaint
Offer	is different from	Assessment

Diagram 10.1

Gaining a Shared Perspective

Nita had been put in charge of establishing the business requirements and priorities for a very ambitious technology project by E.C. Johnson 3d, Fidelity's chairman. The project's goal was to support Fidelity's many different retail and institutional financial service companies through one "logical" system. Nita realized that in a project of this scope, it would be necessary to create much more of a shared understanding between the business people and the systems people than usual. She also saw that, for the project to be completed, each of the dozen different companies had to have a clear vision of their future. Yet, more importantly, to build the system that tied all of those businesses together, it would be necessary to build a shared vision.

Says Nita, "My challenge from the very beginning was to get the presidents of these companies to own the project, and since all of them were extremely busy and some of them were not as technology-oriented as others, this was a real challenge. I saw my role as delivering the project through them, not for them." She told the business presidents "It's important that we all have a clear picture of where we are trying to go. Unless we do, our influence on this system and its design is going to be diminished. It is your system that we are building and you need to drive it."

Next, they began putting together an approach to building the system that they could all agree on. This involved a series of meetings led by Nita.

Structuring Meetings to Elicit Full Participation

I asked Nita how she structured the meetings to be successful. She said "I always put out a draft agenda in advance that said 'These are the things I have heard you all talking about in our conversations. These are the things I think you are concerned about and that we need to deal with over the next period of time. Let me know if you would like to add something or subtract something.' I tried as much as possible to make them the owners of the process at every step."

To make sure that all the different views and perspectives were clearly heard and understood by everyone, Nita prepared herself before each meeting. "I asked myself, 'Where is this person coming from? What is his set of experiences? What does he really care about? What is motivating him? How can I be of service to him?' For example, there may be a person in the group who is running a very large business and needs to get a handle on how to integrate the different parts. Or there may be a person who is running a small business and is concerned with how to eke out a small profit margin. Or there may be someone who sees everything from the cost side.

This tells me a lot about where people will be coming from on any particular issue."

Encouraging Divergent Views and Perspectives

At the meetings, Nita tried to get the different points of view out on the table. "As a facilitator, I have to create a space within myself to hold the divergent views and perspectives that are being expressed without saying 'I agree with this or disagree with that,' which would result in my losing people's confidence and trust. At the same time, I need to make sure that people are able to think about things from a different angle. If this isn't happening, I sometimes will take a person aside after the meeting and say to him, 'You kept saying, *I want this* or *this is what I think*. You need to know that Joe was trying to express something that was important to him, and it's important that you be able to listen to that and to hear it.' This is a key to building common ground and to trying to come up with a shared vision or approach."

Nita got people to speak up by making sure that the things on the agenda were of concern to people. "I stacked the agenda with all the things I knew people needed to say to keep the project moving ahead. We had a number of challenges with the project that not only encouraged learning how to design an incredibly sophisticated system, but how to develop real team skills as well."

How to Be a Facilitative Leader of Collaborative Conversations

Though Nita Kincaid is an excellent example of a facilitative leader, most people do not have her skills. What does it mean to be a facilitative leader? How does one "be" (or not "be") in this role? In general, facilitators need to care about the purpose and goals of the group and want the people in the group to be successful in reaching their goals.

The facilitator's primary role is to intervene in the discussion with the intent of improving how the group thinks and interacts. The facilitator is not there to think for the group members or to tell them the answers, but to help them do their own thinking and discover their own answers.

To use a metaphor mentioned earlier, the facilitator is a learning enzyme that becomes part of the learning system of the group with the idea of improving it. It is often the case that both the facilitator and the group have to learn in order to reach the desired results. The learning processes of both the facilitator and the group are structurally coupled.

For example, group members might be absorbed in such questions as "How do we use this impasse as an opportunity to do some breakthrough thinking?" or "How do I handle my problem with Joe?" The facilitator may be absorbed in questions like "How can I assist people in breaking the grip of their paradigms?" or "How do I enable people to communicate what they are thinking but not saying?" Such questions can make you painfully aware of your ignorance and incompetence and be quite unsettling.

The role of the facilitator is changing against the background of the emerging high-performance, change-oriented learning organization. Traditionally, the facilitator was expected to be "neutral," to not influence the thinking that went into a decision. He or she was often not an expert. Thus, the so-called content interventions that attempted to alter either what the group talked about or their mental models with respect to it were taboo. Only group process interventions that dealt with how the group members talked to one another were acceptable. To a large degree, this made sense.

Today, decision makers are increasingly faced with complex issues and problems that require a deep learning cycle. Facilitators are increasingly being called on to help group members improve the way they think together, not just the way they talk to one another. As a result, the line between process and content is dissolving. The facilitator may directly intervene in people's thinking by pushing them to surface and question their business paradigms or the real causes of their defensive behavior. He or she may also provide new guiding ideas, methods, and tools that help the group members improve both their cognitive and interpersonal skills.

For example, one of the key roles of a facilitator is to help group members become more skilled at public reflection and inquiry. Creating a community of inquiry requires helping group members learn how to ask a question or say "I don't know" rather than just give a pat answer. Instead of giving group members a recipe, like "positive thinking" or "better communication," creating this community is about helping people learn to take a reflective stance: "How does positive thinking block rigorous thinking?" or "What makes it difficult for us to listen to one another?"

Contracting: Creating a Framework for Facilitation

Clarify the nature of the facilitation. Contracting with the group involves clarifying the mission of the group, your role as a facilitator, and the nature of the intervention. This kind of contract is really a social contract or a verbal agreement that states explicitly how the facilitator and client are going to work together. For example, is the group more interested in basic or developmental facilitation? Basic facilitation involves helping a group to produce a desired outcome, to agree on its objectives, to make an important decision, and to iron out conflicts. This usually requires being present at one to four meetings.

Developmental facilitation involves helping the group learn to think and to interact better as well as achieve desired outcomes like breakthrough goals or change implementation. Developmental facilitation usually involves a transformational learning process where people inquire into the nature of group thought and behavior. It also involves creating "practice fields" where people become more familiar with new ideas, tools, and methods such as "fluid framing," "dialogue," "ladder of inference," and so on. My experience has been that this kind of intervention involves working with a group from nine months to a year.

Establish the governing values and ground rules. Once you are clear about the nature of the facilitation, the next step is to establish the governing values and ground rules. The facilitator can be more effective as a learning enzyme for the group if both the facilitator and the group are operating from the same governing values and ground rules.

Clarifying governing values and ground rules establishes a frame for working with the group, one that prepares the ground for high-leverage interventions and helps the group learn as well as produce desired results. This frame shapes how the facilitator speaks and listens to the group members and reshapes how group members think and interact with one another. For example, one of the governing values is "sharing valid information." The facilitator might uphold the governing value by encouraging group members to share all relevant information. Or he or she may encourage people not to simply accept what others say at face value, but to test all opinions and assumptions by asking "How do you know that?"

The facilitator might also uphold the value by giving feedback where he or she not only makes assessments about group members' behaviors but backs them up by carefully describing witnessable events that occurred in the room. In this way, he or she becomes a role model for the group members and teaches them to be cofacilitators.

The governing values of effective facilitation.

★ *Free and informed choices.* This applies to agreeing to the objectives of the meeting, to the methods of inquiry, and to any changes in thinking and behavior.

★ *Sharing of valid information.* People need more than arbitrary opinions and assumptions on which to base a discussion. They need the speaker to provide valid information that can be supported with examples.

★ *Internal commitment to outcomes.* This means that each person feels personally responsible for the decisions that get made because they are intrinsically compelling or satisfying.

★ *Learning is as sacred as results.* A meeting is not over until the group has learned something from it.[4]

Ground rules for collaborative conversations. The following ground rules are especially useful for making effective decisions in situations where the group is trying to reach high-performance goals, introduce change, or deal with complex issues or problems.[5]

1. Share all relevant information.
2. Agree on what important words mean.
3. Suspend your own opinions and assumptions while listening.
4. Test all opinions, assumptions, and inferences by asking for examples.
5. Make statements explaining your reasoning, then invite questions.
6. Focus on interests, not positions.
7. Make decisions by consensus.
8. Feel free to disagree openly with any member of the group.
9. Jointly design ways to test disagreements and solutions.
10. Discuss the undiscussable issues.
11. Avoid making cheap shots or otherwise distracting the group.
12. Keep the discussion focused.
13. Do self-critiques; it's not over until you have learned something.

"I always explain to people that if they choose not to operate by the core values and ground rules," says Roger Schwarz, author of *The Skilled Facilitator,* "I will operate by them anyway, because I believe they work. If people have a problem with that, then I tell them maybe they've got the wrong guy for the job."

When and How to Intervene

It is important to intervene to improve the way the group thinks and communicates when you see that (1) the group is rushing ahead to the next topic and it's obvious that there has not been enough shared understanding built on the last topic; (2) people are advocating a position but discouraging inquiry of the reasoning process by which they came to that position; (3) people are saying things and their meaning is not obvious, is confusing, or is not understood by other people in the group; (4) people are dancing around issues or making them undiscussable; or (5) the conversation is going too fast and there isn't time to question people's reasoning processes.

When you see these things, interrupt the conversation with one of the following:

★ "I think we need to slow things down a bit here and find out what the reasoning process is, otherwise I think we are heading for a breakdown."

★ "What is the data on which you based that conclusion?"

★ "When you said..., what did you mean?"

★ "Is the group really addressing the issues that are on people's minds?"

Giving feedback to the group rather than singling out an individual can often be more effective and cause less reaction. In any case, it is important to give feedback in a way that does not promote a favorite game amongst groups that feel threatened called "kill the facilitator."

Tools and Methods to Help Generate Collaborative Conversations

There is a difference between knowing what to do and knowing how to do it. People often need help in generating truly collaborative conversations, especially when the group is composed of people with divergent views and backgrounds or when reactive or defensive routines are present. The following guidelines for facilitating collaborative conversations can be used in either week-long off-site meetings or in normal business meetings.

1. Create the "container" for a conscious conversation by checking in and out. One of the most important things for a facilitator to do is to create the "container" in which people can engage in a real quality of dialogue. One simple method of creating the container is to "check in" with people at the beginning of the meeting. This involves going around the room and asking people to say a few words about how they feel about being at the session. This helps people let go of the distractions of the day as well as voice concerns that might never come up in the formal agenda. Each person completes his or her comments by saying "I'm in." At the end of the meeting, it is important to let people "check out" by asking them to say a few words about how they are thinking and feeling, what they got out of the meeting, and what it meant to them.

2. Decide collectively what your intention is for the meeting: sharing info, deciding, or going deep. One of the greatest enemies of collaborative conversations is that business groups, often under pressure, try to cover a lot of topics quickly. One very bright executive, Urs Althaus, whom we referred to as the "downhill racer" as he pushed to cover ground, said "We cannot spend that much time on every issue." He then made the suggestion that the group differentiate between issues that required information sharing or a quick decision and those issues where it was necessary to go through a deep learning cycle. If a group has many items on its agenda, take a few minutes to decide how to approach each topic: by sharing information, by making a decision, or by going deep. The topics that require in-depth consideration without time pressure may need to be reserved for a special meeting without an agenda.

3. To build community, trust, and a network of shared meaning, occasionally have a meeting without an agenda. The next time you are bringing a new project team together, take the time to build community before you jump into the task or conduct many highly structured meetings. Make the following proposal: "May I suggest that we put the agenda aside and just talk for a while about ourselves and the concerns that are really facing this group about this project." The result may be that people will sit back and begin to tell stories and talk about themselves and the problems in an open way. These kinds of conversations become the basis for a shared understanding of what is important to various group members, what their views of the project are, and what they want to accomplish. This leads to the ability to solve problems and make decisions with everyone's full commitment and participation.

4. Transform an unproductive discussion into a dialogue. Being aware of the pattern of evolution of collaborative conversations can help facilitators to guide the group and help people in the group to act as cofacilitators. The following are the different stages of a collaborative conversation:

★ *Stage 1. Polite discussion.* People communicate diplomatically to avoid open conflict while at the same time sending mixed messages.

★ *Stage 2. Rational debate.* People put issues on the table, arguing the different sides rationally and suppressing their emotions.

★ *Stage 3. Chaotic discussion or war.* People realize they have both intellectual and interpersonal conflicts that are not easily resolved and that could lead to a blowup.

★ *Stage 4. Community dialogue or embracing the enemy.* People start to communicate with authenticity and vulnerability and empty themselves of biases toward other people or views.

★ *Stage 5. Generative dialogue.* Creating something new becomes possible.

5. Give protocols to create the background for team reflection and learning. The intent of a dialogue is to learn. Learning implies being willing to be influenced and to change one's mind. Often, people cover up the cracks in their thinking by not exposing their thinking processes or the data by which they reached their conclusions. When people expose their thinking processes to public inquiry, it makes their opinions and assumptions available for change and revision. The questions below encourage people to be willing to listen, to share their thinking processes, and to build shared understanding. Pass them out on a printed file (tent) card for people to refer to.

★ *1. Pay attention to my intentions.* What am I we trying to achieve by this conversation? What is on my mind? Am I willing to listen and to be influenced?

★ *2. Balance advocacy with inquiry.* What led you to that view? What do you mean by that view?

★ *3. Build shared understanding.* When we say the word…, what are we really saying?

★ *4. Use self-awareness as a resource.* What am I thinking and feeling? What do I want at this moment, to dominate or to learn? How am I reacting to others' views?

★ *5. Explore impasses.* What do we agree on and disagree on? What does this impasse tell us about differences in basic assumptions?[6]

6. Create a shared interpretation by surfacing, questioning, and reframing assumptions. John Freeman, senior consultant of the CIBC Leadership Center, has developed a simple but practical method for helping people surface and question their opinions and assumptions.[7] "I start out by asking people in the group to choose a key topic to talk about. For example, 'teamwork.' As people begin to talk about teamwork, it becomes evident that it means very different things to different people. Also, as they speak, people automatically reveal their opinions and assumptions. I usually coach one or two people for a while at the beginning to question their assumptions. 'You have a belief that your group would work better if it was a team? What makes you assume that it would work better as a team rather than as a bureaucracy? Does team mean the same thing to you as to the other people you work with?' Soon people pick up on this and learn to question their own and one another's assumptions. As the process goes on, people begin to see that many of their assumptions are completely arbitrary. The effect can be very transformational."

> **P**eople seldom resist learning to change their attitude or behavior when you make accurate assessments and supply observations to validate them.

7. Make the conversation more coherent by asking people to distinguish between observations and assessments. Assessments belong only to the speaker. Observations are based on events that can be witnessed by anyone. In the following statement, what is the directly observable data? "Jill arrived at three fifteen, ten minutes late as usual. She's irresponsible." The directly observable data is that Jill arrived at three fifteen. The assessment is that she arrived ten minutes late, as usual, and that she is irresponsible. Asking people to distinguish between observations and assessments can be very beneficial. On one level, people begin to see where they have jumped to conclusions, made erroneous judgments about others, or talked themselves into getting depressed. On another level, the communication in the group becomes more coherent as people explain their thinking and the reasoning and data behind it.

8. Use the diagnosis/intervention cycle. The intervention cycle has two phases: diagnosis and intervention. The diagnosis phase includes (1) observing behavior, (2) inferring meaning, and (3) deciding whether or not to intervene. It is important to avoid jumping to conclusions, making snap judgments, or projecting your own pet theories onto the group. Carefully observe what's happening in the group, drawing inferences only from directly witnessable behavior. Think about what you want to say before intervening so as to promote learning versus defensive reaction. Keeping these things in mind will prevent you from getting into trouble.

The intervention phase includes (4) describing observations: "Erich, when you disagreed, you got red, pounded your fist on the table, and talked to your neighbor. At that point, all conversation stopped." It is important to confirm whether people agree with your feedback or not; (5) testing inferences: "This behavior seems to be getting in the way of the group moving the conversation forward. Do people agree or disagree with what I have said?" If people confirm the feedback, you will have the opening to go on; (6) helping group members decide whether or not and how to change behavior: If people agree to change, make behavior change requests. "When we have reactions, my request is that we step back for a moment and then ask a question that moves the conversation forward and addresses our concerns." If people do not agree to change, giving advice could result in you falling on your sword.

Note: Though giving feedback assessments to individual group members can be upsetting, people seldom resist learning to change their attitude or behavior when you make accurate assessments and supply observations to validate them.

Creating a Shared Understanding and a Shared Strategy

There is a new kind of leadership emerging in today's organizations, one that represents a fundamental shift from the leader as dictator to the leader as facilitator. Paul Allaire, chairman of Xerox, is a good example of a facilitative leader who creates a community of inquiry in order to penetrate collective illusions; to expand people's ability to learn, think, and interact; and to build an organization that truly functions as a whole.

When Paul Allaire became president of Xerox, he knew that he had to come up with a strategy that would take the organization to the year 2000 and beyond. What usually happens in business is that the strategic planning department goes away and comes up with a strategy. However, the strategy is usually just the finished product of a whole thinking process and is presented "potluck" style for people to buy into. During implementation, it often withers on the vine as there is no shared understanding or community of commitment behind it.

Allaire decided to use a "cook together" model, gathering his executives and spending eleven months developing a shared understanding and then a shared strategy. Allaire, John Seely Brown, director of Xerox's research center in Palo Alto, California, and Ajit Laroia, director of corporate business strategy, generously agreed to be interviewed. Their story illustrates the practical application of the guiding ideas that we have discussed in this chapter.[8]

The need for a shared world view...

Allaire: When I became chairman, one of the first tasks was to undertake a strategic exercise called Xerox 2000, which would define our vision for the 1990s. I had a fairly new management team who came from various backgrounds and had different experiences. One of the things I discovered in our quality process was that, if you try to think strategically or work through issues and you have fundamentally different views of reality, it's very easy to reach different conclusions. It is easy for intelligent people with big egos not to come together if, in fact, their basic views of where they are starting from are different. The issue was how to develop a similar view from which to start.

Shared world view leads to shared strategy, not the other way around...

Seely Brown: It's one thing for a group of strategic planners to go off on their own and create a view of the world that they then pour into people's heads. Frankly, this is kind of a brain-dead idea because all the great thinking, research, and analysis of these very smart people often winds up on someone's desk in a beautiful document that very few people understand the richness of. Also, the people who have to implement that strategy may be in disagreement about the fundamental assumptions it is based on. To me, the most important part of creating a strategic direction is creating a shared understanding. This doesn't come from the planners going off on their own. It comes from what I call coproduction.

Shared understanding is the fruit of coproduction...

Seely Brown: With Xerox 2000, we got the corporate office involved. This included Paul Allaire, his executive and senior vice presidents, plus four or five of us from the outside. We all set aside serious amounts of time—in fact, two days a month—to coproduce the work that goes into constructing a shared view of the world. It wasn't a staff job but a line job.

A methodology based on dialogue and debate...

Larola: The first phase was to assess the external environment and define a set of assumptions concerning customers, markets, technology, competition, and the global economy. This "view of the world" led us to generate approximately sixty assumptions that we then presented to the senior management team for debate. They then narrowed these down to twenty-eight assumptions, based on their relative importance to Xerox. It is important to point out that this occurred only after lengthy dialogue and debate. These assumptions became the basis for a shared world view. Then, from these assumption sets, the senior management team generated a list of actions that they believed Xerox must undertake in order to achieve its strategic intent. (See diagrams 10.2 and 10.3.)

Creating an accurate understanding of the world...

Seely Brown: I think this was a fairly unusual exercise in which we came together as equals to reach a point of view, a take on the world. And there were legitimate disagreements. We took the attitude that we each had our opinions and we could argue them out. But, in the arguing, we got to understand one another's points of view.

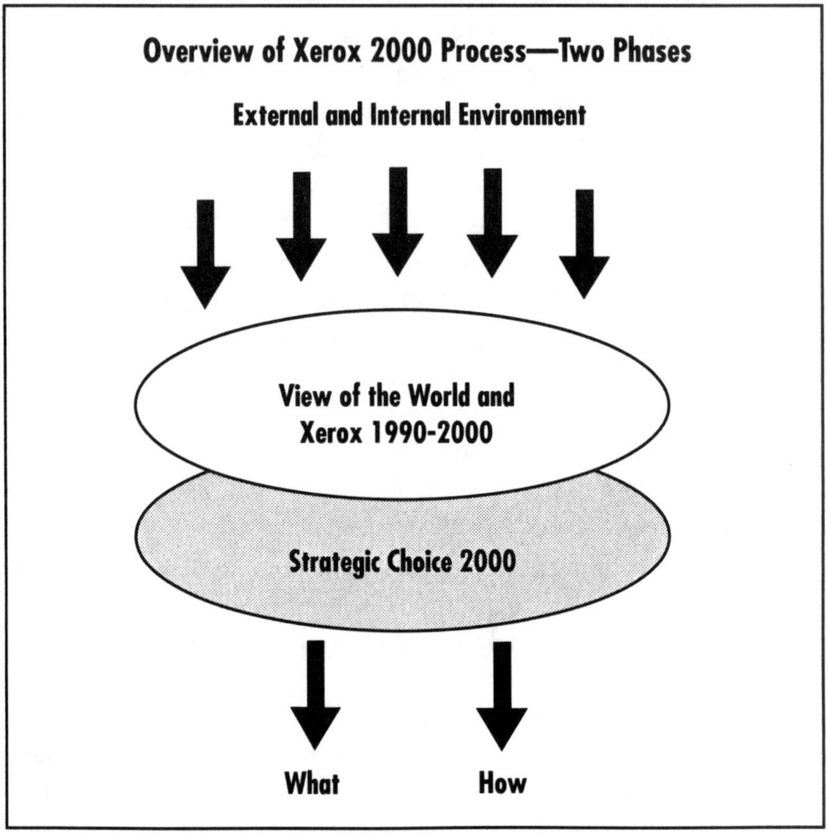

Overview of Xerox 2000 Process—Two Phases

External and Internal Environment

View of the World and
Xerox 1990-2000

Strategic Choice 2000

What   **How**

Diagram 10.2

A real spirit of dialogue fosters the collaboration of different views...

Allaire: You learn, in organizations and in teams, by working with others rather than by working by yourself. We had Roger Levein, who is in charge of the strategy group, act as facilitator. I was just another person around the table but, obviously, even when you try to be just another person, your position does carry some influence. As knowledge oftentimes comes from conflicting opinions, one of the things that I tried to ensure was that we really sought divergent viewpoints and healthy debate.

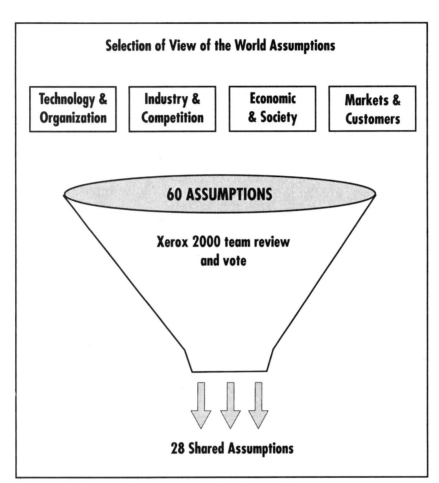

Diagram 10.3

Seely Brown: Allaire was working shoulder-to-shoulder with others, jacket off, sleeves rolled up, and he was willing to take risks and to expose what he did not understand. He was willing to ask lots of questions. He generated a sense of participation, creativity, and risk by his example. He wasn't just sitting back and letting us take the risks by exposing what we knew and didn't know. He would put very tentative ideas, embryonic ideas, on the table, along with other people, and allow these ideas to be evolved.

Learning and reflection are the keys to understanding...

Allaire: In a fast-changing environment, it's not safe to assume that your strategy is correct or that you are doing the right thing. You have to be willing to learn about your environment and be reflective about the assumptions you are operating from. I've learned that the only way you can get people to change is to have them think about and reflect on the real issues. As leadership today is often about trying to get people to work collaboratively to transform an organization, it's important that the learning process reflect this. Generally, business is a very "macho" culture. It is action- and activity-oriented, not reflective. And people tend to move from one mistake to another; we are trying to get out of that. What we were really doing was trying to change the cultural view and to say "It is okay to spend time doing this. In fact, you need to do it. You need to reflect and learn."

A shared strategy based on shared understanding has staying power...

Seely Brown: Creating shared understanding made creating a shared strategy much easier. Our strategic positioning, "The Document Company," is a highly pervasive point of view in the corporation.

Laroia: I personally believe that the reason Xerox 2000 is relevant today, and still driving the strategic direction of the company, is due largely to the focus of these conversations.

CHAPTERELEVEN

Recognize and Disperse Posturing and Defensiveness

It's like an attic in a 100 year old house that's never been cleaned, full of old baggage.

IBM manager, on withheld communication in companies

Why do executives often preach teamwork but act in a dictatorial way without even being aware of it? Why do many managers come to the big meeting and advocate their views in order to win, yet are careful not to upset others? Why is it that every group seems to have a secret that everybody knows but nobody dares talk about—even though talking about it is essential to improving products, quality, or teamwork?

This strange, often bizarre, and frustrating behavior that happens in groups was expressed very well by a cartoon I saw in *The Economist* a number of years back. It showed a group of smiling, sophisticated executives sitting around a conference table discussing an important issue. Under the table were dozens of beasts of a demonic nature with hostile glares, sharp teeth, long nails, swords, and shields that would have made fitting gargoyles for any medieval castle.

While most managers intend to do a good job, they often invest a great deal of energy in what Harvard's Chris Argyris calls defensive routines.[1] This can be very debilitating for people. "I believe we suffer every day, in every single business meeting we go to," says Peter Senge. "Part of us is getting killed, is really getting torn apart. We can't talk about it, we can't even name it."[2] Yet, what can we do?

As one practitioner told me, "The despair that many managers feel about being unable to have an authentic communication where they discuss the undiscussable, talk about problems openly, and overcome the game playing that goes on in most groups is the same as the despair a peasant in a Third World country feels trying to overcome his poverty."

Defensive Thinking and Behavior Is Geared to Avoiding Threat and Embarrassment

For many people defensive reactions are almost second nature. As economist John Kenneth Galbraith says, "Faced with the alternatives between changing one's mind and proving it unnecessary, just about everybody gets busy on the proof."[3] Chris Argyris defines a defensive routine as whatever an individual or group does to avoid situations that are embarrassing and threatening. Interestingly enough, many of the things people do to avoid embarrassment or threat do not eliminate the source of the embarrassment or threat. For example, people may be more concerned with "looking good" than with "being good"; they may protect versus correct their mistakes; they may collude with colleagues to avoid talking about hot issues; or they may not be able to admit that they don't know something.

The price people pay for this is enormous. Although they protect themselves from threat and pain, they are unable to be authentic, to learn, or to grow. The result is that they develop "skilled" incompetence, producing errors as a result of automatic behaviors that are carried out with skill and dexterity. People resist learning because it exposes their incompetence. Yet, at the same time, they remain incompetent and are blinded to this because they are unaware of their defensive behaviors.

What Can a Facilitative Leader Do?

One *ne way the facilitative leader can make a difference in breaking through the posturing and defensiveness that occurs in most organizations is to recognize and dispel it by bringing it to the light.*

This means finding a way to help people talk about things that they generally make undiscussable because talking about them represents a threat or a potential embarrassment. For example, people may try to appear as though they are in agreement even when they are not to avoid a blowup.

Says Senge, "One key to unlocking real openness and honesty at work is to teach people how to give up being in agreement. We think being in agreement is so important. Who cares? You have to bring paradoxes, real conflicts, and dilemmas out into the open so collectively we can be more intelligent than we can as individuals."[4] As people begin to say what's really on their minds, they often hold up a mirror to themselves and others. This can result in people making a shift from posturing and defensiveness to authenticity, creativity, and learning.

Once people experience how good conversations can be, they are often stunned. The German poet Goethe once said "Conversation is the most sublime of human experiences." Many people would say there is no greater joy than to have a real conversation. The issue is how to create the opening or opportunity for this to happen, as well as to develop the skills so it can be done productively.

The Power of Discussing the Undiscussable

The following story about Tom Labrecque and Chase Manhattan Bank shows that one of the most powerful ways to move people beyond their defensive routines is to face them head on.

When Thomas Labrecque, chairman and CEO of Chase Manhattan Bank, summoned his top twenty-four company leaders to a three-day conference without an agenda, there was a great deal of anxiety about what was supposed to happen. Is he angry? Frustrated? What's this going to be about? What the participants found out was that they were being invited to what would later be called a "happening."

Labrecque, a thirty-year Chase veteran, knew what could happen when too many things in the organization become undiscussable. So, before he solicited the views of the executive vice presidents about a mission statement, Labrecque started off by asking the participants a key question: "What are the issues we haven't addressed with one another?" He told them he didn't see the point of leaving the room until these issues were addressed.

Labrecque and an outside facilitator told the group members that the first thing they were going to do was to rate and then discuss their ways of working with one another. They would then break into groups and rate and discuss their own management skills. The members of each group would then critique their colleague's assessments of themselves. It soon became clear that the group members profoundly distrusted one another.

Significant differences exploded amongst the different business-unit leaders, not only about how people perceived themselves, but over the direction the company should go and how it should get there. It was obvious that a raft of defensive routines had been built up over the years. Some executives had built up elaborate strategies for protecting their turf—including office spaces that were barricaded with electronic glass doors and that had three or four armed security guards.

According to one source, "I got a call on the first day of the program from my boss. I asked 'How's it going?' He said 'It's a bloodbath. We had better pack up now and get back to the office before all hell breaks loose.' He did call back, however, the next day to say that things had really turned around."

Another person said "It's not that we don't like one another, it's that we don't like some of the things that the other people have done. Also, it's not just that we don't innately trust one another, it's that we never talked about things, saw things from other people's perspectives, or understood the reasons why people were doing the things that they did. Seeing just this was a real eye opener."

According to Wright Elliot, one of the key people leading the organization change process, "The exercises that we did were not brain surgery. The intent was to improve our competitive position, to improve the way we think and work together, to communicate in a more personal and authentic way."[5]

Everyone I spoke to at Chase stressed that the whole process was very personal. One of the key successes of the program was to develop a customer ethic. It wasn't just a matter of the CEO standing up and waving the flag for customers; it was that the CEO took the opportunity to make sure that everyone, including himself, looked in the mirror and thought about the things they personally did that prevented a real customer focus from occurring. The idea that came out of this was to serve the customers first, even if that means handing them over to another unit.

There were many issues that came up that were controversial. In most cases, after some initial hesitation, the company leaders began speaking to one another and tackling the issues at hand. Some of the issues that came up had to do with structures, executive compensation, and other measurements, especially in regard to who "owned" the customer. Instead of being handled by the product-line czars, customers were to be segmented according to discrete markets, with a senior executive in charge of each. In subsequent months, the executives successfully hammered out a new organization structure and compensation system. Less than half of their pay for performance is tied to what happens in the executives' own areas. "It's amazing how that changes your attitude," said one vice president. This would now ensure that executives would cooperate to make sure customers would be sold the products that suited them best.

According to one executive, "Those were the days that changed Chase." After the original meeting with the top group, 1,100 managers then attended a similar session where they contributed to the crafting of the vision. The program was then rolled out to the other 35,000 people, in sessions led by the 1,100 crafters of the vision, to gain their participation and commitment to the vision. The next step will be the development of leadership and team learning skills. How has it worked out bottom-line wise? Chase still has a way to go to make its transformation and comeback complete, but return on earnings had jumped back up to 18.1 percent as of this writing, way ahead of most of the bank's competitors.

The Source of Defensive Routines

Certainly a committed leader and team can make a big difference in eliminating posturing and defensiveness, but this is only part of the equation. I know of many committed leaders and teams who wound up getting stuck in the same defensive thinking and game playing despite their best attempts to avoid them. Let's take a deeper look at the source of defensive strategies.

According to Argyris, the defensive routines that people operate by in most groups are rooted in a "master program" or what he calls "Model I theory-in-use." The master program tells people to (1) pursue their own purpose, (2) stay in unilateral control of themselves and the situation, (3) maximize winning and avoid losing by advocating your position, (4) be invulnerable and suppress emotions, and (5) avoid the appearance of incompetence by covering up problems and bypassing errors.

The master program leads to face saving (for oneself and others), as well as persuading and convincing through force of argument or subtle pressure. Interestingly enough, this program can only be implemented when people become submissive, passive, and dependent. As this goes against human nature, defensive routines become a vicious circle. Here are some of the most frequently used defensive routines:

1. Avoiding, acting heavy-handedly, or accommodating

2. Suppressing dilemmas by discouraging testing of tranquilizing views and assumptions

3. Advocating one's position in order to win, while not upsetting others

4. Making those issues that represent a threat or a potential embarrassment undiscussable

5. Using fancy footwork to pretend that problems are not that big or to deflect blame

6. Covering up errors and then covering that up

7. Withdrawing and distancing oneself from problems in order to maintain high morale

In many groups, people are aware that these defensive routines are going on but do not say anything about them because revealing them is potentially embarrassing or threatening. As one manager said, "It's like pretending that the emperor has clothes, even though everyone knows he's stark naked." Instead, people seek and extend support for their defensive routines in order not to be exposed. Yet, so that people do not have to feel like they are acting unethically, they often cover up the cover-up by saying things like "think positively," "we don't want to have a blowup in the group," or "you have to be diplomatic." The result is a climate of resignation, escalating error, and an unmanageable organization.

Euro Bank: A Scenario of Defensive Routines

The following story stands in marked contrast to the preceding story about Tom Labrecque and Chase Manhattan Bank. The two banks are in the same industry, compete in many of the same businesses, and

have similar business strategies. Yet, the leadership styles and commitment to transforming the organizations are at sharp variance. The story illustrates the power of the defensive routines that occur in most work groups.

Several years ago I worked as a consultant for a large bank that I will call "Euro Bank." The bank had been highly successful because of the vision and efforts of the previous chairman, but its core business had begun to decline and it needed to reinvent itself. The new chairman hoped to boost sagging profits by selling to core customers higher profit-margin products and services that were being sold by other parts of the bank. This strategy would require teamwork and cross-selling between the different departments. Yet, teamwork was not happening.

Bypassing and Covering Up Issues

I interviewed various people who worked at the bank. I discovered a critical underlying issue that was best summed up in the words of one executive vice president who said, "The chairman preaches teamwork but absolutely abhors the process. He prefers to mandate things, as he has no patience with group discussion."

The chairman, Mr. Team, an ex-military officer, was very good at managing impressions and had a very affable personality. Yet he engaged in subtle forms of domination. He authored a vision statement, but there was not one free and open discussion about it to see if there was any commitment to it. At the same time, he tended to suppress the dilemmas around the complex issues facing the bank by making unilateral statements that left little room for anyone to rigorously question his thinking.

When executives brought up issues that were related to facing these dilemmas or to implementing real change, he would shout them down. He had inherited a successful operation and his basic position was "don't rock the boat." "We have to go global and that's all there is to it," he said to one member who asked about the huge sums of money lost on foreign operations. "It's not appropriate to bring that up here," he said to another who mentioned that the bank had some serious technology problems. "If you have something to say about it, send me a confidential report." One executive drew an apt metaphor about the chairman's tendency to bypass and cover up problems: "He's like a river running into a stone; he goes over it or around it, rarely dealing with it directly."

At first, the group members tried to resolve issues themselves at the chairman's office meetings, advocating their views on controversial topics, but being careful not to upset their colleagues. The chairman would privately mock group members for not speaking with more candor; "pretty smiles and sharp teeth," he would say. Yet Mr. Team himself seemed to be averse to conflict and any time a heated discussion emerged in the group, he would start fiddling with his glasses, making calls to his boat yard, or telling the group to "work it out for yourselves."

Covering Up the Cover-up

Mr. Team was frustrated with the group trying "to run every decision up the ladder" or making side deals with him instead of collaborating. Yet, he was unaware of how he was contributing to the problem by providing no real forum for dialogue and by making so many issues undiscussable. The members of the group were also largely unaware that they were contributing to the problems by allowing topics to be dropped. Said one manager, "If I speak up, I could get in trouble. If I just sit here, they will double my pay at the end of the year as usual."

Some of the issues that needed to be talked about were vital to implementing the chairman's strategy, like the compensation issue. As one executive said, "Why should I sell the other guys products? There's nothing in it for me." Soon the climate of fear, greed, and mistrust began to worsen as a result of shelving issues that were potentially embarrassing or threatening.

Changing the Form Versus Looking in the Mirror

People in the company began to question the chairman's competence and say that the chairman and his executives were a dysfunctional group. Curiously, when Mr. Team started to sense this, his response was to manage impressions. Instead of saying "There is something about the way we think and work together as a group that doesn't work and I think we need to talk about it"—which would have provided a breath of fresh air—he made some threats to show he was strong and fired several weaker members, hoping the rest would shape up. "We've been having some good meetings lately," he later crowed, "people are positive and upbeat and there's lots of esprit de corps."

At the same time, the chairman began spending lots of time on the road on sales calls, withdrawing and distancing himself from problems, and seemed to have exceptionally good morale. One executive vice president said "I can't understand it. We've been on the road with the chairman for a week and he has an empty briefcase. He brought no work to do."

I presented my findings to Mr. Team. I told him that while people wanted him to succeed, they saw a big discrepancy between what he preached and what he practiced. I gave him as many examples as possible. I also told him that his vision wasn't happening because people didn't own it and weren't being held accountable. Key strategic and operational issues were being made undiscussable, in part due to his behavior and in part due to the behavior of the group members. I then made some recommendations designed to transform the defensiveness into learning.

I told Mr. Team that the only way to deal with the controversial issues coming up in the group was to discuss them and that the only way to deal with defensive routines was to focus on them. I suggested that many members of the group wanted a forum for quality dialogue.

After Mr. Team had a chance to digest all this, he asked me to meet with him again. The chairman's response astonished me. He said "Can you find me an organization solution?" I said "You are looking for an engineering solution to a human problem." I explained that if he really wanted to help himself and the company, he had to be willing to hold up a mirror and look beyond changing the form. He had to be willing to ask the tough questions that would allow transformational learning to occur, both for himself and his group: for example, "Is my underlying assumption here to not rock the boat and, if so, what are the unintended results of that? What are the problems that I have with facing conflict in a public discussion? Why do we, as a group, cover up and bypass issues by making them undiscussable?" The chairman chose to ignore these suggestions.

As I watched over the next few years, I noticed that Euro Bank's stock price dropped dramatically, the bank's traditionally high return on earnings (ROE) sank below 18 percent for the first time in years, and serious operational problems began to emerge.

Strategies for Eliminating Defensive Routines

Curiously enough, every person in the story above had a sincere intention to do a good job. Yet they did not have the capacity to deal with the leadership, strategic, or operational issues they faced, especially as these sat on the table like a huge bowl of spaghetti intertwined with personal coping methods, relationships problems, and organizational defensive routines. For years I had been asking myself "How do you sort out the spaghetti?" I talked with Chris Argyris and some of his former students, Bob Putnam, of Action Design Associates, and Roger Schwarz, author of *The Skilled Facilitator*.

According to Bob Putnam, there is a dilemma facing anyone who seeks to do this work. On the one hand, defensive routines are so pervasive that they are taken for granted. On the other hand, the very ways of thinking and acting that create defensive routines also prevent people from engaging productively in the learning activities that are necessary to change those ways of thinking and acting.[6]

Four Steps to Sustaining a Learning Process

Sustaining a learning process in the face of this dilemma requires at least four steps.[7]

The first step is to establish a compelling link between the current behavior of the group and the business results for which it is responsible. For example, the senior managers of a manufacturing company recognized that ineffective strategic decisions were due to rivalry among the leaders of different divisions. If members of the group do not see a compelling link to business issues, few are likely to commit themselves to the learning process. Thus, in most cases, it makes sense to begin with business issues that are causing difficulty and identify whether defensive routines are a key barrier to progress.

A second step is to help people see that despite good intentions, they often produce unintended consequences due to lack of awareness. People are most aware of their own good intentions, of the poor results they seem to be getting, and of what other people are doing to contribute to these results. However, they are often unaware of other people's good intentions and of how their own actions contribute to poor results. This can lead to misunderstandings of motives or actions as well as to unintended consequences. The key is to help each party see how his or her actions contribute to results and how others are thinking in ways that, from their perspectives, make sense and have integrity.

The third step is to help people see that it is possible to learn to think and act in ways that reduce defensive routines and increase effectiveness in dealing with business issues. There are at least two major hurdles here. The first is to help people experience how discussing the undiscussable can be productive. The second is to help them gain confidence that they will be able to develop the ability to do this on their own.

The fourth step is to create a frame for intervening through the governing values and ground rules. As was mentioned in the discussion of shared understanding, it is important to establish governing values and ground rules before you begin to work with people. As

Schwarz says, "This gives me a frame to work from and allows my facilitation skills to be effective. It also gives the participants a different frame to operate from than the master program." The frame emphasizes eliciting voluntary commitment from people versus exercising unilateral control and coercing others, being authentic in one's communication versus suppressing thoughts and feelings, and having a commitment to learning versus bypassing and covering up mistakes.

The following list recaps the governing values: (1) free and informed choice in regard to setting goals, methods, and changing one's behavior, (2) authentic communication and sharing of valid information, (3) internal commitment to outcomes, and (4) learning is as sacred as results. Ground rules include things like "focus on interests, not positions," "no cheap shots," and "separate people from the problem."

The governing values and ground rules are not as hard to learn as they might seem. They can be learned through practice in the process of applying them to business issues and problems. Once learned, they begin to displace the master program. (See diagram 11.1.)

At the same time, helping people break the grip of the old models can bring up emotions; thus it is important to contract with the group about how deep you are going to go. The net effect of this kind of intervention is transforming posturing and defensiveness into learning.

Once these four steps are taken, you have created the readiness to work with the group. There are a variety of ways a facilitator can intervene with the group to move people beyond defensive behavior.

A Conversation With Bob Putnam on Facilitating Defensive Routines

Three levels of intervention: bypass, name, and engage...

Putnam: Suppose you are at one of a series of meetings to review the strategic direction of a company. The head of one line of business

Model I	Model II
• I'm separate and pursue my own agenda	• I'm related and build shared vision
• Seek unilateral control of myself and others	• Be committed to cause; inspire commitment in others
• Maximize winning by advocating my position, yet not upsetting others	• Balance advocacy with inquiring into other's views
• Be invulnerable by suppressing feelings and covering up errors	• Learn from mistakes and see how I contribute to my own problems
• Manage impressions to be acknowledged and avoid looking incompetent	• Being good allows me to look good

Diagram 11.1   Based on the work of Chris Argyris

argues, "Where we have a competitive advantage is in my line of business. That's where we should invest." The head of a different line of business says "We may have an advantage there, but it's a dying business. We've got to invest in growth areas." Others are silent, but past experience gives you reason to believe that several of them may be thinking, "There go Bill and Charlie again. We're never going to get past their prejudices." You think this episode illustrates a defensive routine that reduces the group's effectiveness. You would like to help. What might you do?

If your objective is to help the group make progress in today's discussion of strategy, you might choose to *bypass the defensive routine.* That is, you might craft an intervention that improves the quality of the immediate discussion without naming or engaging the underlying defensive routine. For example, recognizing that Bill and Charlie are both advocating their positions but not inviting inquiry into them and have jumped to conclusions along the way, you might say "When you say it's a dying business, what are the data you are selecting to reach that conclusion?" Later you might ask "How do others read those data? Do you reach similar or different conclusions?"

If your objective is both to help today's discussion of strategy and also to lay the groundwork for altering the defensive routines that prevent the group from working effectively, you might *name the pattern without engaging it.* For example, you might say "Bill and Charlie, I think that you are both advocating your views, but I'm not hearing any inquiry into the reasoning behind your views. When you say it's a dying business, what's the data you are selecting to reach that conclusion?"

If your objective is to alter the defensive routine, then it is necessary to *engage the defensive routine.* The price of engaging is that the conversation shifts away from strategy to how members of the group are interacting. You might say "I hear each of you advocating your view and I don't hear any inquiry into the reasoning behind each view. I'm also thinking that each of you has made the same argument before; we didn't make progress then and I doubt we're making progress right now. Let me check—do others see the same, or do you differ?"

Depending on what other members of the group then say, you might follow up by asking Bill or Charlie, "When Charlie (or Bill) was making his case, what was it that you were thinking but not saying?" As the inquiry continues, it may be possible to identify a pattern. The group members will then be in a position to design corrective action so they no longer get stuck in the pattern. The conversation that is stimulated by engaging interventions also surfaces assumptions that had been undiscussable and makes it possible to test their validity. Done well, engaging defensive routines can help members of a group experience the possibility of genuine team learning.

The "controlled burn"...

Putnam: Once in the early stages of working with a management group, we developed a metaphor that I think is useful for enabling people to discuss the undiscussable without causing a blowup. We were in the midst of discussing a policy issue when a senior member of the firm interrupted somebody else, who became quite upset. The person who had been interrupted said "Wait a minute, I've got to stop and say that you keep doing that, and it makes me angry." This went on for a couple of minutes. Then someone across the table said "That explosion seemed to come out of nowhere. It was like a finger snap turning into a firestorm. This little thing blew up."

I asked, "How can a finger snap turn into a firestorm? It happens when there is a lot of dry tinder. What occurs to me is that we should take a half-hour or so and do some *controlled burns*." The idea of a controlled burn is to deal with an issue that might otherwise lead to an incendiary situation in a slow and controlled way. The objective is to do some work, gain some insight, and then go back to the agenda, not to change someone's personality or make everything all better.

In order to facilitate a controlled burn, I take an active role in asking people to look at the different sides of the issues. This involves asking individuals to give examples, checking to see if others recall the example differently, and inquiring into how people were thinking and feeling both at the time and as we now talk about it. We develop a shared understanding of the dilemmas each person experiences and how these tangles occur. Often members of the group start to understand one another better and identify what each might do differently in the future. Whether they will in fact be able to act differently gets to the next issue, that of longer-term learning.

Developing learning capacity: performance and practice fields or on-line and off-line activities...

Putnam: My partners and I believe it takes a year or so for a group to develop self-sustaining learning capacity. Of course, this varies depending on how diligently people practice and on the difficulty of the issues they face. I recommend a combination of on-line and off-line learning activities. On-line means while you are doing actual work at, say, a budget meeting or regular staff meetings. Off-line means time set aside to reflect and practice. I find that it is vital to do both, and to have each activity inform the other.

For example, in one organization, the business task is developing strategy. On-line sessions are designed to make progress on this task. Then off-line sessions are scheduled where people can reflect on interactions that have been difficult, introduce concepts and skills, and practice using them. Then at the next on-line session, members try to use what they have learned in order to make better progress on the strategy task.

Metaphors, Tools, and Methods

One of the things that can be enormously helpful to a coach or facilitator in intervening in group defensive routines is to have a package of guiding ideas, tools, and methods. Bob Putnam uses three basic tools: the left-hand column, the ladder of inference, and advocacy and inquiry. These are generally introduced in an off-line session or practice field, and then put to use in on-line sessions or regular business meetings.

The left-hand column displays the reasoning process that people use to design actions...

Putnam: The left-hand column comes from a format that Chris Argyris developed. Participants write, in advance, a short case based on an episode that illustrates the kind of difficult situation that they would like to manage better. They divide a page or two in half, and in the right column they write what they and others actually said. In the left column, they write what they were thinking or feeling but did not say. The left-hand column shows what people treat as undiscussable and the right-hand column shows how they design behavior to deal with the dilemmas of undiscussability. The cases are used both as data for participants to diagnose their own behavior and as practice fields for participants to apply new ways of thinking and acting. (See diagram 11.2.)

I encourage people to begin to say some of those things in their left-hand columns. It is important that people speak and listen with good intent so as not to damage relationships. As people say

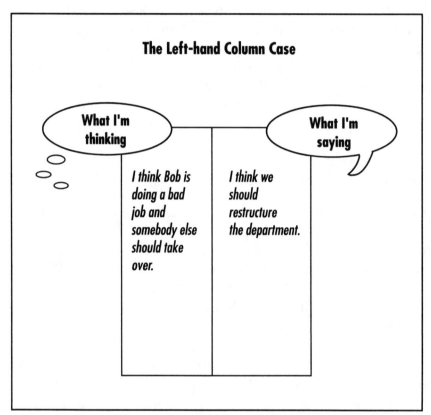

Diagram 11.2

what is in their left-hand columns, it becomes possible to build a shared understanding (or interpretation) as well as for group members to redesign their actions to be more effective. It also becomes possible to recognize and disperse defensive routines that have been kept undiscussable until this point.

The ladder of inference allows people to become aware of the steps in the reasoning process behind their actions...

Putnam: The ladder of inference is a simple model of the steps in our reasoning as we make sense of what is happening in order to take action. (See diagram 11.3.) The ladder of inference is placed on top of a pool of data consisting of everything that people say

MASTERFUL COACHING

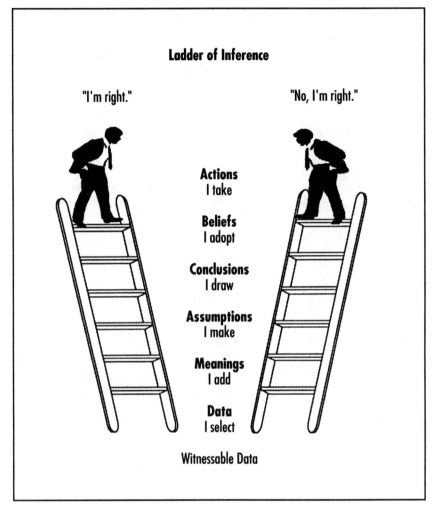

Ladder of Inference

"I'm right."   "No, I'm right."

Actions
I take

Beliefs
I adopt

Conclusions
I draw

Assumptions
I make

Meanings
I add

Data
I select

Witnessable Data

Diagram 11.3

Adapted from Chris Argyris & Don Schön

and do. Our reasoning processes begin with selecting what we will pay attention to and treat as important. That goes on the first rung of our ladder. For example, I might focus on Jack's coming late to a meeting. Then we move to the second rung of the ladder by interpreting or making meaning of what we have put on the first rung. I might think, "Jack doesn't treat this meeting as important enough to be on time." We might go through several interpretive steps. This is done almost instantaneously, without testing our assumptions. Then we draw a conclusion such as "Jack is not a team player." Finally, we take action based on our reasoning process. I might not invite Jack to be a member of the next group I form.

The first lesson of the ladder of inference is that people automatically jump high on the ladder. People are so skillful and quick in their reasoning processes that they do not notice intermediate steps in their thinking or whether they have forgotten to test their assumptions along the way. This is fine and necessary, but it gets people in trouble when they deal with others who have reached different conclusions based on different assumptions. What usually happens when people disagree is that they climb to the top of their respective ladders, hurl conclusions at one another, and explain the other's wrongheadedness by attributing nasty motives. This raises people's defenses.

Facilitating this interaction to bring defenses down involves helping people learn to notice that they have jumped high on the ladder and made attributions or evaluations that are not necessarily true. One way of facilitating here is to ask for examples on which people have based their inferences. "Joe, what was said or what happened that led you to believe that Charlie was blaming you?" "Joe, what did you mean by what you said?" Another approach is to teach people to use this and other tools themselves. One member in a group said when another member jumped to conclusions about a colleague, "Bill, you are so high on the ladder you need an extension."

Advocacy and inquiry—a tool for productive conversations...

Putnam: Advocacy and inquiry are concepts for understanding how people interact. People can create better opportunities for learning from diverse points of view by combining advocacy and inquiry. However, just putting together a statement and a question is not sufficient. If I say "That's a stupid idea. Do you want to wreck the deal?" I have both advocacy and inquiry, but I am not promoting learning. It is necessary to combine high-quality advocacy with high-quality inquiry, "What's your doubt about this deal?"

The ladder of inference is one of the keys to crafting high-quality advocacy and inquiry. People seek to advocate their views by communicating not only their conclusions, but also the data they select and the steps in their reasoning. People inquire not to sway others to their point of view, but to discover how others move up and down their own ladders of inference. And people encourage others to help them see gaps in their reasoning. (See diagram 11.4.)

Roger Schwarz on Eliminating Defensive Routines

Roger Schwarz has some excellent ideas on facilitating groups that have been accumulated both by study and practice. Roger named four things he does as a facilitator that produce results in helping people move beyond defensive behavior.[8]

1. Help people examine defensive thinking and behavior.

Problems in Balancing Advocacy With Inquiry

High Advocacy/High Inquiry	Low Advocacy/High Inquiry
• Communicate: conclusions, data you select, steps in your reasoning • Inquire to discover steps and gaps in one another's reasoning	• Asking questions but not revealing your views *"What costs do you have in mind?"*
High Advocacy/Low Inquiry	**Low Advocacy/Low Inquiry**
• Advocating your view but not inquiring into other's views *"What we've got to do is cut cost!"*	• Silent withdrawal • Not revealing your views or questioning other's views

Diagram 11.4

2. Ask questions that surface and test assumptions.

3. Help people see the unintended consequences of their actions.

4. Help people learn to alter their assumptions and redesign their actions.

1. Help people examine defensive thinking and behavior. People often think and act defensively when they are in a high-stakes situation that is potentially threatening or embarrassing to themselves or to others. When people start trying to save face, win the argument with unilateral statements, or answer the question "How do I avoid losing?" it's a sure sign that "productive reasoning" has been replaced by "defensive reasoning."

Other signs of defensive reasoning are that people seem to be distorting reality in order to cover up mistakes, attributing negative motives to others, or drawing conclusions in an illogical way (logical to them, but not to others). This is all due to the fact that defensive thinking and behavior is usually based on very subjective opinions, untested assumptions, or soft data. The assumptions people are making may or may not be true, but people act as if they are true. The reason people do not check out their assumptions is that this often involves a high risk of embarrassment or threat.

For example, a boss in an architectural firm sends a mandate to a person who has not been demonstrating leadership to make some big changes. The person wonders whether the boss is asking him to do this because he wants him to make changes or because he wants him to mess up so that he can have a reason to fire him. Based on other people's speculations or his assessment of his boss's behavior over the years, the person makes an assumption that his boss just wants to "ease him out."

He does not test the assumption because asking his boss directly represents a potential threat or embarrassment. So, let's say his assumption is inaccurate and he does what he thinks is reasonable and cautious, whereas it was the boss's intention for him to take more risks. By not carrying out the boss's request with vigor, he loses his boss's trust. By not checking out his assumption, he acts in a way that creates exactly the conditions that he is trying to avoid.

He may reason that "If I test my assumption by asking him, he might think that I'm incompetent. Or if I test it, he might know something I don't want him to know." We can see that defensive reasoning based on untested assumptions and soft data tends to become a self-fulfilling prophecy, as well as becoming self-sealing. It is self-fulfilling because it creates the consequences he is trying to avoid. It is self-sealing because his reasoning prevents him from learning information that could prevent the self-fulfilling prophecy.

2. Ask questions that surface and test assumptions. One of the key roles a facilitator plays is to help people break the hold of defensive reasoning. You can do this by paying close attention to what people are saying and by asking questions designed to help people surface and test the assumptions underlying their statements and opinions. It's important to keep in mind that every opinion has an assumption behind it. "Hold on a minute, when you say 'x,' it sounds like you may be assuming 'y.' Do you agree? If so, what led you to the view that...?" Use your wisdom, intuition, and insight to develop a sense for the assumptions embedded in people's statements.

Says Schwarz, "I often work with the managers who report to elected officials and the managers are often given mandates by their bosses that they don't agree with. This presents them with a dilemma: 'Do I tell my direct reports that I disagree with my boss and risk being seen as unsupportive by my boss, or do I just go along in order to maintain a united front when I present the mandates to the supervisors at the next lower level?' In this case, the facilitator might point out that the dilemma is more complex than they imagined: The manager's direct reports are likely to see the same problems the manager saw with the decision. If the manager doesn't share his concerns or denies them, his direct reports may question his judgment."

Schwarz goes on to tell how one manager in this situation said that he decided not to question the elected official. He reasoned that by hiding disagreement in front of the supervisors, he would get their commitment. Schwarz said, "The question I might ask is 'What led you to conclude that? What, if any, assumptions are you making there?'"

3. Help people see the unintended consequences of their defensive behavior. In many cases, people develop a theory of action assuming it will get results they want. In most cases, people are acting in a way that is rational based on whatever assumptions they have made. Yet as we have seen, when defensive reasoning is involved, people often do not check out the assumptions their theory is based on. Thus, they are often not aware of, and do not anticipate, how their actions are designed to produce unintended consequences. In most cases, the things people do to avoid embarrassment or threat do not eliminate the real cause of the embarrassment or threat.

For example, in the case above, the manager thinks he is doing the right thing to get commitment. Yet the supervisors may be thinking, "Wait a second. This man is either lying or doesn't see the problem and is incompetent." Then they say to themselves, "Do I raise the issues or play it safe?" The supervisors, as well, decide not to question the manager, assuming that it is better not to question the boss. In this case, neither the supervisors nor the manager can anticipate the unintended consequences of their actions because they are blinded by their defensive reasoning.

If you can help people see that their behavior might be getting them into trouble and producing unintended consequences, you can create the readiness to change. In the case of the boss, his defensive behavior and untested assumptions may produce what he doesn't want—the loss of the commitment of his reports. In the case of the supervisors, who would like to make a difference, they may lose any possible influence that they might have.

4. Help people learn to change their assumptions and redesign their actions. As one of the values of effective facilitation is free and informed choice, it is not the facilitator's role to give people the answer or tell them what to do. Rather, it is to help them decide whether they want to change, and if so, to help them. In most cases, helping test assumptions and interrupting defensive routines involves encouraging people to "discuss the undiscussable" or say what they are thinking but not saying. For example, a boss gives an employee a huge number of assignments to do in a short time. The employee can say "yes" or "no." If she says "no," she thinks her job is in jeopardy. If she says "yes," she thinks she could wind up looking incompetent.

Alternatively, you could discuss the undiscussable with your boss. For example, the employee in the above example might say "You are my boss and I have some tough issues to raise with you and frankly I'm scared as hell because I don't know how you'll react. If we take on all these jobs, I believe clients will suffer. If I just say no, then I think you might say that I'm not a team player. Do you agree with my assessment of the situation?" In most cases, it is important for the facilitator to remind people of the ground rule to jointly design ways to test disagreements and solutions.

Oftentimes, people do not say the things that they are hiding because they are afraid of the emotions and that people will strongly disagree. Paradoxically, two ground rules that help people express difficult thoughts as well as handle their emotions are (1) make statements and then invite questions, including disagreement, and (2) be specific. Use examples. By saying "I observed that you do…. Do you agree or see it differently?" you reduce the chance of drawing false conclusions that will anger others.

Another powerful tool that can help in preparing for a difficult conversation is for the facilitator and coachee to role play the conversation in advance. The facilitator can play the role of the boss and the coachee can play his or her own role. This enables the person to realize where his or her own thinking or behavior has been defensive and based on untested assumptions. The coach can also switch to the coachee's role at times to model effective behavior.

Tools Can Create New Possibilities

Over the years, I have noticed that people appear to think they only have two possibilities: the possibility of the oppressive silence that comes from making things undiscussable or of speaking up and saying their thoughts and feelings and having them blow up in their faces. However, these ideas, tools, and methods show that people do have other possibilities and choices and that, as a coach, the more you work with people on these tools, the more they will see this and, at the same time, the more skillful they will become in exercising their possibilities and choices.

CHAPTER TWELVE

Go for Results Now!

We have to understand the world can only be grasped
by action, not contemplation. The hand is more impor-
tant than the eye, the cutting edge of the mind.

Jacob Bronowski

Outrageous goals, shared strategies, cutting through defensive routines in groups—many of the coaching strategies suggested in this book are designed to encourage more creative and productive conversations. The only way to utilize the insights gained from such conversations, however, is to take action. Yet, individuals, teams, and organizations often spend too much time discussing things or making elaborate plans and preparations and then do not take the action necessary to see the process through. To quote an old saying, "After all is said and done, a lot is said and not much is done." Here's how a masterful coach can get results.

Sidestep Elaborate Planning and Go for a Result Now

Experience shows that when people skip elaborate planning and preparations and go for an immediate result, they can produce breakthrough results that no one could have predicted or scheduled. You can see evidence of this when there is a challenge or crisis. Several years ago Motorola Chairman Bob Galvin became convinced that only by selling directly in the home marketplace of the top Japanese firms could Motorola learn how to compete on a better or equal basis. Then an opportunity arose.

> *Their success revealed that no matter how desperate the need for better technology, resources, or cooperation, people can get results with what they have.*

Motorola's communication sector was given the chance to supply Nippon Telephone and Telegraph with a particular pager. The good news was that Motorola was one of the few companies outside Japan to be able to compete for the job. The bad news was that the time allowed for developing the product was less than two-thirds of what Motorola considered a normal product development cycle. Also, the quality requirements were so high, even for a company like Motorola that was already famous for its "Six Sigma" quality program, that the managers considered them impossible. The tight schedule precluded any search for new technology, elaborate planning and preparations, or specialized training. Success would depend on people learning to work together as a team and to leverage the knowledge that they had.

A team was formed that immediately began to look for innovations. The group decided to take a "zero defects" approach. In other words, any defects in the product were unacceptable. No repairs on faulty equipment would be permitted. Conventional wisdom and standard operating procedures were thrown out the window. The team used many innovative methods for success—and succeed they did. Here are some comments from team members: "The team was turned on by the challenge of doing something that was absolutely impossible to do." "Engineers were working 100 hours a week and getting calls at three o'clock in the morning." "It was the most exciting time in my life."

When a pager was started down the line, a small green sticker was put on the chassis. The sticker remained unless a defect was discovered. The first time the hundredth consecutive pager reached the end with its green sticker on, the production line stopped and everyone cheered. How did they do it? The bottom line is that the team did not have a chance to do the usual. They didn't have any time to attend to strategy or the perfect organizational structure. Their success revealed that no matter how desperate the need for better technology, resources, or cooperation, people can get results with what they have. The question is how to make such miracles routine.

The Breakthrough Technique

Is there a coaching method for obtaining peak performance from your team? Is there a coaching technique for making sense out of ten-year strategic stretch goals or reengineering projects whose complexity is mind boggling? Is there a way for people who feel overwhelmed by the discouraging complexity of their situations to experience a sense of significant accomplishment?

Most of us are skeptical of self-contained management philosophies, cure-alls, and quick fixes. Yet there is a technique that can be used to answer the questions posed above—it's the "Breakthrough Technique" developed by Robert Schaffer, author of *The Breakthrough Strategy*.[1] The Breakthrough Technique is an approach that gives people a sense of accomplishment, that naturally leads to a feeling of collaboration between people of different views and perspectives, and makes everyone feel that they can make a difference, not in some far-off future—but today.

Set Compelling, Urgent, Short-term Goals

Many companies set big goals, make a plan, and lay out the steps—yet by the time they get started, they are often months behind in their goal. According to Schaffer, "It's good to set big, breakthrough goals, but companies often kid themselves about what it is they can accomplish. Furthermore, they get stuck in the planning and analysis phase and often don't achieve anything at all. Experience shows that achieving breakthrough projects through smaller goals or 'small steps' often proves not only to be more realistic but more powerful."

When Schaffer talks about a breakthrough project, he's talking about a short-term goal or a step where people can experience some success. For example, going to the moon involved solving certain engineering problems along the way. Each of these represented small successes in the scope of the project. Without those small successes, the rocket ship would never have gotten off the ground.

Schaffer said, "I am working with a financial institution that has set an ambitious goal of creating a 50 percent increase in its business over the previous year. That's pretty powerful and significant in terms of a target. Yet, what I have discovered is that everyone is milling around trying to figure out how to get the 50 percent. They set the goal in January and now we're into March, and they are not moving adequately toward it."

You can set a big, long-term goal and mandate that people achieve it, but unless you carve off short-term pieces, it often turns out to be just hot air.

According to Schaffer, "It's interesting that nobody said 'Instead of getting paralyzed by the idea of increasing sales 50 percent, why don't we pick one line of business and try to increase sales 10 percent in the next four weeks?'" The idea is that by producing some tangible results, the company will build momentum, as well as learn something that might create an opening for further progress.

Focus on What You Can Do Now

One of the most important aspects of this approach is to take advantage of the existing readiness for change. Instead of people saying "That's not realistic" or "We tried that," you want people to say "This is what we have all been waiting for." Just as important, if not more so, is to have people focus on what they can do with existing resources and authority. "Anyone can make a grand slam at bridge with thirteen spades," Schaffer says, "but how can you win playing with the cards you have?" That's the game of management.

Most groups say they would like to get better results, but they often preface their remarks with "But first...." They go on to say that the boss has to change, they need a bigger budget, or the corporate culture has to be transformed. The coach has to have the confidence to say "Yes, I can see how getting all of those things sorted out might lead to better results, but possibly there are some things that you can do on your own."

Schaffer tells of a good coaching method for these situations. Tell group members to make two lists. On the right side of the paper, have them write down all of the things that are needed from the boss or the ways that the culture or situation must first change to help produce better performance. On the left side, have them write down all of the things that can be done right now. These lists help people see that to succeed on the right side, they have the difficult task of persuading others to change the culture. The coach needs to say to people "On the left side, it is *you* who can make it happen. If you identify those things and start on them, no one can prevent you from making progress." It doesn't matter if it's not a perfect solution. When people start accomplishing things, top management starts to get on board and the culture starts to loosen up.

The next step is for the coach to suggest that people select something to get started on. Which one of the things that the individual or team has identified would they most like to try? Where could they make the most progress with the least amount of effort? This is not just to get people moving but to have them break out of the "I can't" mindset and into the "I can" mindset.

Think in terms of weeks not months. After this kind of dialogue, the coach might ask the manager and team to select a concrete first-step goal that could be achieved in a matter of weeks rather than months. The very act of carving off something that they can commit to, where success is near and clear and where there are no "outs," creates excitement. Team members will look at one another like they are about to invest themselves in something that they know will require initiative and risk.

An early success will build momentum, creating additional readiness for change. People will then feel ready to set new, more challenging breakthrough goals. To encourage people to greater heights, a coach might well say, "You know, that product improvement is something our customers will appreciate; it gives me an idea of how we can do the same thing across the whole product range."

The Breakthrough Technique is based on designing each project for success by building in what Schaffer calls "zest factors." These automatically elicit the fun and excitement of high-performance teams.

Zest Factors

* ★ A sense of challenge and risk
* ★ Urgency
* ★ Near and clear success
* ★ Collaboration
* ★ Cutting through bureaucracy
* ★ Fun and excitement

"What about teamwork?" says one manager who tried this approach. "You can talk about teamwork all day long, but people will not really understand what you are talking about until they actually start to accomplish something." The fact is that teams are a vehicle for getting something done. They develop by facing a real challenge, by taking disciplined action, and by struggling to produce results. We saw this in the Apollo project to put a man on the moon. We see this as any sports team makes a run for the championship. To generate excitement and fun, some companies turn Schaffer's notion of a breakthrough project into a worldwide competition.

At Motorola, teams with names like *Flexperts, Mission, The Ronamakers,* and *Cycle to Success* compete each year. These teams become examples of excellence that help inspire the rest of the company. For example, the *Flexperts* group of manufacturing and process engineers dramatically improved a changeover bottleneck in a pager assembly line. They reduced conversion time from eight hours to only one-half hour in only a few weeks while greatly improving quality. The *Cycle to Success* team, made up of administrative people, reduced the time to process an invoice by 125 percent and saved the company $750,000 in processing and materials costs. On a human scale, the results are impressive too. Teams from Motorola worldwide who were doing breakthrough projects competed to see who could achieve the most outstanding results and learning. One team member who went to the Motorola world finals competition said, "This was the most profound experience of any in my career, and the first time in my life that I have felt truly recognized."

Just-in-time training. The same approach goes for elaborate training efforts and other preparations. Says Schaffer, "Training needs to be presented on a just-in-time basis to help people take the next step in the project, not by sending people off to abstract training programs in quality or empowerment that don't lead to concrete results." While writing this, we heard of a Fortune 100 company TQM manager who worked for eleven months on an elaborate plan for introducing the company's total quality program. According to the plan, there would be no visible results for over two and one-half years. It would take that long just to get everyone trained!

Launching the Breakthrough Technique

So, how do you get started with the Breakthrough Technique in an organization? Following is a model that coaches can use in almost any situation. The model was developed by Charlie Baum, a masterful facilitator and a former colleague of Schaffer's. It grew out of work done with companies like Motorola, Dun & Bradstreet, and others, where it was applied to furthering the success of those companies' quality and customer programs.

Launching the Breakthrough Technique in a group or organization requires some preliminary steps. First you must persuade someone in senior management or line management to use the approach. Once there is buy-in and an understanding of how the process works, the next step might be to review your group's overall strategy and then to ask the different department heads to identify performance opportunities in their areas. These become the places where people can sponsor a team to work on a specific breakthrough project. Start with designing a pilot project for success and then use small, incremental steps to build on that success. Baum says that "If you are tight on the following four points, you can be loose on everything else."[2] (See diagram 12.1.)

The Four Step Breakthrough Technique

1. Find a sponsor who identifies a performance opportunity. Once the leader defines a performance opportunity—and has made sure it's in an area that is measurable, like cutting product development time, reducing the number of product defects, or increasing sales revenues—it's important to find a local sponsor.

The Sponsor's Role

★ Identifies what performance is today
★ Takes a stand for the opportunity
★ Brings the team together
★ Presents the opportunity to a team to see if they want to go for it
★ Gives the team the confidence to move across traditional functional boundaries to get the job done
★ Reviews the team's short-term goals and work plan and removes obstacles

---

2. Choose a team leader and team. It's important to choose a team leader with a proven record of achievement as well as good people

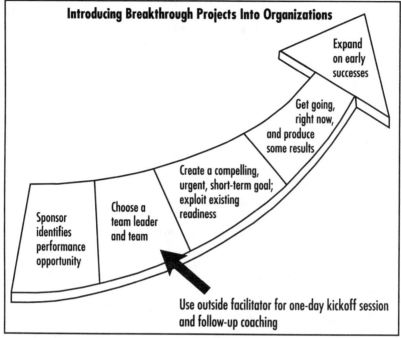

Introducing Breakthrough Projects Into Organizations

Expand on early successes

Get going, right now, and produce some results

Create a compelling, urgent, short-term goal; exploit existing readiness

Choose a team leader and team

Sponsor identifies performance opportunity

Use outside facilitator for one-day kickoff session and follow-up coaching

Diagram 12.1

skills. Team members are selected based on their knowledge and capabilities, not on their personalities or status. Invite everyone to attend a *breakthrough briefing session* where you generate enthusiasm about the project and invite them to set a specific goal. Make use of facts that show where the company's performance is today. For example, "The competition has a defect level of 3.4 per million on consumer electronic products. Ours is 3 per hundred thousand."

Team Leader and Member Qualities

★ Have a proven performance record
★ Know how to get along with people
★ Treat everyone on the team as a colleague
★ Have demonstrated necessary and relevant knowledge and capabilities

---

3. Design a breakthrough project by creating an urgent, short-term goal. The next step involves setting a goal that is clear-cut and attainable as well as one that represents a significant step up in performance. This tends to quicken the pace and generates a sense of teamwork. It's also important that the goal be based on existing resources, authority, and readiness for change. The response from others should be "this is what we have all been waiting for," not "that's not realistic."

Goal Qualities

* ★ Razor-sharp and measurable
* ★ Accomplished in two to twelve weeks
* ★ Have clear conditions of success—who, what, by when

---

4. Bring in an outside facilitator for the one-day kickoff session and follow-up. To help the team to design a breakthrough project, it's a good idea to organize a one-day, kickoff session. Use an outside facilitator to work with the team on this day to set the breakthrough goal. This needs to be in keeping with the shared strategy of the organization. For instance, you might focus on the design of new products or improving work processes that have direct customer impact. The breakthrough project can be a discrete project or part of a larger project. You might decide to build a particular component of a new high-definition television in the next six weeks.

During this day, the facilitator also helps the team create a written work plan. The facilitator meets with the team on the second, fifth, and eighth weeks of the project to see if the project is on track. The projects are usually completed by the eighth week. At that point, the facilitator meets with the team to harvest the insights that have been gained from the project and to see how these insights could be applied to expanding the scope of the project or to institutionalizing the success that has been achieved.

```
┌─────────────────────────────────────────────┐
│        The Facilitator's Responsibilities     │
│                                               │
│  ★ Makes sure goals are razor-sharp          │
│  ★ Assists in creating the work plan         │
│  ★ Ensures that work plan includes diverse   │
│    views and perspectives                     │
│  ★ Monitors progress at weeks two and five   │
│  ★ Harvests opportunities with team at week  │
│    eight                                      │
└─────────────────────────────────────────────┘
```

Action Learning

One of the big pluses of the approach is that achieving the breakthrough goals often results in people learning how to think and act differently as they take action. The combination of thinking about solutions and taking experimental action has a multiplier effect on learning as progress toward the target is made.

One of the most important steps in the process is to take time out to capture the insights that are gained along the way. This is one of the purposes of the follow-up sessions with the facilitator. If you experiment with this approach a few times, you will discover that breakthrough expansion routes are naturally clarified as the goal is reached, management development happens by management achievement, and the organization naturally expands its capacity to create the desired future.

The breakthrough strategy is also easily applied to larger reengineering projects or where a stretch goal has been set. Again the advantage is that people create momentum and new openings for action by building on early successes. (See diagram 12.2 for how the breakthrough projects fit into reengineering projects.)

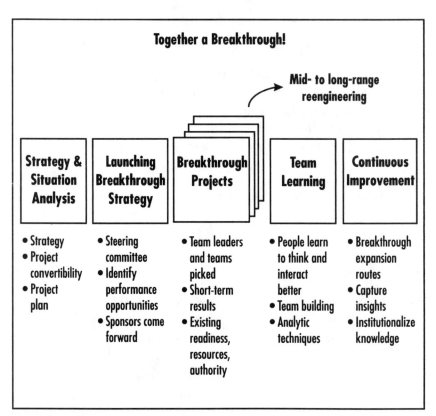

Together a Breakthrough!

Mid- to long-range reengineering

Strategy & Situation Analysis	Launching Breakthrough Strategy	Breakthrough Projects	Team Learning	Continuous Improvement
• Strategy • Project convertibility • Project plan	• Steering committee • Identify performance opportunities • Sponsors come forward	• Team leaders and teams picked • Short-term results • Existing readiness, resources, authority	• People learn to think and interact better • Team building • Analytic techniques	• Breakthrough expansion routes • Capture insights • Institutionalize knowledge

Diagram 12.2

The Breakthrough Technique at Dun & Bradstreet

To find out how breakthrough projects work in the real world, I spoke with three people involved with breakthrough projects at Dun & Bradstreet (D&B): Mike Berkin, Charlie Baum, and Sharon Shelton. Berkin, a senior vice president of performance quality at Dun & Bradstreet Information Services, has set up hundreds of breakthrough projects. Baum acts as an outside facilitator. Shelton was the team leader for a project called Operation Clean Slate at D&B's Greensboro, North Carolina, facilities. She is now an assistant to the president of D&B and has acted as a facilitator for many breakthrough projects.[3]

Finding out what worked and what didn't work in quality programs...

Berkin: When we started in 1991, my role was to take us from the design stage into action. From a study we had conducted over a ten-month period of time, we found that seven out of ten TQM efforts fail for various reasons—lack of senior management commitment, lack of business performance gains, overinvestment in training at the expense of measurable results, etc.

Thus, we designed our Performance Quality Program based on five key characteristics: (1) business performance gains based on measurable goals, (2) early successes—getting something meaningful done in a matter of weeks, (3) fast team formation, (4) just-in-time training—giving people just the right kind and amount of training needed to take advantage of a specific opportunity, and (5) a nontraditional launch. For example, we knew that if we launched quality in the typical fashion with a big leadership kickoff and lots of education, there would be many cynics in the company who would say something like "This, too, shall pass." So instead, we decided to launch some breakthrough projects and, after a while, people started hearing informally about these projects, got excited, and wanted to hear more about them.

An example of a successful breakthrough project...

Berkin: One of the most successful breakthrough projects was called Business Scope. It had to do with our business analysts selling products to businesses about which we were gathering information for our credit reports. The idea bubbled up from the Pittsburgh office, and a team was immediately formed. The team soon realized that they had to build a business plan. So, we brought some people in from marketing who showed them how to come up with a product design, a forecast, and pricing. Well, the team defined the market, defined the product, and figured out the pricing and forecasts. In a matter of weeks, the product was being offered; first in Pittsburgh, then nationally. Since it was launched, it has contributed over $8 million in revenue to our business.

Finding performance opportunities...

Baum: In another instance, Doug Nay and Tal Phillips, two street-smart managers from the New York-area office, were responsible for collecting information for credit reports on companies. They discovered that too many customers had been calling for credit reports on companies not in the D&B file and then disappearing without buying anything. It was taking seven days to create new reports on companies not in the D&B file, but the customers needed them much sooner. Doug and Tal got on the phone and asked the manager of the Greensboro office if he would help sponsor a team to dramatically reduce turnaround time. The manager at the time, John Hubben, said, "Okay. I've been working on a plan." Doug and Tal said, "You don't know what we mean. We want this to be a bottom-up project, with the people on the front line setting the goals and coming up with the solutions."

A team leader and a team set a breakthrough goal...

Baum: Doug and Tal flew down to Greensboro, and Sharon Shelton was chosen as a team leader. Sharon is an exceptionally bright person, but at the time didn't feel like she was being creatively challenged. In fact, she was getting worn down by having to fight day-to-day battles.

A team was then selected from all of the functions that would be necessary to meet the goal. I spent one day with the team helping them to carve off a short-term, measurable objective and to create a written work plan. They were enthusiastic participants as we went through the process of brainstorming and problem solving. They knew that that evening they would have to present their goal and plan to Doug and Tal and were excited about it.

The team jumps into action...

Shelton: Once we defined our goal, we immediately began creating a work plan. Our freewheeling idea-generation session lasted until late in the afternoon. By the end of the session, the conference room walls had been covered with a blizzard of suggestions for eliminating waste or unnecessary steps. We had developed an action plan by grouping the best ideas into categories that we called "action cells." Individual team members assumed responsibility for the cells, and we were ready to roll. It wasn't long before results were realized.

Baum: I got a call later from John Hubben, the manager of the group, when I was in New York. He said, "It seems like the team is running the place now. All I seem to be doing is ordering lunch. In fact, I just walked into the meeting and asked if I could help, and they asked me if I could get some sandwiches brought in." "Well John," I said, "You'd better make sure that the sandwiches are good." He laughed. At that moment, John had begun to make the shift from a top-down middle manager to a team cheerleader.

Shelton: We soon realized that the reason it was taking us seven days to process the reports was because we were operating under an old paradigm. A big part of the problem was that we just had too many customer requests waiting at various stops in the process. We started decreasing the inventory, as well as making other paradigm changes in rules and procedures. In a matter of weeks, we were able to get the processing time down to three days. We developed contingency plans for fluctuating inventories so that we could continue to serve customers within three days.

Not just breakthrough results, but breakthroughs for people…

Shelton: After participating in this project, I have a very different attitude about myself. I think this has something to do with the fact that we not only accomplished our goal, but we shared our insights with other offices across the country who, in turn, reduced turnaround time to three days or less. I also became a facilitator for other breakthrough projects. The biggest difference for me is that I believe I, as an individual associate, can make a significant impact on a large corporation. This impact is felt in day-to-day activities and outcomes, the corporate culture, and the bottom line. Instead of hearing people saying things like "Why doesn't somebody do something?" and "What's the matter with management?" you now hear people saying "Let's change this," even if it's a whole work process and it's always been done that way!

D&B starts small to win big...

Berkin: We have initiated over 1,000 breakthroughs like this since we started our Performance Quality Improvement effort. This has had a significant financial impact with approximately $19 million in annualized cost savings and $34 million annually in additional revenue.

CHAPTERTHIRTEEN

Add Value by Design

To love what you do and feel that it matters,
how could anything be more fun.

Katharine Graham, Publisher, *Washington Post*

People Have a Deep Need to Add Value

Each of us wants to have the experience of being lovable and capable and to know that our existence is a real contribution. One of the ways that human beings attempt to be the "source" of this experience for themselves is to look for ways they can create or add value for other people or to their situations. This value can be derived from people's way of being—being caring, helpful, or supportive. It can come from using knowledge and skills to help others solve bothersome issues and problems. In a way, the desire to add value is part of each human's quest for significance.

If you are running a company or team, and people are just going through the motions, it's usually an indication that something about the environment is inconsistent with human nature. You know the signs. People are doing their job, but that's all. Every day they come in and do more or less the same thing, over and over again. They demonstrate hardly any commitment, creativity, or flexibility. If it's not in their job description or regular routine, they don't do it. They come at nine and leave at five. They take the required number of sick days and the required number of paid vacations. They do things to make it look like they are participating but, in fact, you believe they are not really participating. This can be very frustrating. What do you do in this situation? A masterful coach helps build an inspired environment in which a person's natural tendency to create and add value is called forth.

The Importance of Adding Value

The guiding principle behind coaching individuals or teams to add value is to ask them to put themselves in the customer's place. They need to think about all the things customers think about when making a purchase or contracting for a service. The same idea applies not only to external customers but to colleagues within the organization.

> **A**dding value not only means that people must learn to do something new but also unlearn something old.

The value-added equation asks "What value do we have to offer?" "What does it take to satisfy a customer with a specific need?" and "What role can our company, team, or any individual play in fulfilling these needs?" It's critical to offer the customer the "whole solution" rather than thinking only in terms of what you do. This could include not only a new product, but intangibles— like a knowledgeable sales force, responsive deliveries, or flexible billing.

Once people understand the term "adding value," you need to explain why it's important in terms that speak to them personally. For individuals, it's an opportunity not only to bring more of themselves to the job, but to see an opportunity that no one has seen before and to step into it and make a contribution they can truly be proud of. In the future, employability will not be based just on being able to do a job but on being able to walk into an unfamiliar and undefined situation and create a way to add value. Charles

Handy, in his book *The Age of Unreason*, uses the metaphor of a doughnut to get this concept across. The center 15 percent represents your normal job. The 85 percent around the center of the doughnut is your desire to make a contribution. That's where the work of the future will be done.

The individual must learn to ask "What are my personal interests?" "How can I create new ways of satisfying customers?" "How can I find ways to improve the business operations?" It is answering these three questions all together that is the key for success in business today. Adding value not only means that people must learn to do something new but also unlearn something old. Start by having a brainstorming session where you deal with these questions in the first half of a day. Then in the second half of the day, look at barriers that keep people from bringing their passion, commitment, creativity, and caring to work: for example, a dominating boss, visions and goals that are not visions but a set of instructions, job descriptions and procedures manuals that keep people in lockstep. Pay close attention to the things that people say are obstacles to adding value and then work with them to systematically remove these obstacles.

Defining Value: The "Four P's"

To give people a framework for understanding what adding value means, talk about the Four P's—four ways we can define value: personal, perception, performance, and people.

Personal. Just as everyone has a unique fingerprint, so also does everyone have their own personal definition of value. To some, it's innovative products; to others, it's quality; to others, it's service. Each person defines value in his or her own way. For the last ten years, I have been flying Swissair to Europe, always preferring it to any other airline. The reason is that one time ten years ago, I forgot my ticket and my wallet and credit card as well. I had to get to Zurich to make a speech the next day, but didn't have money to pay for another ticket. I appealed to the Swissair station manager, Mr. Brady. He said, "Don't worry about the money. Just write your address down and we'll bill you." He didn't even ask for identification.

Perception. The second part of value is perception. What matters is not whether you think you have the greatest product in the world, but how people perceive the value you have to offer. Peter Drucker tells an interesting story about a time early in his career when he worked for a British company that sold padlocks in rural India. The company was taken over by a new owner who decided to make improvements. The quality of the locks was greatly improved without increasing the price. The new padlocks were harder to break into and were much smaller. Unfortunately, the lock sales in rural India almost completely dried up, and Drucker was sent to investigate. It turned out that the old padlocks were big and imposing and scared thieves away. Also, they could be opened easily by anybody in the family with a stick or screwdriver after the key was lost. The moral of the story is that while the company thought it was adding value, the customer perceived the opposite.

Performance. The third aspect of value has to do with constantly improving performance. It's the notion that the product or service or continuous improvement idea that you have to offer must do something that outperforms whatever is currently on the market. Dennis Ester, quality vice president at Motorola's Two-Way Radio Division, says that the company uses a process mapping technique for increasing performance: "We map all the steps in the process and assign values of time and quality. Motorola's line workers then study the map and look for disconnects, white spaces, and redundancy. Then, they map the process as it should be. We basically get the processes down to just those things that add value. When we do, it's amazing to see the dramatic performance improvements that we get in products, services, or administrative functions."

People. The ability to create a customer-focused, value-driven organization can only come when managers know how to create a positive work climate and to interact with people in such a way as to bring out the best in them. This is why coaching is so important to the value-added equation. One employee on the payroll can either produce "one X" of added value or "ten X" or "one hundred X." The issue is that getting people to add value isn't just a matter of giving people a set of instructions, a set of guiding ideas, or a technique. If adding value is a personal thing, it's also a holistic thing. It can't be separated from the organization's basic culture. Does the organization honor its people or put up with them? Does it allow people to bring their whole selves to work or not? Does it invest in education that allows the employees not only to do a better job but to create a better future for themselves?

The Leader Creates an Adding Value Context

Telling people that they should add value, selling them on the idea, and even developing the skills that go along with it is important. Yet, the issue of adding value is inseparable from the company culture. This is the basis of using a "pull approach" rather than a "push approach" to get people to add value. What that often comes down to is a leader who takes a stand for certain governing ideas that mean a lot to him or her and who then strives on a daily basis to create a healthy work climate and a passion for creating new ways of satisfying customers. Ned Johnson, chairman of Fidelity Investments, is a good example. I had the opportunity to meet many people at Fidelity during a consulting stint there and to find out how Mr. Johnson uses his leadership role to promote adding value.[1]

The Fidelity Story

The secret of Fidelity's success is creating a spirited, entrepreneurial, innovative, learning environment where people are continuously looking for new ways to satisfy customers.

Ned Johnson

Headquartered in a very understated building on Devonshire Street in Boston, Fidelity Investments is the largest mutual-fund company in the United States. With managed assets of almost $300 billion as of March 1995, the company, on any given day, trades 5 to 10 percent of all shares on the New York Stock Exchange. Fidelity has an unusual management culture that focuses on constant innovation and self-renewal—preemptively changing everything about itself before the market or competitors force it to. In fact, you could say that the company left the Twentieth Century back in 1946 when Edward C. Johnson 2d founded Fidelity Management & Research Company and began creating one of the country's first learning organizations.

Edward C. Johnson 2d had an all-consuming obsession with the stock market. For fifty years, he kept a daily journal containing his observations of the market, once comparing it to a beautiful woman that men could seek to know but never really understand. This created a management culture at Fidelity that not only produced exceptional investments like the Magellan Fund but, in the words of one former fund manager from the 1960s, an environment where people seemed to have a hunger for learning about any new investment idea. According to him, "We were literally paid to learn from each other."

According to Bob Beckwitt, who manages Fidelity's $10 billion Asset Manager Fund, "The company encourages you to do something that you find to be a real personal calling and then it extends a lot of trust to you and lets you test your wings—which is very empowering." Yet, to make sure people succeed with their dreams, as well as produce tidy returns for Fidelity's shareholders, people like Bob Beckwitt are provided mentoring by world-class investment experts like Peter Lynch who, since retiring from running the Magellan Fund, spends a good deal of time coaching young fund managers.

Edward C. Johnson 2d ran his business always looking for an opening in the opposing line of scrimmage that he could exploit to help take the business forward. For example, Johnson didn't invent the mutual fund business but he came up with the idea of putting a single individual, rather than a committee, in charge of a fund—an idea that had a dramatic impact on performance. There were many other firsts as well.

Fidelity was the first investment company to hire ethnic minorities—its first fund manager being Jerry Tsai, a Chinese immigrant. Later, Johnson's son Ned blazed many new trails as well—like check writing on money funds (something that people at that time thought was crazy). They were the first company to set up 800 numbers and 24-hour service.

"In effect, what resulted from this was a management culture that said you must break new ground," says Fidelity executive Leo Dworsky, "with a strong underlying belief that if you don't break new ground, you will whither and die." At the same time there is latitude to pursue personal interests. As a former Fidelity executive, the late Rab Bertelsen, told me, "Fidelity is an environment where, if you have a dream that is burning a hole inside you, and you want to try an idea, it's unlikely that anyone will tell you 'no,' even if it's been tried several times before. Rather, what they will say is 'let's do an experiment to test it.'"

According to Ned Johnson, the key to Fidelity's success is creating a spirited, innovative, learning environment where people are constantly looking for new ways to satisfy customers. Just how is such an environment created? For one thing, the Johnsons' entrepreneurial zeal, innovative attitude, and perpetual sense of curiosity set the tone for others in the company. "You may go in and make a big presentation about something, and it makes Mr. Johnson think of something that he is interested in," says Nita Kincaid. "He will digress and talk about it, possibly making comments about a broad range of things in the process. Then he will come back to what you were talking about and ask, 'But have you thought about this?'

"At Fidelity, people tend to always be thinking about the next change or improvement," says Nita, "the next fund, the next technology, the next marketing innovation." Mr. Johnson reinforces this constantly through his emphasis on the Japanese concept of "kaizen," which means continuous improvement. "He's always looking for people who can come up with new, good ideas that can improve the company—even if that means the 'creative dismantling' of what we already have. Where there is a gap, we move very quickly to fill it with initiative or action that brings value to the table."

As one technical analyst said, "I have the opportunity to work in one of the most incredible pools of learning and activity in the world, as well as to earn significant incomes at a fairly young age." And, again, people are often expected to invent their jobs. "When I first came here," said the thirty-year-old technical analyst, "I had a general charter for what area I was supposed to work in but absolutely no clearly defined job. I just took a look around and experimented until I found a way to add value." He came up with a special stock market report that is prized by all of Fidelity's fund managers.

If you ask people what they are interested in doing and then give them the tools and encouragement to try it, they will come back with something extraordinary.

Though not all experiments pay off, there is a value placed on learning. "Ned used to stick his head in my office door and talk about all kinds of ideas," one fund manager said. "Then he would ask about what I was learning and how I was applying it." Johnson says "At Fidelity, we may make mistakes, but we never waste learning." Johnson is hungry for learning at every turn. "If you go to talk to him about how a major project is going," said one highly placed executive, "you naturally want to make a good impression. He listens, but after the overhead presentation is over, he really digs in. He is intensely curious. What are the issues? How are we thinking about them now? How does our thinking need to change? What's the next step? The result is that he adds value through his every interaction with people."

Perhaps this story by Darla Hastings sums up Ned Johnson's coaching style best. "He told me once that if you tell people what to do, they will come back with something average. If you ask people what they are interested in doing and then give them the tools and encouragement to try it, they will come back with something extraordinary."

> ### Coaching Lessons to Be Learned From Fidelity
>
> ★ Continuously look for new ways to satisfy customers.
> ★ Hire smart people who don't quite fit the mold.
> ★ Provide jobs that are unstructured, but expect people to add value.
> ★ Look for openings to take the business forward and take action.
> ★ Create a culture of preemptive change and creative destruction.
> ★ Challenge people to think outside the box when they say "It can't be done."
> ★ If someone wants to try a zany idea, say "Let's do an experiment."

A Nontraditional Perspective

One day, I visited the financial district of New York to meet with people at the Chase Manhattan Bank. The Chase building sits in a large plaza and its architecture is very tall, formal, and imposing—not the kind of place you would want to apply for a loan if you missed your last car payment. As you walk into the lobby, you see a statement emblazoned on the wall. It says, "Our purpose is to provide financial services to those companies that support the well-being of our customers whether they be individual, companies, communities, or countries."

What caught my eye, and made the rest of the message stand out in that imposing lobby in the heart of New York's financial district, was the word "well-being." It told me that there was a new era emerging where business was not just about making money or making and selling products and services. It was about contributing to the well-being of people, communities, and the planet that we share. The people whom I talked to in the bank said that when Chairman Tom

Labrecque first saw the message, it was only a small banner. He insisted that it be put in huge letters. Labrecque believes firmly that if the company contributes to the well-being of people, communities, and customers, it will have a very profitable relationship with them.

Every coach should ask the question "Does our work contribute to people's well-being?" As we've seen, it is important to create a work environment that allows people to delight customers and to improve operations. But it is hard for a company to add value if it is not supporting the ecosystems, educational institutions, and other institutions that it touches. The following stories illustrate how companies like Reebok and Bally encourage their people to make a difference in the world. (See diagram 13.1.)

Reebok: Bringing Your Whole Self to Work

If people feel good about themselves, they are more creative and productive.

Over the last one hundred years or so, a macho management culture has evolved, based on the belief that the only thing that matters is work and that the business of business is business, that is, to make money. The personal parts of people's lives were supposed to be checked at the door when people showed up for work. Yet, a growing number of powerful executives, many from the baby boom generation, have found that while making money matters, the other things that people care about matter too. One of these executives is Sharon Cohen of Reebok. Cohen joined the company in the early days when there were only twenty employees and later wound up working for CEO Paul Fireman as Reebok's vice president of advertising, a powerful job in the competitive, frenetic world of athletic footwear and apparel.[2]

Says Cohen, "I came to work for Paul Fireman because I liked his values. He talked about honesty, about taking a stand for the things you believed in, about keeping your word, and about family." At 45, Cohen's life changed: "I had a baby girl." She left her job in

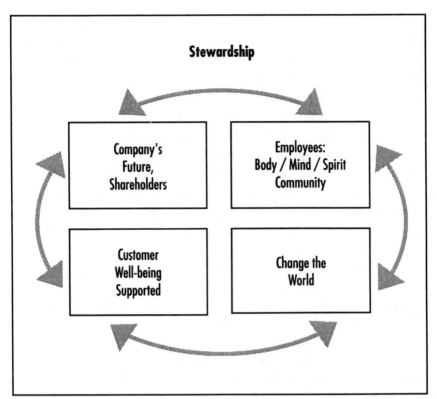

Stewardship

Company's
Future,
Shareholders

Employees:
Body / Mind / Spirit
Community

Customer
Well-being
Supported

Change the
World

Diagram 13.1

Reebok's marketing area and became vice president of public affairs and executive director of the Reebok Foundation. One of her roles is to help Paul Fireman create an environment where people can bring their whole selves to work.

"You have to look at the person as a whole," says Cohen. "People spend a lot of time at work. You can't compartmentalize personal life and work life, individual and family concerns, personal concerns and social concerns. People are not just workers by day and good parents by night. In the same sense, you can't pretend that people just bring their minds to work and sit at a desk all day. They also have a body, a spirit, a soul."

CEO Paul Fireman is a believer in corporate responsibility. "I doubt if there are very many CEOs, if there are any at all, who would admit to social irresponsibility. But there's a long way between the rejection of irresponsibility and the acceptance of responsibility. If you think of a bell curve, what you will find under the bell of the curve, where most companies gather, is what we might call social indifference. That's all those companies and managers who don't regard the matter of responsibility as part of their corporate mission."

According to Cohen, "The things that we do in the area of social responsibility—like the Reebok Human Rights Award and Human Rights Program—make people feel proud of the company and good about themselves. When people feel good about themselves, they are naturally more creative and productive. They add a lot of value to their jobs. You can't measure it, but you can feel it when you take a walk through the halls. It's not coaching in the traditional sense, but it's a kind of indirect coaching." What does the company do in the human rights area? In the fall of 1994, Reebok found out that a factory in China was housing its employees in an unsafe building. Reebok called the factory and said that the employees would have to be moved. The factory manager said, "We will have them out by the end of the month." The Reebok representative said, "That's not good enough." The factory workers were in better housing by the end of the week.

Then there is the Reebok Human Rights Award. Each year, the program recognizes four young people on the front line of human rights work who, early in their lives and against great odds, have had significant impact in their communities. Another Reebok human rights program, "Witness," is designed to arm the human rights movement worldwide with the weapons of mass communication, such as hand-held video cameras and fax machines. "A video camera in the hands of the right people is more powerful in stopping the violation of human rights than a tank or a gun," said musician Peter Gabriel. President Jimmy Carter has hailed the company as doing more for human rights than any other company in the world.

Reebok also has a volunteer program that provides opportunities for people to be of service in the community. According to Cohen, "We do a big effort with the City Year Serve-a-Thon—a youth development program that has become the new urban Peace Corps. Our employees get together on the day of the Serve-a-Thon and paint the school or do whatever the project happens to be."

"We also do other things," says Cohen, "like serving Thanksgiving dinner to the homeless in our cafeteria. We know that this is creating a real benefit for our employees, not just the guests. It is great for employees to see themselves not just as people doing a job to support themselves, but as people who are doing something to make a difference in the world. We don't do these projects for economic reasons, but we know that whatever good it does for people to be able to make a real contribution, we get it back tenfold. It's part of what makes the Reebok environment one of commitment, caring, and possibility. It becomes part of the way managers interact with the people who report to them and this becomes part of the value that people create and bring to customers. Can you see it in profitability? Yes! How do you know? We can't measure it...but you just know it."

How does this all add up in dollars and cents? Reebok's performance over the last ten years has been 30 percent compounded in sales and almost the same in profits. According to Cohen, who has a marketing person's ability to zero in on a single phrase that says a lot about a company, "Someone referred to our brand about a year ago as 'pure performance plus humanity.' When I heard that, it clicked."

Bally: Creating a Value-Added Context

It is one thing to be able to create a context that inspires and empowers people to add value if you are the CEO of a large company, but how do you do it if you are a middle manager or a team leader? John Egan, marketing and sales manager for Bally shoes retail shops in the United Kingdom, found a way. Egan not only has a philosophy and a system but knows how to inject it with fun and excitement.[3]

Bally's U.K. management has nurtured a particular business culture where employees pay attention to personal needs, ask customers what they think, and send thank-you notes. According to Egan, "I've learned that for people doing front-line jobs, it's not the salary and it's not the benefits package that make a difference, it's the small things—a bit of recognition or a bit of praise or a bit of sharing in success."

The key to creating a value-added culture is to have a philosophy about people. One thing that Egan has realized is that most so-called ordinary people are capable of extraordinary things.

> *One of the biggest mistakes that managers make is seeing people as ordinary just because they are doing ordinary jobs, and therefore they expect ordinary things from them.*

Egan strongly believes that if you look after the staff first, they will look after your customers. A lot of companies introduce a customer-focused approach but don't take into account that employees are angry and resentful because they haven't had a day off in three weeks. "We teach our managers," says Egan, "to look after the needs of the staff in every single way. For example, we tell them to put themselves in the other person's shoes if someone has to pick up a child, or has a doctor appointment, or is taking a class and wants to leave the store early. We teach them to say 'yes' instead of saying 'no, it's a busy afternoon and you are going to have to wait until the normal time.' If you do look after the small things, like letting people go ten or fifteen minutes early, they'll come back and work late or forgo their lunch break, not because they have to, but because they want to. Furthermore, their happiness will come through in their smiles or in their eyes when they are actually talking to a customer and trying to sell them a pair of shoes."

It helps, says Egan, "to just talk to people on an individual basis. The first thing that we would do when we go into a Bally store is to greet everyone in a very enthusiastic way to make sure people know that we think they are important. Then we find the opportunity to ask them how the job is going, what they've done previously, what they like, what they don't like, if they found the training useful.

"Once you've had a chat with this person, make it clear how much you think he or she can contribute. 'Have there been any problems and how can we improve that?' or 'If you owned your own shop, what would you do?' We all share the philosophy of recognizing people and making them feel part of an organization, no matter what part they play, how big or how small. Even if the cleaner walks by while I am there, I will ask him what he thinks."

One of Bally's reasons for success is training, which is headed up by Susan Wellman. "We know that people aren't going to want to work in a shoe shop for the rest of their lives," says Wellman. "We recognize that if people do want to progress and do want to develop as people, we've got to give them the mechanics to do that." Bally makes sure that the courses it runs are not just for the company's benefit, but for the employee's development as well. This includes courses in creative writing, leadership, and interdisciplinary management.[4]

Along with asking people for their ideas and providing training, recognizing performance is very important. "We also do things," says Egan, "to recognize the average performers, not just the superstars. Sometimes, it's finding out snippets of things—someone might have had to work on her day off just to solve a problem in the store. Usually what we do is send her flowers, a bottle of champagne, or a note." Personally, Egan believes that as long as recognition is sincere and honest, it's impossible to overdo it.

"I was at work one day and we were looking at the absence and sickness record. We noticed that we had quite a few people who had 100 percent attendance records. These were people who instead of turning over and staying in bed when they woke up with a headache decided that they were going to work. We felt we should recognize this achievement, so we sent beautiful boxes of hand-made chocolates to over seventy people. We sent the chocolates straight to their homes, right out of the blue. When they arrived home, there was a mysterious box and a letter from me saying 'Thank you very much for your perfect attendance record over the last twelve months.' And the next day they went to work and said 'Bloody hell, look what happened!'"

A Final Reflection

This book is really about how to coach people to achieve high-performance results and introduce transformational change while bringing out the best in them. Bringing out the best in people involves creating an environment that is consistent with the things that people care passionately about. On one level, this is about coaching people so that they expand their ability to realize the future of their dreams, experience higher levels of accomplishment, and have the soul-satisfying experience of being part of a real team. It's about holding the line on basic human values, like honesty and fairness. As Coach Lou Holtz of Notre Dame football says, "Do it right" and "Do your best."

On another level, the things that people care passionately about transcend the desire for personal success, the need to belong to a group, and the goal of making next quarter's bottom line. They include things like personal self-renewal, concern for community issues like education, and a world where we honor the values of human beings and allow our natural environment to flourish. In writing this book, I met many men and women whose definition of leadership, coaching, and teaching went beyond the usual parameters and included the notion of social responsibility. These were often men and women whose personal and corporate commitment to stewardship involved investing in a common cause and giving their time and energy as an integral part of their lives, not just as a mere gesture. As one executive elegantly put it, "I invest in the recognition of the unity of the world, my connectedness with all people, and my own highest human aspirations."

About the Author

Robert Hargrove, author of *Masterful Coaching,* is the founder of Transformational Learning Inc., which offers consulting and training services. According to Robert, "Our business is to inspire, empower, and enable people to make a difference, whether in the life of one person, a group, or the world at large."

Robert Hargrove is an internationally sought after speaker on the topics raised in *Masterful Coaching*—stewardship, executive reinvention, collaboration and communication, building learning organizations and communities of commitment. These talks are laced with wisdom, compassion, and humor.

Robert Hargrove and his colleagues also offer in-depth coaching programs on these and other topics that are based on transformational learning. These programs enable people to see themselves and their situations in a new way, one that reveals new possibilities and choices. They also enable people to go through the deep learning cycle needed to learn new skills and capabilities and unlearn old habits that are counterproductive.

For more information about masterful coaching, public speaking, and training and consulting services, contact Transformational Learning Inc., 39 Harvard Street, Brookline, Massachusetts 02146, (617) 739-3300, fax (617) 738-9149.

Notes

Introduction

1. From the Harvard Business Review article "The Knowledge Creating Company" by Ikujiro Nonaka (November-December 1991) in the *Learning Imperative: Managing People for Continuous Innovation,* a Harvard Business Review book by Robert Howard, ed. (Boston: Harvard Business School Press, 1993).

2. Paul Allaire, "The New Productivity: Using Quality to Enable Our People to Create Value," speech to the Executives' Club of Chicago, May 29, 1992.

1. The Journey to Masterful Coaching

1. I am grateful to Peter Senge for telling me this story about Royal Dutch Shell in South Africa.

2. I appreciate getting permission to print this story about Fidelity's founder, E.C. Johnson 2d.

3. I am grateful for permission to print this quote from Fred Kofman of MIT's Organization Learning Center. Some of the ideas in this section have been based on writings of Fred Kofman and Peter Senge. See "Communities of Commitment: The Heart of Learning Organizations," *Organizational Dynamics,* Autumn 1993.

4. M. Scott Peck, *A World Waiting to Be Born* (New York: Bantam Books, 1993).

5. I appreciate friend and colleague Erich Weber, chairman of Job Design, Switzerland, for sharing his thoughts on coaching with me.

6. The governing values are adapted from the work of C. Argyris and D. Schön. See C. Argyris & D. Schön, *Theory in Practice: Increasing Professional Effectiveness* (San Francisco: Jossey-Bass, 1974).

7. The notion of double-loop and single-loop learning is the work of Chris Argyris and D.A. Schön. See C. Argyris & D.A. Schön, *Theory in Practice: Increasing Professional Effectiveness* (San Francisco: Jossey-Bass, 1974).

8. Again, appreciation for permission to quote Fred Kofman.

9. Ibid.

10. See Edgar H. Schein, *Process Consultation: Its Role in Organization Development,* Volume I (Reading, MA: Addision-Wesley Publishing Company, 1988).

11. I am grateful to Fred Kofman for permission to use the idea of the learning enzyme from his paper entitled "Leading Learning Communities."

2. A Coach Is Something That You "Be"

1. Jacob Bronowski, *The Ascent of Man* (London: British Broadcasting Corporation, 1973).

2. John Feinstein, *A Season on the Brink* (New York: Fireside Books, 1989).

3. John Wooden with Jack Tobin, *They Call Me Coach* (Chicago: Contemporary Books, 1988).

3. Coaching Happens in Conversations

1. I am grateful to longtime colleague and friend Michel Renaud, of Renaud Pemberton International, Montreal, Quebec, for his contribution to this chapter based on his work coaching individuals and teams.

2. Dawna Markova, Ph.D., coined the words "river story" and "rut story." See D. Markova, *No Enemies Within* (Emeryville, CA: Publishers Group West, 1994).

3. I am appreciative of conversations with Sara Schley, of the MIT Organizational Learning Center, whose insights on coaching individuals contributed greatly to this chapter and the methodology for coaching people to take successful action.

4. The ladder of inference was developed by Chris Argyris who is a James Conant Professor of Education and Organizational Behavior at Harvard University. He is the author of numerous publications and has developed many tools for management learning; see C. Argyris, *Overcoming Organizational Defenses* (Needham Heights, MA: Allyn and Bacon, 1990), C. Argyris, *Strategy, Change, and Defensive Routines* (Boston: Pitman, 1985), and C. Argyris, *Knowledge for Action* (San Francisco: Jossey-Bass, 1993).

4. Stretch Goals, Yearning, and Learning

1. Commentary from the *Boston Business Journal,* August 5-11, 1994, 15.

2. Charles R. Day, "Go Find Yourself a Crisis," *Industry Week,* July 4, 1994, 23.

3. Shawn Tully, "Why to Go For Stretch Goals," *Fortune,* November 14, 1994, 148.

4. Gary Hamel & C.K. Prahalad, "Strategy as Stretch and Leverage," *Harvard Business Review,* March-April 1993.

5. Robert Fritz, *Creating* (New York: Ballantine, 1993).

6. Peter Senge graciously shared his insights on learning organizations. See Peter M. Senge, *The Fifth Discipline* (New York: Doubleday, 1990) and P. Senge, C. Roberts, R. Ross, B. Smith, & A. Kleiner, *The Fifth Discipline Fieldbook* (New York: Doubleday, 1994).

7. Hirotaka Tekeuchi & Ikujiro Nonaka, "The New New Product Development," from *Managing Projects and Programs* (Boston: Harvard Business Review Book, 1989).

8. From the Harvard Business Review article "The Knowledge Creating Company" by Ikujiro Nonaka (November-December 1991) in the *Learning Imperative: Managing People for Continuous Innovation,* a Harvard Business Review book by Robert Howard, ed. (Boston: Harvard Business School Press, 1993).

9. Ibid.

10. Tom Peters & Robert Waterman, *In Search of Excellence* (New York: Warner Books, 1982).

5. The Unwritten Rules of the Game

1. Paul Allaire, "The New Productivity: Using Quality to Enable Our People to Create Value," speech to the Executives' Club of Chicago, May 29, 1992.

2. Peter Scott-Morgan of Arthur D. Little, Inc., graciously shared his work about the "unwritten rules" that is the basis for this chapter. See Peter Scott-Morgan, *The Unwritten Rules of the Game* (New York: McGraw Hill, 1994).

3. Brian Dumaine, "Mr. Learning Organization," *Fortune*, October 17, 1994.

4. Permission to reprint this diagram from *Prism*, Second Quarter 1994, published by Arthur D. Little, Inc., Cambridge, MA.

6. From Theory of Action to Practice

1. Permission to reprint this diagram from *Prism*, Second Quarter 1994, published by Arthur D. Little, Inc., Cambridge, MA.

2. Gary Hamel & C.K. Prahalad, "Strategy as Stretch and Leverage," *Harvard Business Review*, March-April 1993.

3. I am appreciative of conversations with John O'Rourke, president of Pony USA, and his insights into coaching individuals and teams.

4. Again, special appreciation to Peter Senge for conversations about his work in the MIT Organization Learning Lab. A number of his ideas are expressed in this chapter.

5. My appreciation to Fred Kofman of the MIT Organization Learning Center.

6. I appreciate Fred Kofman, of the MIT Organization Learning Center, for sharing his work in creating learning communities.

7. P. Senge, C. Roberts, R. Ross, B. Smith, & A. Kleiner, "Creating a Learning Lab—and Making It Work" from *The Fifth Discipline Fieldbook* (New York: Doubleday, 1994), 558.

8. T. Goss, R. Pascale, & A. Athos, "The Reinvention Roller Coaster," *Harvard Business Review*, November-December 1993.

9. This dilemma exercise is from Bill Isaacs and Dia Logos in Cambridge, Massachusetts.

7. Observing and Giving Feedback

1. Edgar H. Schein, *Process Consultation: Its Role in Organization Development*, Volume I (Reading, MA: Addision-Wesley Publishing Company, 1988).

2. Action maps are another tool developed by Chris Argyris. See C. Argyris, *Knowledge for Action* (San Francisco: Jossey-Bass, 1993).

3. David Ogilvy, *Ogilvy on Advertising* (New York: Crown Publishers, 1983), 16.

4. Pat Riley, *The Winner Within* (New York: G.P. Putnam's Sons, 1993).

8. Teaching New Skills and Capabilities

1. Robert Fritz, *Creating* (New York: Ballantine, 1993).

2. I am appreciative of conversations with Philippe Chéhab, division manager of Swissair, on the truly inspirational work he is doing at Swissair with systems thinking and shifting people's mindset and identity from separate to related.

3. This is based on a model from Innovation Associates, Framingham, Massachusetts.

9. Trigger Breakthrough Thinking

1. I am grateful to Peter Jackson of Royal Insurance for sharing how Royal has used breakthrough thinking to create a point of view of the future.

2. George Lois with Bill Pitts, *What's the Big Idea* (New York: Doubleday, 1991).

3. Andrew E. Serwer, "McDonald's Conquers the World," *Fortune*, October 17, 1994, 112.

4. From a film by Joel Barker and Wayne Burkan, "Paradigm Prism Video Workshop," Aurora Productions, Minneapolis, MN.

5. P. Ranganath Nayak & John M. Ketteringham, *Breakthroughs!* (San Diego: CA, Pfeiffer & Company, 1994).

6. Robert W. Galvin, *The Ideas of Ideas* (Schaumburg, IL: Motorola University Press, 1991).

7. William Taylor, "Message and Muscle: An Interview with Swatch Titan Nicolas Hayek," *Harvard Business Review*, March-April 1993.

8. From the Harvard Business Review article "The Knowledge Creating Company" by Ikujiro Nonaka (November-December 1991) in the *Learning Imperative: Managing People for Continuous Innovation,* a Harvard Business Review book by Robert Howard, ed. (Boston: Harvard Business School Press, 1993).

9. Ibid.

10. Susan Caminiti, "Can the Limited Fix Itself?" *Fortune,* October 17, 1994, 168.

11. I am grateful for the conversations with Stephen Pook, Sr. vice president in charge of information technology, who led a task force that spearheaded a breakthrough at Engelhard Corporation. I am also appreciative of colleague Fernando Assens for his initial interview with Stephen Pook.

10. Build Shared Understanding

1. David Bohm has researched and written extensively on dialogue. See David Bohm, *On Dialogue* (Ojai, CA: David Bohm Seminars, 1990).

2. Fernando Flores has done extensive work in the area of action language. See also Terry Winograd & Fernando Flores, *Understanding Computer and Cognition* (Norwood, NJ: Ablex Publishing, 1986).

3. I am indebted to Nita Kincaid of Fidelity Investments for the time she spent sharing ideas on masterful facilitation.

4. The governing values are adapted from the work of C. Argryis and D. Schön. See C. Argyris & D. Schön, *Theory in Practice: Increasing Professional Effectiveness* (San Francisco: Jossey-Bass, 1974).

5. The ground rules are selected and adapted from Roger Schwarz, *The Skilled Facilitator* (San Francisco: Jossey-Bass, 1994).

6. The protocol for team reflection and learning is from P. Senge, C. Roberts, R. Ross, B. Smith, & A. Kleiner, *The Fifth Discipline Fieldbook* (New York: Doubleday, 1994).

7. I am appreciative of the time John Freeman, senior consultant for the CICB Leadership Center, spent sharing about his successes with dialogue sessions at CICB in Canada.

8. I am grateful for the time that Paul Allaire, John Seely Brown, and Ajit Laroia spent with me sharing the process of creating a shared world view at Xerox. (April, May 1994)

11. Recognize and Disperse Posturing and Defensiveness

1. Many of the ideas in this chapter are based on the work of Chris Argyris, whose work in the areas of getting people to discuss the undiscussable is documented in many publications. See C. Argyris, *Overcoming Organizational Defenses* (Needham Heights, MA: Allyn and Bacon, 1990) and C. Argyris, *Strategy, Change, and Defensive Routines* (Boston: Pitman, 1985).

2. Brian Dumaine, "Mr. Learning Organization," *Fortune*, October 17, 1994, 154.

3. Michael Hammer & Steven A. Stanton, *The Reengineering Revolution* (New York: Harper Business, 1995).

4. Brian Dumaine, "Mr. Learning Organization," *Fortune*, October 17, 1994, 154.

5. I am appreciative of conversations with Wright Elliot of Chase Manhattan Bank about the change process the bank has been going through the past few years. Also see "A Chastened Chase," *Business Week*, September 26, 1994, 106; "Chase's New Vision: Putting Teamwork First," *American Banker*, Wednesday, June 16, 1993; and "Still Waters Run Deep," *Forbes*, October 25, 1993.

6. Bob Putnam, of Action Design Associates in Newton, Massachusetts, graciously shared about his work of facilitating groups to move beyond defensive routines and design effective actions.

7. The first three steps to sustaining a learning process are from Bob Putnam. The fourth step comes from Roger Schwarz, professor at the Institute of Government at the University of North Carolina at Chapel Hill. See also Roger Schwarz, *The Skilled Facilitator* (San Francisco: Jossey-Bass, 1994).

8. I am grateful for the time Roger Schwarz made for conversations about his experience of working with people to disperse defensive routines.

12. Go for Results Now!

1. I am grateful to Robert Schaffer for sharing his ideas and expertise on developing high-performance teams using the Breakthrough Strategy. Many of the ideas in this chapter are based on his work in this area. See Robert Schaffer, *The Breakthrough Strategy* (New York: Ballinger Publishing Division, 1988).

2. Charlie Baum graciously shared his insights about high-performance teams and how to introduce these teams into an organization where there is no ready-made slot for them.

3. I am appreciative of the time Mike Berkin, performance quality manager of Dun & Bradstreet Information Services, and Sharon Shelton spent with me sharing about the breakthrough projects they have successfully initiated at D&B.

13. Add Value By Design

1. I am grateful for permission to write about Fidelity Investments and especially grateful to Bob Beckwitt, Leo Dworsky, Nita Kincaid, Darla Hastings, Roger Servison, and Rab Bertelsen.

2. I am grateful to Sharon Cohen for conversations about Reebok and its inspiring work in the area of social responsibility.

3. I am appreciative of conversations with John Egan about what Bally is doing to nurture a culture where people can add value.

4. Thanks to Susan Wellman from Bally for her comments on the educational programs for employees.

Acknowledgments

Firstand foremost, I would like to acknowledge my partner in life, Susan Youngquist. She brought inspiration, lots of encouragement, and unflagging effort to this project. I provided some of the ideas, content, and writing. She provided a road map for where I was going and made sure all the pieces fit together to make a whole.

Carl Kaestner, a long-time colleague of mine at Transformational Learning Incorporated in Brookline, Massachusetts, played a very pivotal role in helping to elicit key ideas that I knew on a tacit level from all my years of coaching but could not express in words. Carl also was extremely helpful in finding the best coaching methods and techniques that would give the layman access to the possibility of masterful coaching.

I would like to acknowledge Peter Senge of the Organization Learning Center at the Massachusetts Institute of Technology (MIT), author of *The Fifth Discipline*. Peter has established the vision of the learning organization and connected it to the highest human values. In doing so, he has established the notion of the learning organization as a powerful new tradition, and this book is in many ways part of that tradition.

In addition to Peter, who contributed greatly to the book through his inspiring example, conversations, and writings, I would like to acknowledge two other people at the MIT Organization Learning

Center. The work of Fred Kofman helped a great deal in articulating the ideas of transformation and learning as they apply to bringing about real change and results. In the same group is Bill Isaacs, whose stand to improve the quality of dialogue on the planet inspires me and whose writings have furthered my understanding of the nature of collaboration.

In addition to these people, I would like to acknowledge a whole community of professional coaching and teaching practitioners who are masterful in their work and whose presence is inspiring and uplifting. Duly acknowledged are Charlie Kiefer, president of Innovation Associates in Framingham, Massachusetts, who opened the door for me to doing the work of transformational learning within organizations years ago when it was virtually unheard of and Michel Goodman, also of Innovation Associates, who contributed the importance of the idea of methods and tools to help people speak with greater openness and honesty and for the idea of structuring ways for teams to learn on the job.

Another powerful and influential source for the book has been Chris Argyris of Harvard University. He is a gutsy person with a fighting spirit and an incredibly precise intellect. He has opened many new horizons of possibility for coaching and learning within organizations, especially as it pertains to recognizing and dispersing defensive routines. His colleague, Bob Putnam, of Action Design in Newton, Massachusetts, provided a great deal of insight into how to create the bridge between transforming individuals and transforming groups. Another Argyris colleague, Roger Schwarz, professor at the University of North Carolina and author of *The Skilled Facilitator,* also helped in providing some of the methods and tools.

Robert Schaffer, of Robert Schaffer and Associates in Stamford, Connecticut, helped to provide the notion of the small steps to strategic successes through the vehicle of short-term breakthrough projects. Schaffer is a street-smart, practical, gentle man of wisdom. A big acknowledgment to Charlie Baum, a former colleague of Schaffer's for showing how to introduce "Breakthrough Technique" in organizations.

Other people who have made big contributions are Sara Schley, of the MIT Organization Learning Center, and Michel Renaud, of Renaud Pemberton International in Montreal, Quebec. Sara was extremely helpful in teasing out the distinctions of coaching, as well as in providing a framework for coaching individuals. Michel was also essential in shaping the chapter on coaching individuals and in communicating how to set the context and design of an ongoing coaching relationship.

Dr. Peter Scott-Morgan, a director of Arthur D. Little, Inc., in Cambridge, Massachusetts, provided the insights on the unwritten rules of the game, a new discipline in organization high performance and learning. I appreciated Peter's boundless enthusiasm and willingness to pitch in and help whenever asked.

I would also like to acknowledge Rob Gass, director of Arc International, for his ideas on transforming corporations by starting out with setting a strong context and David Korkosz, a good friend, for embodying the whole spirit of inquiry and reflection, as well as for his ideas on the subject.

There were many coaches in the book who were senior or local managers in organizations and, again, each of these people provided ideas, generosity of spirit, and a shining example. One that provided enormous inspiration was Paul Allaire, CEO of Xerox. His attempt to create a shared understanding in formulating the vision for Xerox for the year 2000 was a courageous example of how innovative, "outside the box" thinking applies to management practices. Also extremely helpful in this case was John Seely Brown of the Xerox PARC Institute in California and Ajit Laroia of the Xerox Strategy Planning Offices.

U.S.: Other senior or local managers who made outstanding contributions were Stephen Pook, senior vice president of Engelhard Corporation; Nita Kincaid of Fidelity Investments; Sharon Cohen, executive director of the Reebok Foundation; John Rheingold, business unit leader of Microsoft Project, Microsoft; Tom Kaiser, president, Energy Group, AIG; Mike Berkin, senior vice president of performance quality at Dun & Bradstreet; Sharon Shelton, presidential assistant,

Dun & Bradstreet; Wright Elliot, executive vice president of Corporate Communications, and Elaine Dinn of Chase Manhattan Bank; John O'Rourke, president of Pony USA; and Kenneth Patterson, publisher, Motorola University Press.

International: John Egan, vice president of marketing, Bally Shoe UK; Peter Jackson, executive vice president of marketing, Royal Insurance, London; Fritz Autenreith, vice president of human resources, Ascom, Switzerland; Andreas Spahni, CEO, and Herbert Kahlich of Credis Mutual Funds, Credit Suisse, Zurich; Erich Weber, Job Design, Switzerland; Hans Jurg Bauer, CEO, Erima, Germany for suggesting that I write a book on coaching; and Peter Odermatt, Ciba Geigy, Switzerland, B.J. Lemmich, Ciba Geigy, South Korea, and of course my colleague, Andreas Roman—their coaching contract with me led to a coaching manual which in turn led to an early draft of the book.

Finally, the most special acknowledgment to my son Roc for his total support, endless patience, and interesting feedback on various things I asked him to read and review during this project.

Index

Ideas   9/16/00

P.130 Use several young "designers" for new design
— Encourage students to write papers on (w/ citations)
                    Family Leadership
                              Planning
                              Decision Making
                              Team Bldg
                              Mgt
                              Prob Solving

Plot   9/16/00.
        What it is I want to accomplish:
            Increase P.I.N + help Families manage
                              Successfully in changing
                                          times

Key Tasks + Probs to be Solved	Kinds of Approaches to use + what I Know + don't know
1. Share ideas ie neutral frameworks, Rsp mgt, frameworks: ldrshp	1. Book — need producer
→ Child Dev — Planning Theory — Dec	& Family Coaching: Changing times
2) Mgt — mgt	2. Web Site — need producer
3) Myers- — Team	Org + Change
Briggs — Prob Sol	3. Newsletter Family + Change
Personality	4. Teaching
4) Religion	
5) Englishting (2+3	
Prob - Competition Book to be written	Learn about coaching + other approaches
3 Prob Time - need time to research + finish Book	Put rest on Website / + Web newsletter
4. Prob - Retirement - Time Consuming - (after 2 weeks will be over)	Parenting Knowledge Mgt,
5. Prob + Time w/ Husb / fam Family Teaching	
— Come 1st ; Will give balance	re Fam. + Change: Coaching for Helping Profs? + EE Profs?